THE
NEW LEARNING
INFRASTRUCTURE

EDUCATORS WITH THE *COURAGE*
TO *REFORM LOCAL SCHOOLS*

STU ERVAY

LIGHT·YEAR
PRESS

Dedication to the
Work of the National Teachers Hall of Fame

• • • ● • • •

Exceptional and Courageous Teachers Inspire and Lead

The inception of this book comes during a time American schools are suffering. They are reeling for many reasons: misguided governmental policies, a devastating pandemic, inadequate funding, mismanagement that allows organizational priorities to supersede academic excellence, and a misunderstanding of what quality learning is and why it is important to the health of our nation. Most egregious is the diminishment of the teaching profession from a dynamic force for guiding students toward authentic and multifaceted achievement, to a group of civil servants expected to comply with expectations from special interest groups, lawmakers, and bureaucrats.

Many organizations recognize those problems and attempt to find ways to solve them. The most influential is the National Teachers Hall of Fame because it attacks today's issues, not by starting with top-down structural reforms such as better funding, higher salaries, more enlightened laws, and other kinds of administrative tinkering.

Ken Weaver
Executive Director

Those changes *are* necessary. But the essential kind of rethinking must focus on who teachers are and what they do. The Hall of Fame recognizes and honors exceptional career teachers, encourages excellence in teaching, and preserves the rich heritage of the teaching profession in the United States.

The Teachers Hall of Fame also enhances the public's awareness of the vital role of education in society by working collaboratively with national

Carol Strickland
*Immediate Past
Executive Director*

education organizations and building linkages with other national teacher recognition programs. It recognizes and celebrates the accomplishments of exceptional career teachers, preserves their careers in museum and virtual formats, and utilizes their skills and experiences to elevate teacher quality and student learning through integrated programming.

This book, *The New Learning Infrastructure: Educators with the Courage to Reform Local Schools*, is an effort to examine schools from the inside out, looking at school reform as a people endeavor, not just organizational restructuring. The author offers the background of challenges schools encounter but uses key characters in a fictional story to show how their transformation is essential to upgrading educational effectiveness and quality.

While the story is fictional, the plot is based on over thirty years of working with real public schools and educators throughout the nation. All those people are remarkable and inspiring, much like the teachers selected as members of the National Teachers Hall of Fame. This book is dedicated to those classroom-based leaders, what they have done and continue to accomplish as models of active service to their profession and students.

To illustrate why this book is dedicated to the 150 members of the National Teachers Hall of Fame, here a few examples of what these extraordinary career teachers continue to do inside and outside the classroom:

Jennifer Williams (Class of 2016), a high school art teacher from Nampa, Idaho, created a classroom to inspire creative thinking, self-discipline, dignity in work, doing something well, and promoting curiosity and respect. She related the knowledge to the lives of her students while planting seeds that giving back to society was important and art was the perfect way to do that. Her "Project Van Go" offered art lessons to thousands of students in rural schools in Idaho for four decades. Williams allowed students to be teachers of the day using art to bridge age and ethnic barriers. Even after retirement, Williams and her former students, now art teachers them-selves, continue to share the joy of art with a new generation.

Christopher Albrecht (Class of 2019), a fourth-grade teacher from Brockport, New York, infuses his classroom with core ideas. Creativity allows for the expansion of ideas, breaks the rules of conventional thought, and prepares students for complex problem-solving. Students must take productive risks as failure is an effective pathway to learning. Productive learners will come to have faith in themselves. Learning should build a student's willingness to work hard. Effective teaching focuses on how students learn best rather than teaching the standards. Working together is a valuable way to learn.

Andrew Beiter (Class of 2020) a middle school social studies teacher from Springville, New York, and his students started the Springville Students for Human Rights in response to the genocide in Darfur. This group was the catalyst for the Summer Institute for Human Rights and Genocide Studies for Buffalo-area high school students. The summer institute morphed into the Academy for Human Rights (academyforhuman-rights.org), which focuses on putting knowledge into action for students and educators in western New York. In addition, Beiter co-founded the Educators' Institute for Human Rights (www.eihr.org), devoted to supporting educators who rebuild communities around the world.

Dr. Melissa Collins (Class of 2020), a second-grade teacher from Memphis, Tennessee, and her students educated the community through active engagement such as "carnival physics." Participants, dressed as marchers during the Civil Rights era, learn about physics through carnival rides and a civil rights march from the Civil Rights Museum to the Lorraine Motel, where Dr. King was assassinated. Dr. Collins collaborated with teachers around the nation and the world. She brought the world into her classroom through Zoom sessions with teachers and student-to-student exchanges.

Donna Gradel (Class of 2020), a high school environmental science teacher from Broken Arrow, Oklahoma, and her students became change agents in their school district and around the world. Based on student research, the board of education approved a district-wide energy policy and installed energy-efficient lighting and a new ventilation system. In Kenya, Gradel and her students brought clean water and protein to orphans. They constructed an aquaponic system to raise tilapia for food. After learning the fish food was too expensive, they obtained a grant from MIT and invented low-cost sustainable fish food and the system to produce the ingredients. Subsequent classes created affordable designs for chicken coops and cost-effective chicken food to provide protein at a Kenyan school that rescues victims of sexual abuse. Gradel and her students traveled to Kenya to build the coops and the system for the food, extending their classroom across the globe.

Kareem Neal (Class of 2022), a high school special education teacher from Phoenix, Arizona, transforms his classroom into a strong community of learners. He builds on his student strengths and inspires them to give their full effort as they make progress toward the goals of the Individualized Education Program and learning employment skills. For fourteen years Neal sponsored a student organization that aims to eliminate the biases/pre-judgments that prevent people from connecting with peers and fellow humans. Neal's belief in his students gives them the skills and confidence to find sustainable employment and not have to be cared for by others. His goal is to make all his students feel welcome, wanted, and valuable.

Robert Fenster (Class of 2022), a high school history teacher from Hillsborough, New Jersey, creates "labs" in his classroom where students are given a set of learning goals and a variety of options about how to achieve them, including working individually and in groups. The option gives students choices about their learning. At one of his labs Bob teaches mini-lessons to help students struggling to grasp a subject. At another lab students create podcasts about race in the United States. One of Fenster's collaborations resulted in an exchange program with teachers in Sierra Leone to create global connections between students on slavery topics.

Gary Koppelman (Class of 2014) taught fifth grade for forty-six years at Blissfield Community Schools in Blissfield, Michigan. His classroom, which he called the "World of Wonder," featured challenging, creative activities connected to the BELL, a climatically controlled greenhouse at the cutting edge of life science investigation. He envisioned and raised the funds to create a hands-on, minds-on approach to learning. Koppelman continues to oversee its care and growth, even after his retirement. The BELL lab challenges young people to explore new worlds of plants, animals, and habitats, resulting in many scientists and science teachers added to our society. Koppelman received the 2013 National Science Teaching

Association Shell Science Teaching Award, and he continues to serve the 4-H community in Blissfield.

Rebecca Palacios (Class of 2014) taught early childhood and dual language education for thirty-four years in Corpus Christi, Texas. She now serves as the Senior Curriculum Advisor for Age of Learning, the premier online learning tool for students in preschool through high school. Palacios mentors area teachers and is a cofounder and former vice-chair of the National Board for Professional Teaching Standards. She is a nationwide professional development presenter and served on committees for the National Science Foundation, the Education Development Center in Boston, and Scholastic. Palacios is a published author, with her latest book titled *Being Your Child's Most Important Teacher: A Guide for Families with Young Children*. She retired from teaching in 2010, but she has not retired from the education profession.

Linda Evanchyk (Class of 2010) taught English and journalism for thirty-eight years at Choctawhatchee High School in Fort Walton Beach, Florida. After retiring in 2017, she decided to continue her dedication to the district that provided her own education as well as her teaching career. She was elected to serve on the Okaloosa County District School Board in 2018. Evanchyk was recently reelected for another four-year term. She was one of the first Okaloosa County teachers to attain National Board Certification, designated as a Master Journalism Educator by the National Journalism Education Association and named Florida's Journalism Teacher of the Year in 1995 and 2009. Evanchyk coauthored the book *Those Who Teach Do More: Tributes to American Teachers*. The community appreciates her passion for the district as she attends school activities, supporting the students and staff.

David Lazerson (Class of 2008), more affectionately known as "Dr. Laz" to his colleagues and students, is still in the classroom after forty-five years. He is a special education teacher and music director at The Quest Center of the Broward County Public Schools in Florida. Lazerson is one of the founders of Project CURE the World, a racial harmony group that became a force for positive change regarding racism and stereotypes. Dr. Laz and the group were selected as recipients of the 2022 National Education Association's Rosa Parks Memorial Award, awarded each year to an individual or organization who inspires others to champion the cause of human and civil rights. The Showtime original movie *Crown Heights* is based on Dr. Laz's book *Sharing Turf*, which documented the New York race riots of 1981 as he helped bring the people together with music. He continues performing and using music to enrich the learning process for his students with autism and Down syndrome. His latest project, the H.E.ARTS Project, focuses on empowering individuals with special needs through the expressive arts.

Norm Conard (Class of 2007) taught high school social studies for thirty-one years in the small town of Uniontown, Kansas. His hands-on, minds-on approach to learning history challenged his students to explore history through the eyes of unsung heroes. His students inspired him through their research to find little-known people who changed the course of history. When a student found the name Irena Sendler in a footnote, she became interested in the woman who saved Polish children during the Holocaust. Discovering the woman was still alive but living in poor conditions in Poland, the students and Norm worked to bring attention to what a hero Sendler was. The Polish government took note and provided for Sendler until her death in 2008. The story brought attention to the difference one person can make. That attention led to the creation of the Lowell Milken Center for Unsung Heroes in the nearby city of Fort Scott, Kansas. Today the center features a museum and park, training teachers to help students explore all facets of history. Under Conard's direction, the center has reached three million students in its fifteen years of operation through virtual and on-site presentations. Since retiring from teaching, Conard's classroom has grown exponentially.

Francis Mustapha (Class of 1994) taught biology and life science in Fort Wayne, Indiana, for twenty-seven years. He believes all students can learn and should be lifelong learners. He confronted students who did not have confidence in themselves to succeed in science classes, igniting the love of science in young women who felt that it was only a man's world. Mustapha mentored dozens of aspiring science teachers and passed along his love of the subject matter into the future. Born in a small village in West Africa where no one could read or write, Mustapha's life changed when he attended a new school that opened in a nearby village. His dream of providing a new school in the village where he was born became a reality in 2013. He now serves as the executive director of Madina Village School in Sierra Leone. He and his wife, Bobbie, now residents of Sierra Leone, are building a hospital in the village to further the idea that teachers can indeed change the world.

Recognizing selected teachers for their outstanding contributions to students and the profession is important and well deserved. These excellent models show how the practice of teaching impacts students and their world.

The purpose of this book is to systematically close the gap between exceptionality and standard practice, making stories such as those above closer to the norm. A New Learning Infrastructure makes that happen by removing bureaucratic hobbles and limitations on teacher professionalism.

Contents

• • • ● • • •

Foreword

C hallenges in the work of schools today are complex and confusing. It takes courage to have new ideas and make plans for their implementation. It takes no small amount of courage to just show up every day, let alone to try changing and improving systems that are so complex, to communicate about them, to plan for their implementation, and to stay the course long enough to see the work bear fruit and create desired outcomes. It takes courage to work through the "slump" that always occurs in changing initiatives, situations in which the players lose sight of the purpose. Frustrations emerge, impatience dims the visions, purposes flatten, and energy dissipates.

People outside of education, some well-meaning, advocate account-ability with the statement "It's not rocket science." Well, of course not. This is education science, which is complicated. It is about systems—systems within a system, systems outside the system, and self-generated systems.

When No Child Left Behind (NCLB) became reality, it challenged just about everything educators believed about the role of the federal government and states in terms of control over local schools. It challenged everything about how decisions would be made and who should make them. It challenged the roles of administrators and teachers. It upended administrators' roles as leaders of the system and of teachers as integral parts of the instructional team. Both were kicked to the curb.

NCLB challenged a fundamental belief of what educators were trying to live and wanted to see bear full fruit. That belief was that schools led by teachers and supportive administrators (and boards) could create the kinds of schools and classrooms we wanted for our students.

Bravery and courage (more courage than bravery) meant first having a clear sense of purpose and a mental model of what good practice, quality schools, and effective leadership should be. Teachers lead. Administrators support (and from Fullan, "love their teachers"). Superintendents support principals, and boards support superintendents. This mental model eventually became "High Performance Learning." At its center lay the students' reasons for doing the work of learning.

Having a clear mental model made it easier to fight off opponents and saboteurs. Nebraska's state model invited data collection about effectiveness. Success stories the data revealed convinced state policy leaders of the model's efficacy. Even leaders at the federal level were convinced, those who believed a single state test promised the cheapest and most efficient way to collect data about how schools were doing.

Nebraska's better way energized teachers. It redefined the roles of teachers and administrators. It brought significance to the work of being an educator. It promoted energy in the classroom because student learning was measured in an ongoing way, at the time and point the learning took place and within the classroom.

The "heroes" in this book are real. Names are fictitious, but their professionalism is authentic. They make a difference where their feet are planted. They spread their expertise to others and share the work of creating a new world of learning. They deserve recognition and should be remembered as we embrace a redirection in education—a redirection that begins at the foundational level: the classroom and the teachers.

This book is a great place to start. Read it. Reflect on it. Use it to guide what you do and what you think.

—Doug Christensen, PhD
Commissioner Emeritus, Nebraska Department of Education
Professor of Leadership in Education, retired

Introduction

A s a teenage boy I considered my vocational options. The process started with crossing off jobs I did not want—mowing lawns, pumping gas, or sacking groceries. As a hobby I enjoyed shop and mechanical work, but my father said my skills were marginal.

The military interested me because it was orderly and challenging. It also promised opportunity, albeit associated with considerable risk. Church work was an option, and the *Perry Mason* television show made the legal profession seem cool. Journalism looked attractive since writing and research appealed to me.

Education was not anywhere near the list of my career options. School was something I tolerated. My parents remained neutral on the topic. While scholastically capable high school graduates, neither attended college.

Eventually my involvement with the YMCA and church youth organizations brought the realization that working with young people proved an interesting and important pastime. So I became a leader in both church youth organizations and YMCA camps. Making a career of youth development work required a college degree. So I earned a teaching degree along with a commission in the United States Army.

Leadership opportunities in the army involved instruction. That responsibility opened my eyes to possibilities. After fulfilling active-duty obligations in the military, I obtained a graduate degree in educational leadership. Afterward I taught in high schools and middle schools, believing I was destined to become a principal, then a district superintendent.

But slowly I became obsessed with a problem in American public schools. Unlike in the military and other vocations, advancement in professional education did not seem inherently linked to how well one performed the institution's core purpose.

Teaching

In the 1960s most school administrators were men, often ex-coaches, skilled at overseeing an organization in much the same way they managed sports activities. The system worked reasonably well in terms of orderliness, personnel supervision, public relations, and compliance with regulations.

Teachers were both monitored and inspired by building-level leaders. They measured teacher success by their ability to manage children and young people, conduct instruction competently, maintain good relations with parents of students, and cooperate with colleagues as expected.

It all seemed to work—somehow.

But I could not come to terms with teaching as an isolated activity where I experienced—

- One adult in a room with many children or young people
- No working with other adults in any consistent way
- No colleague approval of my work beyond hearsay
- Feeling successful *only* in the context of positive student responses
- Little appreciative supervisory feedback from building administrators

As a secondary social studies teacher, I felt like an assembly line worker, adding to the "product" as it moved along the academic belt called grade levels. Disenchanted with only textbook-focused instruction, I developed programs that featured simulations, role-play, and panel discussions using debate as a teaching technique.

Debate taught students how to think—how to research, use evidence to support arguments, see both sides of an issue, cooperate with a partner, and learn the meaning of true effectiveness as a community member and a scholar.

Students seemed to appreciate the opportunity to view social studies as stimulating and relevant to their lives. Nevertheless, it was not enough to make me feel *part of a profession.*

I did not feel like an essential member of a team, in which each fulfilled a role while collectively supporting the defined mission, in contrast to how I felt as an army officer—appreciated and fulfilling a significant role.

Those who never served the military in leadership roles may think everyone is required to follow orders. But officers are commissioned to think, collaborate, and work together in accomplishing their mission—the definition of accountability for an officer, unlike the recruit or private, who is expected to do nothing more than comply.

No matter what I did as a public schoolteacher, I could never shake the feeling my work was more like that of a private than an officer, more like an assembly line worker than an executive. While public schools remained tied to the assembly line mentality, the business world was beginning to see a problem with that model.

The impetus behind the revised thinking came from an industrial statistician named William Edwards Deming. He created a new method referred to as Total Quality Management (TQM). The Deming Management Method (later TQM) changed industrial decision-making and action-taking by giving assembly line workers greater collaborative authority.

To Deming, his process was necessary to upgrade the quality of product and service. Deming's ideas resonated with me in terms of how schools and districts should work. But the process would be much more complicated for schools than for business and industry.

"Bringing teachers to the table" involves more than teaming assembly line workers at the local automobile plant. It involves a complex array of curriculum development, instructional design, and continuous assessment strategies.

How could educators find a model that somehow managed this array of functions to work in concert? Would this model allow teachers to play key leadership roles to make everything operate smoothly?

Between 1969 and 1971 I decided to seek a doctorate and focus my research on the professional status of teachers. Hypotheses I developed for my dissertation study revolved around the word *autonomy.* The premise underlying my approach included a definition such as *Professional autonomy means having the authority to make decisions to act in accordance with one's professional knowledge base.*

Research findings taken from secondary teachers working in Texas school districts indicated that nearly all teachers did *not* perceive themselves as having professional autonomy. Rare exceptions came from one district with a militant union and one school that employed the wife of a powerful local politician and member of the board of education. From all accounts, she ran the school.

All other teachers in the study said they had limited authority in their classrooms but did not have personal or collective authority in any larger venue. This sample population of secondary teachers did not possess professional autonomy, which led to the conclusion that teaching is *not* a profession.

This research was conducted long before the No Child Left Behind era. My dissertation began a quest to find or develop a new model for inclusively managing district academic programs. As a professor in a respected teacher education institution closely connected with public schools and with the help of many others, I created and implemented such a model. This book is based on that model and the insights gained over thirty-five years working in hundreds of school districts around the country.

1

Bridges and Schools—
Rethinking Infrastructure

An infrastructure lies below and supports everything above. It typically includes physical structures that make human communities work. Infrastructure is usually thought of as something tangible, like a bridge. Bridges are especially important. Upgrading them means rethinking their purposes.

But infrastructure can also be a service, like education, something that supports our daily lives in ways that make everything else possible. Like bridges, schools are essential for making society work. Upgrading them also means rethinking their purposes, planning for something other than the status quo.

Bridges allow us to move conveniently from shore to shore. Schools help us move from the ignorance of childhood toward a productive and fulfilling adulthood. Schools are essential to the service infrastructure. Rethinking infrastructure is necessary and ongoing.

Bridges are constantly being reconceptualized to meet the needs of a growing and diverse population. Planners invent new ways to be ready for a different future, based on evidence and imagination. Bridges still facilitate the moving of people from shore to shore. But they are now magnificent structures, designed to accommodate large and fast-moving vehicles.

Schools have done the same thing with larger buildings and more educators working to enlarge curricular content and make instruction more efficient. The status quo of the past has been replaced with an updated utility, a different kind of usefulness. We human beings struggle with this phenomenon because we love what is comfortable: the aura surrounding that little covered bridge down the road, the closeness of teachers and young friends in the safe little school on the hill, growing and becoming together—imbuing our memories with a meaning so precious that they cannot be adequately described, a reconceived utility.

We humans are conflicted. The comfortableness of what *was* fights the convenience of what *is*. We cannot have both. One dominates the other, with convenience and efficiency coming out on top. But maybe there is a way to change that scenario. Maybe there is a way to have both comfortableness *and* convenience. Perhaps a reconceptualization of the practice of utility is the new challenge—and thus a new opportunity.

As humans we employ the gift of imagination. As George Bernard Shaw said, "You see things as they are and say, 'Why?' But I dream things that never were, and I say, 'Why not?'"

People of the twenty-first century are beginning to question the utility of convenience and efficiency. Mass- and Internet-based social networks are more distractions than fulfilling experiences. Feelings of purposelessness are rampant. Depression and suicides are blights on communities. Loneliness is an epidemic.

Can bridges and schools be reconceived to address these problems? The question might seem silly, but maybe not. What if a bridge can also be a building or even a village—like the Ponte Vecchio Bridge over the Arno River in Florence, Italy, where people live in apartments and meet in coffee shops or work together in small studios; sit on verandas and enjoy the setting sun over the river; read, study, reflect, create, build, and become more than hordes of strangers going from one shore to the next, pausing to become an inherent part of the environment and humankind? Why not?

What would happen if we disrupted the factory-like academic assembly line and superficial means of determining learning quality in schools?

Past experiments with those goals in mind have been attempted and eventually disappeared. Those experiments failed because they were merely an overlay on an existing system—cosmetic changes in schedules, teaching techniques, assessment of learning, and other behaviors that never specified updated outcomes in terms of student growth, as in upgrading a bridge by building a modern village above an existing substructure, a substructure that eventually buckles under the increased weight and activity above.

In schools the inadequate substructure consists of an old and poorly designed academic program. Teachers are not prepared to work collaboratively to modify curriculum. They have not been trained to connect a new curriculum to a better instructional design.

Curriculum and Instruction Are a School's Infrastructure

What and how schools teach undergirds everything else so that infrastructure must be substantial and enduring. Patchwork "fixes" such as high-stakes tests, officially developed accountability standards, and the occasional tweaking of the system do not work, as with a bridge with rusted trusses and rivets that cannot be repaired by a guy on a scaffold replacing rivets and welding on plates.

The bridge, whether repaired or replaced, must be substantive. And if a bridge is to do more than provide a way for people to get from shore to shore, it must be *extremely* substantive, strongly reinforced in every detail, not only to keep everything stable on top but also to ensure the entire superstructure lasts a long time, quality throughout and perpetually significant in terms of human and cultural utility. Bridges are for crossing. Schools are for learning.

But as with bridges, quality schools and learning must also be perpetually significant in terms of human and cultural utility. Students must acquire understanding, knowledge, skills, behaviors, values, attitudes, and preferences—now and over time, perpetuated by curiosity and a cognitive substructure that induces engagement throughout a lifespan.

To make those things happen, schools must rethink and rewrite curriculum, actions that have been tried many times. The flaw in those previous efforts was in *who* was doing the rethinking and rewriting—curriculum specialists no doubt, like bridge architects who create artistic renderings and specifications, then turn them over to workers untrained or unmotivated to implement such sophisticated plans.

In education the disconnect between curriculum experts and classroom teachers is only part of the problem. Too often the curriculum experts are authors of textbooks and other instructional materials touted as cutting edge, commercially produced materials advertised as being solutions, when in fact they are only as good as local teachers think they are, which is not always positive. Or the curriculum experts are district-level administrators greatly influenced by external mandates for achieving accountability via high-stakes tests. Accreditation and the need for ongoing funding loom over the decision-making and action-taking process like a heavy cloud.

Conversely, competent designers and implementors sit in the same room during the planning stages. They merge the hypothetical with the practical, using the popular "yes—and" approach for turning dreams into reality.

Teachers and administrators who are *both* curriculum designers and talented classroom conductors can work together to maximize the *full* definition of learning for American students.

A New Learning Infrastructure

Infrastructure can be an essential service, not just a physical subsurface. As a service, the learning infrastructure is not dependent on one kind of driving force, such as educational institutions. A physical infrastructure contains many more parts than just bridges, but also roads, electrical grids, water and sewer lines, communication links, ongoing maintenance, and many more.

The same is true of the learning infrastructure. It involves much more than schools. It also includes other community groups, families, work-related training, and the myriad of experiences of individual human beings within life's sphere.

Much of the learning infrastructure is unmanageable for obvious reasons. We human beings are complex learning organisms, influenced by a wide variety of experiences, responsive to conditions of living such as personally felt obstacles, culturally imposed attitudes, and both psychological and physiological quirks. Inside our skin and brain are hidden values and priorities that we act on in sometimes unpredictable ways. A learning infrastructure must recognize and be built on that understanding.

Today's professional teacher is an employee of the state or a private educational organization with the following expectations:

- Properly prepared and credentialed
- Regulated in terms of assignment and professional expectations
- Overseen and evaluated by superiors who are also properly prepared and credentialed
- Paid by taxpayers represented on school boards, legislatures, and governors' offices; or boards of directors in private schools

Today's professional teachers are servants of the public they serve, expected to legally act *in loco parentis*—in place of the parent. *In loco parentis* works well when the culture served by a school is rooted in common beliefs. But in today's multicultural and socioeconomic environment, *in loco parentis* is hard to pin down. A partisan political environment places the meaning of *in loco parentis* all over the attitudinal map.

Enormous pressures fueled by a pandemic exacerbate frustrations even more, preventing our being in proximity of each other, thereby demanding heavy reliance on virtual instruction. Schools and districts, as organizations reliant on buildings and the supportive environment they provide, were not ready for virtual instructional programs. No one expected that all-consuming challenge to our existing learning infrastructure.

Creating a New Learning Infrastructure will mean a dramatic change in the way we think about teachers and teaching, schools, and districts, about organizational management structures and administrative hierarchies.

During the progression of the COVID-19 pandemic, many sacred cows associated with our society and economy were forced to transform. Small-business owners and other traditional organizations pivoted dramatically.

Churches initiated more online services. Health and the sciences were thrust into the spotlight, and a small number of schools and colleges altered their systems.

"Necessity is the mother of invention, is an old English proverb that likely has roots in the sayings of Plato. We invent new ways to survive when the old ways no longer work. In the last decade or two, technology companies changed old corporate rules to be more creative and thereby more competitive.

One of the more intriguing examples was explained in the September 2020 book *No Rules Rules: Netflix and the Culture of Reinvention,* by Netflix cofounder Reed Hastings and culture expert Erin Meyer. Hastings and his managerial team changed the corporate infrastructure, dumping dozens of old assumptions about how employees should be regulated and encouraged to perform their work better—in order to become more creative.

Innovation is both individual and collaborative. So how can Netflix or any other organization encourage both individual reflection and communal invention at the same time?

In schools, the New Learning Infrastructure could earnestly and authentically employ those same ideas and principles, to accept and even applaud the idea that teachers are not subordinate employees but rather fully functioning professionals consulted for their knowledge and skills in terms of *what and how* students are taught and how they learn.

Why not go beyond administerial and managerial oversight, which is the traditional infrastructure? It either highlights or implies that teacher involvement in decision-making and action-taking should be limited only to advice.

In the New Learning Infrastructure everyone on the school district's professional team feels his or her contributions are being valued. This effort becomes a three-pronged design. Educators are encouraged to reflect (think deeply), talk with each other in positive ("yes—and") ways, and feel valued to their core. Perhaps this sounds like an unrealistic and blissful utopia in which employees sit around a fire and mumble incantations of peace and harmony. Some may believe that real people in the real world need assertive leadership and guidance, required if anything worthwhile is to be accomplished.

Once I felt that way, and in some ways I still do. A little of the army officer still resides in my soul. But even in those army days, I quickly realized leadership is a two-way relationship. I was as dependent on my tank commanders as they were on my ability to make intelligent decisions. All tank commanders needed to be smart and decisive. To function as a team, they needed the ability to communicate. As with all soldiers, they needed to know I valued their lives and well-being, just as they did mine as their company commander.

The usual analogy is sports related, because the conditions are similar. But in the army it is often a life-or-death situation. A football team loses a game. Military units lose or destroy lives. The stakes are much higher.

The stakes are higher in education too. This New Learning Infrastructure has nothing to do with loss of control or voodoo mysticism. It has everything to do with lives gained or lives lost, not in a battle involving armies but in a future world in which challenges or enemies are of a different sort.

The New Learning Infrastructure is designed to build student mastery on many levels, not just in STEM (science, technology, engineering, and mathematics), not just in being able to write and read in a cogent manner. Mastery in the twenty-first century relates to our ability to think innovatively, to communicate clearly, and to value the importance of both self and others. All other skills are technological necessities in the context of available tools and databases. STEM and baseline communication skills *are* critical, but only when considered in the realm of human values, priorities, and interactions.

The New Learning Infrastructure requires skills that transcend the mundane, with teachers who see both sides, understand the ramifications of embracing knowledge, and possess the kind of wonder that promotes curiosity in students. Then they evaluate the pros and cons without unreasoned bias but with the power of insight and academic discipline. Such teachers demand as much of themselves as they do their students and realize life is more than what we do.

It is *how* we think and believe while doing it.

2

Professional Discipline

The New Learning Infrastructure requires strength and lasting endurance. It must be built with sterner stuff than the ways schools and districts are structured today. The vertical and unitary chain of command process now prevalent in K-12 districts must become more horizontal, making professional accountability less a matter of supervisory expectations—more like mutual support systems and disciplined team dynamics.

Horizontal management in schools is typical of the way hospitals work, with administration taking care of finance, maintenance, personnel, and other operational needs and with professional medical personnel concentrating on the care of patients, coming together when organizational and professional needs require it, such as when patient care requires facility upgrades, increased budgets, and equipment purchases. Replace "patient care" with "student learning," and the same setup can be true for schools.

Professional discipline assumes the existence of personal accountability, overseen by senior members of a staff. As in hospitals, the horizontal organizational configuration in schools advances the idea that teachers are employed with the expectation that they will adhere to excellence by their new associates, excellence in terms of curriculum-design expertise as well as effective instructional prowess.

The New Learning Infrastructure will succeed only if professional discipline is visibly active, evident in student learning quality as measured by many types of performance. The best way to explain how that system works flows through the eyes of a fictious young teacher. Mary Chapman learned the meaning of professional discipline and tried to adhere to its principles.

The meaning of professional discipline:

Mary's preparation for teaching includes more than subject matter expertise and instructional methods. Inclusive of mastery definitions, precise curriculum development, and strong formative assessment techniques, it also notes the strong emphasis on the use of teaching teams to build and critique programs.

My name is Mary Chapman, and this is my fifth year of teaching seventh-grade science. In the 2020–2021 school year I taught using three different configurations. In-classroom instruction used staggered schedules to accommodate social distancing for the COVID-19 pandemic. During part of the school year I incorporated virtual instruction. A hybrid model for brief periods incorporated both on-site and virtual instruction. Then I attempted "normal" classroom configurations late in the school year.

This kind of teaching presented a significant challenge for many reasons. The first was my own safety and that of my students. I avoided being infected by the virus. Students who tested positive were quarantined. Diligent school officials made certain only students and teachers who tested negative were allowed on campus or in the classrooms. Nothing about teaching during a pandemic was easy. But fortunately, the stability of my early years and my internal confidence helped me move through the challenges.

My loving and supportive middle-class family remained a positive influence during my childhood and teenage years. I qualified for college admissions and remained socially active with involvement in sports, particularly tennis. After college I married my husband, who works as an accountant. We have a two-year-old daughter. Our family life is quiet yet fulfilling.

I am thankful for my unique teacher preparation program and the modus operandi of the school district that hired me. My good fortune became evident during professional conferences and interactions with teachers from other districts. They helped me understand why I am so lucky, especially after the COVID-19 pandemic hit.

Vast differences exist in the quality of teacher education programs, and the same holds true for how public schools and districts are managed. Those two facts keep me appreciative of my past and current life as an educator. Both my undergraduate preparation and the policies of the district I joined represent professional and organizational quality.

My professional preparation for teaching gave me the skills and self-discipline to handle difficult situations. And the school district that hired me operates a decision-making and action-taking system that keeps everything in place. Professional discipline means a simple compliance with directives issued by those in authority, the external manifestation of strongly held internal values.

My Preparation for Teaching

Standard teacher education programs for elementary-grade instructors stress sufficient expertise in core subjects, grades K-6. "Self-contained" classrooms at those levels require teachers to become acceptably proficient in each of the big four disciplines: mathematics, science, language arts, and social studies.

Typically, elementary teachers qualified to work in middle school grades seven and eight must take additional courses. In my case I earned fifteen credit hours in specified science courses. Students prepared to teach grades nine through twelve must major in one or more subjects, earning a minimum of forty-five semester hours in each. Add to that the methods of teaching courses. Those prepared to teach high school sometimes also teach grades seven and eight within their certified fields with no additional requirements.

Except for an orientation course offered in the first two years of a college program, no professional course is typically taught before the third year. All required teaching courses occur in the junior and senior years, including on-site field experiences in area schools.

My preparation followed much the same pattern—the exception underscored in methods classes. In my case, professional discipline remained key. Professional discipline gives allegiance to principles established as hallmarks of integrity. I agree with that definition, but my understanding of the term expanded in my teacher education program. I entered teacher education with neither the narrow nor expanded professional discipline already in place. My upbringing and other positive influences over time readied me for the values that support both interpretations.

The "expanded" version includes the following:

Who a teacher is in terms of honesty, curiosity, creativity, conviction, openness, commitment, dependability, and drive to serve is more important than any other personal characteristic.

What a teacher believes about the purpose of education informs and underscores the instructional process and subject matter learning, making *what* an essential supplement to the inculcation of student skills and knowledge areas.

Why a teacher seeks employment in a school or district, to seek opportunities to encourage the personal, academic, and vocational growth of students over a lifetime is important, then being part of a team of educators who share those same convictions.

How teaching accomplishment is determined by student readiness is seen in mutual engagement with and excitement in learning as a human gift that results in a more satisfying and worthwhile life.

Where and *when* are both key considerations, especially during a pandemic or other social crisis. Teaching and student learning occur anywhere and anytime, not just in a school's classroom during prescribed hours.

When one looks at how most universities teach methods courses, the focus on instructional strategies takes precedence. Some also delve into personal characteristics of the prospective teacher and examine a novice teacher's beliefs. But they do not always explore what lies behind the strategies and beliefs by examining the potential that lies within and finding ways to pull that potential to the surface, by helping aspirant teachers become more than they ever thought they could be.

Methods courses in my university turned me into a different person, forcing me to rethink educational purposes and commit to seeing possibilities instead of accepting a stagnant status quo.

For years the gold standard of instruction underscored The Madeline Hunter Model of Mastery Learning. As a direct instructional model, it included good points. But my professors believed focusing everything on the "how" was not enough. Teachers were not just intermediate agents between curriculum and student learning. The error came in assuming that the "what" (curriculum) always emerged from a textbook, other printed resources, or published standards.

This revolutionary thinking seemed to ask too much of mere public school teachers. Could they control both curriculum *and* instruction? Surely curriculum remained the purview of researchers, scholars, professors, and other recognized experts in their fields.

My teacher education professors thought differently, which transformed me in ways I hope now transform my students.

· · · ● · · ·

Mary received an enlightened professional preparation, and her school district both supported and took advantage of her skills and beliefs about the purpose of education. Her unique qualities enabled her to participate in the creation of a dynamic curriculum *and* teach it in an engaged manner. Her school district became an even more active learning infrastructure, not simply an inert subterranean system but also one that contributed and responded to the society it served.

Mary and her colleagues gave life to learning, thereby exciting their students to learn. Both teachers and students with real opportunities to explore learn deeply, acting on their learning in productive and creative ways.

These actions must be authentic and purposeful in the context of societal expectations, fully accountable to everyone who trusts and depends on what and why students learn. The essence of professional discipline is to serve the larger good. Mary and her colleagues design curriculum and use it as the basis for teaching. Their students and the long-lasting quality of their learning measure the effectiveness of this infrastructure by multiple types of performance.

Real learning happens in various places and ways and under a variety of circumstances.

Mary continually realizes that real learning, the kind that changes our behavior and ways of thinking, often happens in non-school settings and situations. She begins to see how that truth also affects the classroom.

Mary continues her story:

Brain-based learning was a unit of instruction offered in my teacher preparation. How funny! What else should learning be based on?

But I began to understand that education traditionally treated the human brain as a neutral repository of information considered important to society by those who decided what was necessary for us to learn, with the assumption that we teachers just push buttons to open a cognitive trap door and pour in prescribed knowledge. Smart students retain and use that knowledge. Those not so smart allow it to leak out. That simplistic view interferes with the real learning that stimulates creativity and new ways of behaving.

As a highly active organ, the brain processes information in extremely complicated ways. It becomes more powerful by making all kinds of connections made by emotions, prior memories, concepts we manufacture through other experiences, and remembering details acquired from previous learning. Real learning occurs when a new understanding attaches itself to something previously learned, the famous "aha" when we feel something reformulate inside our heads: "I never thought of it that way before."

This new way of thinking about teaching and learning offers huge implications for curriculum and instructional design, for how we teachers assess student progress, intelligence, and aptitude.

We now realize intelligence is unique and changeable, not a single condition identified and recorded once or twice. And formal research verifies what we know almost intuitively. We learn things in parallel, and our entire body can be involved. Information is significant only if it is meaningful and makes sense. For something to make sense, a pattern or structure must fit.

Emotions can override learning. A brain attacked by depression, grief, or anger is not ready to learn something new. Research elaborates on the brain's complex and unique way of remembering and processing as it operates holistically.

One finding particularly struck me because I recognized it so quickly. People learn best when *challenged* but not when *threatened*.

Our methods included how to make brain-based learning part of the learning infrastructure. We learned *why* we needed to practice professional discipline in making curriculum and instructional design reflective of the new understandings, especially during formative (ongoing) assessment of our students' academic and intellectual growth.

Not all public schools or their patrons accept these new understandings. No institutions in America are more traditional than public schools and how they function. Tradition is hard to break. "What was good enough for me is good enough for my kids."

Finding a school district that understands the kind of change advocated by brain-based learning presented a real challenge for my fellow students and me. In fact, it was downright risky. If we did not have the geographic flexibility to find a district compatible with what we were learning, we could be disillusioned. After all, in the traditional infrastructure new teachers do not lead change. They learn "how things are done here" and how to "get along."

I was lucky to find a compatible district that appreciated my training and perspectives on teaching and learning, willing to fully use my skills in curriculum and instructional design. My teacher education program taught me that the nuts and bolts of curriculum and instructional design are critical—another essential part of professional discipline.

The most intense aspect of professional discipline involves how to operationally define mastery of student learning in ways that reach beyond test scores and meeting other requirements, authentically and formatively measured. The definition of mastery is essential—both generically and specifically. What do we educators expect our students to know, do, and become after graduating from school and after completion of each grade level? What do we expect them to master—now and for the future?

Most public schools struggle with something that seems so simple. The old view of curriculum prevails. It is something to be *covered*, based on the belief that human nature dictates that some young people cognitively capture bits and pieces of knowledge provided in the classroom. Others fail or do poorly. Such is life.

That philosophy no longer applies. Too much is at stake. Letting students fall through the cracks is unacceptable.

My professor drilled us on the creation of three mastery statements: a general one for a fictitious district, one specific to a subject area, and one more for a subject we would likely teach at a particular grade level.

We created a general mastery statement in small groups, as in a real-world school district. We accomplished that task in three class periods, but the frustration around the complexity of the assignment underscored the enormity of the task. How could K-12 districts nail down what they aspire their students to master in concrete and holistic terms?

Many districts ignore mastery declarations. Instead, they resort to the use of mission statements with a few flowery sentences. Text for brochures, web pages, and other media represent their aspirations, not specific mastery goals. The challenge comes in recognizing the impact of *scope*.

Scope is the amount of time available in the instructional timeframe, such as a school year, to accomplish intended learning goals. Aligning scope with such considerations as student readiness, content difficulty, and instructional time available is necessary for students to master anything.

Virtual instruction during COVID complicated everything. Mastery represents more than an aspiration. It is a realistic intention, and achieving mastery is critical. A curriculum that emphasizes brain-based learning cannot be taught quickly. It requires soak time—essential reflection. Discerning the achievement of mastery requires ongoing formative assessment using subjectively accurate measures, created and administered by teachers while making judgments based on evidence and intuitive observations.

The New Learning Infrastructure requires trust in teachers to make those judgments, moreover, for teachers themselves to feel confident in doing so.

• • • • • • •

Mary's teacher education experience included four elements not typically found. The definition of learning mastery is infinitely more inclusive than doing well on tests. It also includes precise curriculum development, powerful ways to assess learning formatively, and the importance of professional collaboration among teachers. Mary discovered that the New Learning Infrastructure includes many parts not previously taught in teacher education or professional practice.

3

Trust, Respect, and Attention to Detail

In her teacher education program Mary Chapman understood what it takes to build a New Learning Infrastructure. Anything created to support surface functions must be trusted.

Trust comes from people who respect those who build and maintain the infrastructure. For bridges, respect is based on a knowledge that highly competent architects, engineers, and skilled workers make something substantive, safe, and enduring—with great attention to detail. For schools in the New Learning Infrastructure, trust and respect go to the teachers. In this reinvented education system, they also practice attention to detail.

Mary's introduction to this principle showed her the importance of mastery learning and being able to articulate what it means in concrete and holistic terms, "concrete" in connection with specificity, "holistic" in the context of learning as multifaceted and interconnected brain functions. Defining mastery is just the beginning. While essential, it rests on the big picture. The *real* work begins with the professional discipline to achieve that big picture—no detail overlooked, no mistakes tolerated.

Mary now moves into curriculum content and design, researched and written in usable and measurable ways in every classroom, encouraging quality student performance and sequenced through the grades to achieve learning continuity, fulfilling the quest for student mastery. An important aspect of building curriculum meant that Mary worked closely with colleagues, a necessary skill to achieve the continuity of student mastery.

The meaning of attention to detail

Mary's preparation for teaching was built on trusting and respecting her professors and associates, understanding the imperative that anything lasting and substantial became that way because its construction was precise and detailed. Mary learned to create curriculum and instructional programs based on precision.

Mary's story continues:

Our professors told us that mastery is the top of a locally developed curriculum pyramid. A mastery statement describes a specific definition of what students are to know, do, and become after graduation from the school district.

Each subject area and grade level builds blocks toward the achievement of the final set of expectations with separate mastery statements for each subject area and grade. For example, I teach seventh-grade science. My first task consists of collaboration with all others who teach science in every grade. We establish a mastery designation that aligns with the general district statement *and* the study of science as a discipline.

Mastery statements establish what my students are expected to know, do, and become after completing the full subject area program, as well as each academic year. Grade-level statements must be identical across the district.

When compared to science mastery statements in sixth and eighth grades, the seventh-grade statement needs to show a logical connection. I reinforce sixth-grade learning in my grade, and the eighth-grade teachers reinforce what I teach in seventh grade. Curriculum experts call this process *sequencing* or *spiraling*. Schools and districts have long depended on the services of commercial publishers to develop what they called scope-and-sequence charts or blank templates, sometimes referred to as curriculum maps or mapping.

Mastery is a function of curriculum content and design. It may not be detailed in terms of covered content, but it paints a broad picture of the kind of human beings we ideally want our "grade completers" and graduates to be. A mastery statement encompasses past public school experiences. We research all ideas about what a truly educated person should be and include those ideas in our statement. We capture a holistic and current real-life essence in the statement. Check out what we created:

Students completing the full program of studies at XYZ School District will demonstrate skills that expand their understanding of reality. They will continuously express a deeper understanding of themselves and how they fit into the world. They will solve complex problems, think and act creatively, and manage their own needs responsibly.

Graduates will explain and act on principles associated with entrepreneurship, the ability to become lifelong learners through knowing how to learn and being motivated to do so.

They will use curiosity to stretch boundaries into new and different realms and reveal an inherent drive to learn continuously, to ask good questions, and become part of diverse communities with vigorous and stimulating feedback.

They will demonstrate and articulate the importance of self-confidence, gained through experience with widening groups, taking meaningful initiatives (reaching out), and accepting and acting on consistent encouragement from respected associates.

Each day students and graduates will practice mindfulness in terms of clarifying priorities and actions. They will exhibit openness and acceptance of others from different backgrounds. They will articulate and work to achieve self-discipline and personal values. They will create and maintain the convictions to pursue these values.

Students participating in and completing the full program of studies at XYZ School District will speak and write effectively. They will make people feel at ease, those from every walk of life. Students and graduates will enter conversations with others and show genuine interest in their ideas and activities.

While each academic discipline is important, graduates will grasp the idea that problem-solving is associated with a complex and interactive system. Solving problems requires collaborative skills that allow all disciplines to work in concert. Students and graduates will exercise and respect the meaning of intellectual passion, a passion not simply for attaining more knowledge but also for comprehending its significance and value. They will communicate expressively both orally and in writing, demonstrating that life is more than a single dimension but an assortment of experiences that make it worth living.

After we finished and proofed the mastery statement for our fictitious school district, its substance and tone stunned us. Then reality hit. What school district, board of education, administrative staff, patrons, or parents of students would understand and dare to accept our mastery statement?

The challenge of creating a mastery statement for a full science program and each year's course felt personally daunting. Where in that simulated district mastery statement would the discipline of science fit for my seventh grade? As I slowly read the simulated district statement, certain words and phrases popped out. All these points made my subject much more than the procedural "scientific method"—

- Problem-solving
- Inventing new solutions to human problems
- Maintaining a sense of wonder and interest in new ideas
- Working closely with others to discover new worlds on the earth and beyond

Middle school kids are fascinated in themselves, the changes they experience in their bodies and minds. Biologically, what makes them become who they will someday be? How do the biographies of others link to how they feel as preteens and teens? What intellectual passion captured those people and how did it happen? How can it happen to them?

Biology, geology, physics, geography, anthropology, and all other facets of life on earth need further exploration. They need collaborating with others who share that kind of personal excitement for the greater good.

Even before we created our simulated science mastery statement, I decided that my middle school mastery statement needed a biographical focus to enable my students to project themselves into an imagined future in all facets of science to include environmental concerns and a deep dive into skills needed to make a difference for both ordinary people and our nation's economy.

In my imagined course I used field trips, role play, panel discussions, and debate. We built connections with adults in careers associated with scientific discovery and social improvement. My biggest challenge was to make the imagined mastery statement fit the time or instructional circumstances involved. Little did I realize my task would be impacted by a worldwide virus, which turned out to be both a liability and an opportunity.

When I left the university and taught virtually, it was tough. But with science front and center in the news every day, its importance now and in the future could not be more dramatic—essential for twelve-year-old kids as they considered their future adult roles.

• • • ● • • •

Dedication

At first Mary Chapman understood little of the scope of mastery statements. Her dedication to becoming a teacher underscored her enjoyment of young people and learning. She was committed to helping others learn. Her own experiences with school remained positive with memories created by inspirational teachers or activities.

In her third year of college Mary enrolled in professional teacher education courses, where the professors in her program introduced a New Learning Infrastructure. Mary took risks as a participant in the creation of a new kind of enhanced learning milieu. The New Learning Infrastructure focused on student mastery but also debated three vital questions: (1) Mastery of *what*? (2) *How* is mastery officially met? (3) *Who* would make that decision and be held accountable for doing so?

The New Learning Infrastructure placed responsibility for answering all those questions on teachers, individually and collectively. Updated teacher preparation underscored attention to detail as never before, substantively not just tinkering with the existing system. Mary's professors did not mince words about how this change would happen.

First, college courses must change. Professors introduced change to the best of their abilities.

Second, field internships must align with the content of those courses, finding partner school districts that accepted principles adopted by the university's preparation program and actively supported them.

Third, a school district that hired Mary must have a decision-making and action-taking system that aligned with the goals of her college preparation program.

That scenario and sequence of events would fortunately occur with Mary, but mostly for serendipitous reasons that need to become universally intentional for Mary's story to become indicative of what happens everywhere.

Attention to detail begins with good wordsmithing.

Precision of expression in the form of writing is critical. Mary, like most of us, learned the wordsmithing skill through trial, error, critique from others, and creating actions based on what was printed. Often the original conception as expressed in words and phrases needed changing, and those changes made better actions possible.

Mary's story continues:

Our teacher education professors grouped us again, this time in terms of a particular subject. Four of us selected science, with the task to create a simulated science mastery statement for a fictitious district in two ways: draw key words and phrases from the fictitious general mastery statement and then find other good examples.

We decided to use the excellent material produced by International Baccalaureate (IB), which uses words and phrases such as *curiosity, conceptual understanding,* and *inquiry*. It stresses the following:

- Investigation and evaluation of scientific evidence to draw conclusions
- Accurate communication of scientific ideas, arguments, and practical experiences
- Analytical, critical, and creative thinking used to solve problems
- Linking scientific knowledge to technological development
- Understanding the interdependence of science, technology, and society

We examined ideas associated with STEM: science, technology, engineering, and mathematics. But we used them in the framework already established by the other considerations.

We included all those areas of concentration in our science mastery statement for the imaginary XYZ School District. Our professors drilled us to ensure we understood and were committed to the points in both the general and subject area mastery statements:

- Attention to detail
- More attention to detail
- Never letting up
- Restating, defining, giving examples
- Making us more than teachers who taught science, but almost science itself

When it came time to write my simulated course mastery statement, I pitched the ideas to my fellow students and professors. I needed to convince my peers and instructors that a biographical approach was correct for a middle school grade. My argument came from extensive research on middle school students' need to explore their world and their developing interests and abilities. I addressed district and subject mastery statements to more than simply lecture students about great scientists and how they got that way.

My students would learn to think like those scientists, with introspection through role play, simulations, and use of debate to make my students feel science and what it means, utilizing rigor, accuracy, intensity, patience, and ongoing determination with transformative exercises.

The old ideas of teaching as lecture, discussion, participation in activities, a little group work, and other traditional methods are not replaced—but dramatically embellished to challenge students to think and grow as never before, never to threaten them but to appreciate the efforts of students who struggle and give them additional opportunities.

As my university courses continued, we learned a mantra that stays with me to this day: "Design down and deliver up."

In the physical world, buildings and bridges are meticulously designed. Elaborate plans are sent down to engineers and crafts-people, who deliver up in terms of making designs reality. Both the design and the effort to transform it into reality must give attention to the smallest details.

In school districts, subject area and grade level mastery state-ments are worthless if there is no process in place for "delivering up." The difficult collaborative process challenged us to create those statements and make sure they had an impact.

One of our professors loved talking about the American Constitution as an exquisitely written document, fundamental to our democracy and freedom. Yet for over 234 years we still argue about the meaning of its principles and provisions. The Constitution designs down well enough, but the delivering up gets bogged down by opinions, attitudes, prejudices, and all other foibles human beings carry around. To control that phenomenon, we pass laws and procedures. Though not always perfect, they make the Constitution work.

In schools, curriculum and instructional design are what make mastery statements work. Since my grade already aligned a well-defined science mastery statement, all I needed to do was create a curriculum and instructional process that fulfilled the grade-level statement in science. But how? By doing the same thing designers and builders do. Start with a plan based on an idea of what constitutes excellence—student mastery. Then write down that plan piece by piece, making sure everything includes a result we can be proud of.

We used chunking to break down our grade-level statements. First we needed a statement to "chunk" from, the district's science mastery statement. Based on research and discussion, my teacher preparation classroom created the following:

XYZ District Mastery Statement for Science

Students will explain how scientific investigation is conducted, describe each step in the process, and demonstrate how it is done in various components of science, such as biology, botany, geology, physics, anthropology, chemistry, and others.

They will explain and demonstrate how scientists evaluate findings by using the scientific method and draw conclusions from evidence. Students will use scientific terms and data to communicate ideas, argue in favor of a particular conclusion, and prove the practicality of those observations.

They will define systematic analysis and demonstrate its strategies by solving problems using critical and creative thinking. Students will explain and demonstrate the relationship between and among pure and applied science and technological applications. They will depict the interdependence of science, technology, and society, using multiple examples from the past and present.

• • • ● • • •

At first blush, the words in our mastery statement sounded wonderful to us. But translating those words and phrases into reality seemed like an intimidating charge to novices and even more seasoned teachers. These ideas needed both input actions (the teaching act) and the formative (ongoing) assessment process. The last sentence alone was a challenge for both students and teachers to assess on a regular basis.

Thus begins the detailed work of creating the New Learning Infrastructure, with the dedication of young teacher novices who think deeply and remain dedicated to professional growth, who understand that the use of words is not to be taken lightly.

Words and Wordsmithing

Words and wordsmithing are the tools and skills necessary to design mastery statements and a curriculum that ensures quality teaching and learning. People not well acquainted with vocabulary and how words can be strung together to stimulate action might not understand mastery statements and their intentions. Mary's professors and Mary herself recognized the challenge. Some of her fellow students struggled with the necessary verbal complexity.

Our twenty-first century struggles with wordsmithing. The dominance of mass and social media reduces almost everything to sound bites and emotionally charged phrases. Commercialism and marketing ploys glorify simple descriptors and even outrageous remarks. Nuance is dominated by an either/or type of thinking and acting.

Reflection, as a necessary way to improve the quality of human life, is considered by some to be a waste of time and effort, which makes it even more difficult to institute a New Learning Infrastructure. But we persevere because we must, to improve the quality of schools and schooling.

4

Design Down and Deliver Up

Mary's next task is to create a mastery statement for the simulated middle school science class she identified. It must align with the district and subject area mastery statements. To create that alignment, she must examine words and phrases: content fields, nouns, adjectives, and especially strong verbs.

Special attention must be given to Bloom's taxonomy because it ranks learning bottom up, from remembering things to understanding something about them, applying them to real life, analyzing their effectiveness, evaluating their worth, and creating something better from what was learned earlier.

Creativity sits on top because our century expects it. Creative people succeed and live well. They imagine, improve, and upgrade. Yet today's school programs still concentrate on remembering and understanding. COVID-19 made that condition abundantly clear, because creative people danced around the status quo and found ways to survive.

Doing what you say you will do.

Mary discovers that flowery and powerful words and phrases are valuable only when they depict reality: past, present, and future.

We again join Mary as she learns how to design down from comprehensive mastery statements to mastery statements she must use for her own course.

My idea set up a middle school science program based on the biography of scientists and included characteristics instructive to my students. Classroom strategies included role play, simulations, debate, and other interactive techniques to help my students feel what science is and who scientists are.

At the end of the year I wanted them to know that scientific means rigor, accuracy, intensity, patience, and ongoing determination. The starting point examined the fictitious district's mastery statement for science. I pulled out a few key words and phrases:

- Steps in a scientific investigation
- Techniques for evaluating findings using the *scientific* method
- How a scientist gets to the point of drawing conclusions
- Processes used by scientists to prove their conclusions are practical
- Analytical thinking done systematically through problem-solving
- Defining and using critical and creative thinking
- Explaining and demonstrating the relationship among pure science and applied science
- Explaining the relationship between science and technological applications
- Depicting the interdependence of science, technology, and social needs

As I reflected on those key elements in the district's science mastery statement, I attempted to frame them in a biographical context. The Oxford Dictionary defines the term *scientist* as "a person who is studying or has expert knowledge in one or more of the natural or physical sciences." Scientists are usually thought of as being expert researchers. They speak and write about their work, because what they learn in the research must be shared with, examined, and evaluated by other scientists in a peer review. The findings of one scientist are always subject to the critical analysis of other scientists. Some scientists use their time and financial backing to think about and research whatever comes to mind. Others are given a task, such as finding a vaccine to prevent COVID-19. They concentrate their attention on that one goal.

History's most famous scientists were those who, through experimentation and deep reflection, came up with theories that changed human life directly or indirectly. Their stories ranged from heroic to tragic, but buried in those stories was the drive to make a difference in their time on earth.

I focused on that *making a difference* goal to keep attacking ways all of us think and act as scientists, whether we assume that mantle or not. The subtitle for my simulated middle school course was "People Who Think and Act like Scientists Make a Difference." My proposed mastery statement follows.

Students will—

- Define science as a scholarly activity and explain how it is the best way to study.
- Explain and demonstrate how quality research is conducted.
- Describe each research technique in terms of why it is important.
- Select two famous scientists from history and explain why they were chosen.
- Relate those scientists' stories in terms of what motivated them.
- Choose a vocational pursuit scientists might follow as adults and explain why.

- Defend conclusions made by one prominent scientist from today or in history.
- Create and present an argument for how a particular scientific finding can improve technology or the quality of life.

Each of us presented and defended our course mastery statement in several ways:

- Student readiness. Alignment with both the general and subject-area mastery statements
- Logical spiraling considerations with other grade levels
- Scope in the context of time allotments and instructional configurations
- Examples of curricular components
- Preliminary ideas of what and how student assessment would be conducted to ensure mastery
- The kind of evidence accumulated to prove student mastery at an acceptable level

The answers I gave in my oral defense had to square with action verbs in each sentence, as well as adequately address the content field. Coverage of Bloom's taxonomy was also important, especially in consideration of how well the course attended to the top four goals: applying, analyzing, evaluating, and creating. Those verbs need not appear in the mastery statement itself, but the actions they called for needed to be inherent to the instructional program. Most of all, elements of the mastery statement must follow the intent of the course theme: scientists making a difference.

The critique from my professors and fellow students said I did not thoroughly think through two problems. The first problem was "spiraling" in concert with previous and subsequent grade levels, which everyone admitted was difficult in a simulation. In a district a subject area committee would resolve what gets taught and where, what gets introduced and reinforced.

The second problem was that "scope" might be too "pie in the sky." Discounting new problems associated with virtual instruction, typical school year contact time with middle-level students equals a total of 165 clock hours—or fewer, exclusive of homework time.

How could I cram everything in my mastery statement into that timeframe if I had an average of twenty-five students in each class, especially if my "mastery" expectations were so high?

Some of the elements of the mastery statement should be moved to another grade or dropped altogether, especially those that failed to speak directly to my theme of "People Who Think and Act like Scientists Make a Difference." This project differed from what happens in most teacher education programs, in the context of depth and intensity.

My professors candidly spoke to the reasons that many teacher preparation programs fail to include this kind of intense training. Some professors are not acquainted with the process themselves. Governmental regulations in some states do not allow universities to require more than the minimum number of semester hours in professional preparation. Education deans in many states are hamstrung by legislatures and state boards of education with powerful people who assert their belief that teachers need only a strong subject area background. Such thinking hinders what my professors call the New Learning Infrastructure.

The Design-Down and Deliver-Up Mindset: Taking Mastery Seriously

The expertise of those who perform essential and valued work in society is never thought of as mediocre. These are the people we depend on for our health, safety, and well-being: medical doctors, commercial pilots, cruise ship captains, and others.

We assume they all learned a mastery equated with exemplary performance, a mastery so pervasive it carries into their ongoing professional work. Sometimes we pay a heavy price for misplaced trust. Agencies attempt to regulate that possibility through accreditation, certification, licensing, managerial oversight, inspections, testing, and a myriad of other ways to ensure authentic mastery.

But nothing is better than exceptionality as recognized by learners and the people who hire them, by clients, patients, and students; by subordinates, colleagues, associates, and protégés known intuitively by the contributions they make every day. They are recognized as being conscientious, mindful of others, carefully analytical, and almost sagaciously accurate.

True mastery, as a teacher or student, is achieved via both emotional and intellectual engagement. People who master something care about it. They hone their skills for the purpose of becoming more precise and accountable. What they do means something. It is not simply a job or hobby, never just going through "the motions." They are fully engrossed and fascinated, and they constantly try to do better. Those kinds of teachers support the New Learning Infrastructure as the way of inspiring their students.

The adage "Good teachers are born, not made" is nonsense. Human beings contain the capacity to be both good learners *and* teachers. With few exceptions, nurture is capable of overcoming nature, depending on the quality of the "nurture." The quality of nurture depends on caring, determination, and precision in how the academic environment is developed and maintained over time. Making intentional mastery statements into a program of studies that inspires and uplifts students is the next step, creating a curriculum and instructional process that is precise and sensitive, as well as accurate and stimulating.

Defending what one creates can result in clarity and real improvements.

Mary discovered that curriculum-building and instructional design can be improved through vigorous critique given by others. Creating dynamic teaching teams in every school is essential to the success of the New Learning Infrastructure.

Mary's story continues:

The intense process of creating and defending a grade-level mastery statement in science was one of the most difficult things I have done. Criticism by my professors and fellow students was hard to take, but it began changing me.

Working through the introspection and agonizing how to overcome shortcomings was no fun. Oddly, though, I began seeing through my dismay and realized a potential never felt before. Something about the discomfort I experienced uncovered much about myself. My professors and fellow students did not threaten me. They told me I could meet this challenge and do it better.

Isn't that real learning? It's being pinned to the wall by criticism and coming out of the experience stronger and smarter, more resilient and more willing to take future chances and grow from them.

My fellow students were forced to go through the same drill as I professionally criticized their mastery statements in math, language arts, social studies, and others. We all began to understand that school is not just about discrete subjects. All subjects, when considered holistically, become part of each other. Science needs language arts, math needs social studies—and beyond.

In the real world everything intertwines and is mutually inclusive. School represents just one way to make our society better. We teachers help our students to be open to new ideas. We inspire them to become significant contributors.

We finally finished work on the mastery statements at the district level for each major subject and for our course/grade levels. But our professors said, "These mastery statements were just the beginning. Now you must take 'design down and deliver up' seriously."

My primary goal integrated with similar goals in grades before and after mine, a biographical focus with the goal of causing students to believe that people who think and act like scientists make a difference. The defense of my statement jolted me into a serious reality. The most significant related to scope.

One of those who attacked my statement said he counted eight parts of my course, all of which needed to be taught and learned to mastery. That fellow student and others asked me to describe what mastery looked like for each of the eight elements listed.

"Just tell us what you are looking for in the first one. It has two verbs you will measure—a student's ability to 'define' and 'explain.'"

I said, "The 'define' gets into what scholarship is."

"Okay. What is scholarship?"

I fumbled around a little but finally came up with 'systematic study.' Not good enough.

This was getting ugly. I said, "Scientists develop and test hypotheses."

"What is a hypothesis and why is its use the best way to study?"

Geesh! "A hypothesis is an educated guess. An educated guess is a theory derived from reading and earlier experiments, a kind of pre-research type of research."

That satisfied him for a minute or two.

Then another student asked about my "explain" part. "Why is that the best way to study?"

I felt ready for that one. "Just reading or listening to garner knowledge does not engage the brain. New information does not connect to anything that already resides there, as with the adage 'Learning does not occur if answers are provided for which there are no questions.' The development of a hypothesis must come from an intellectual itch that must be scratched. For example, What caused the Civil War? What motivated Thoreau to write *Walden*? Why is a knowledge of algebra important in statistical analysis?"

The second student asked more serious questions. "What does that piece of the course have to do with the idea that scientists make a difference?"

Easy. "Because they speak and write about their work, their findings. They interact with others who want or need to know, something all of us should be willing to do, usually on a smaller stage."

Then came the zinger: "Let's say your students respond to your insistence that they define and explain, and they can do that both orally and in writing. How much classroom or virtual instruction time will that take for twenty-five students in a class? How will you know every student has mastered that element of the statement?

"Will mastery entail just quick and simple answers? Or will it necessitate students giving examples from history or real life? Will you ask them how that new knowledge will be used by them in the future? And how much of the 165-clock-hour pie (in a standard or virtual classroom) will that require if you have twenty-five students in the class? Five hours? Ten? And what are your thoughts about how skills learned in that first element of the course should be reinforced throughout the remainder of the school year?"

His pickiness annoyed me at first, but I later learned how important it was to answer those questions. The devil is in the details. All those questions and more would need to be answered to create the curriculum and instructional designs.

There were times I wanted to scream, "This is just school, guys, not a PhD program!"

But our professors steered us away from those feelings. "The New Learning Infrastructure is no longer just school. We're no longer introducing stuff you'll forget later or material you feel is unimportant."

In later years COVID-19 caused all of us to be more sensitive to that principle. Even those of us not directly involved with science could understand how its practice, and our sensitivity to it, improved or saved lives.

With those confrontations behind me and what I learned from them, I felt ready to get serious about the "design down and deliver up" part—the curriculum.

* * * ● * * *

Mary began understanding that the expansion of academic insights does not occur in a single dimension or cognitive universe. It is relational and *always* subject to justification. Everything in the curriculum must be justifiable for students ("Why do we have to learn this stuff?"), colleagues, parents of students, and community patrons—and especially to those who will someday depend on these students to become adults with responsibilities for serving our world.

5

Curricular Precision with Tools, Skills, Accountability, Quality

Designing down in creating curriculum requires "chunking" to break apart the mastery statements. Chunking starts with disassembling the district's general mastery statement into mastery statements for each subject.

Mary used the word *chunking* instead of *deconstruct*, because when national standards were popular, they used the term *deconstruct*. While external standards have value, they are *not* a starting place for the New Learning Infrastructure. Government attempted to micromanage curriculum through external subject area standards.

The New Learning Infrastructure considers external standards later in the developmental process, mostly as a litmus test, a check to see any miscues in the internal development of mastery statements and the curriculum they engender.

Proof of alignment in the New Learning Infrastructure involves thorough examination of words, phrases, subliminal meanings, and connotations. The study of science is not in a domain by itself. It crosses over into other intentions for student learning, and vice versa, because the study of science is dependent on language, social needs and wants, mathematical analysis, and other skills.

The district's science mastery statement is chunked into course/grade-level mastery statements, as with the one Mary Chapman created in her teacher education program, then defended to the point of exasperation. Although frustrating, that experience taught Mary the importance of giving attention to detail.

Giving attention to detail does not stop there. The curriculum for Mary's course contains three elements:

1. The course mastery statement
2. Unit outcomes that spell out in greater detail each element of the mastery statement
3. Components that break down the unit outcome into teachable and learnable pieces established for each period of instruction

A "period of instruction" may be one on-site class fifty-five minutes long, up to four or five such classes, or virtual contact with students via Zoom or another platform. The use of components communicates with students where that program of studies heads and what is expected of them. Unit outcomes and their components present the best evidence for a precise curriculum. Preeminent tools used by teachers focus on measurable student knowledge areas and skills.

Curricular precision is the opposite of subject area coverage.

Mary learned the opposite way from how colleges and schools have functioned for decades, how the instructor's job provided information and stimulated thinking from the front of the classroom, then expected students to replicate that content to a certain level of proficiency on examinations. Some students would not meet the expectation and therefore failed or performed below expectations. Curricular precision reveals its importance when delivered and when received by students. The New Learning Infrastructure offers no wiggle room.

Mary's story continues:

> After our professors taught us the intricacies of creating mastery statements at the district, subject area, and course levels, we worked on curriculum development. Demands were just as stringent to accomplish that task. Because of the allegiance to the design-down and deliver-up principle, the mastery links looked like the following:

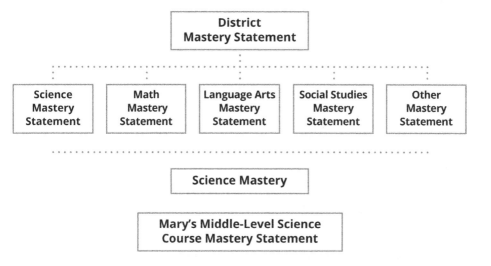

My professors said the next step in design-down expanded on the course mastery statement in ways it could be taught—piece by piece. Over the timespan allocated in course scheduling, we divided the pieces into unit outcomes and components.

At first I failed to understand the logic behind it. So I asked my professors, "Why can't we just list the areas of learning indicated in the mastery statement and teach those elements one after the other?"

"Ignoring the interchangeable and interactive aspects of Bloom's taxonomy would keep everything at the remembering and understanding levels. In other words, the first element of the course mastery statement that calls for students to 'define' and 'explain' can be covered and assessed in thirty minutes."

As I learned when defending a portion of my course mastery statement, the New Learning Infrastructure involves more than "covering" basics. While the verbs *define* and *explain* fall into the mere understanding level of Bloom's taxonomy, the content fields become much more substantive.

The two content fields answer these two questions: Why should we think of science as a scholarly activity? Why is the use of the scientific method the best way to study?

The professors said, "The unit outcome should be written using as many categories in Bloom's taxonomy as possible."

So I developed the following:

Unit Outcome Number One: Students will **define** science as a scholarly activity by **describing** its emphasis on acquiring background or contextual information, **using** that information to **formulate** reasonable theories, **creating** hypotheses based on those theories, and **conducting** experiments to either **support** or discard a **hypothesis**. Students will **extrapolate** from those techniques a way to study any subject, **explain** why it is effective, and **create** an example of how new information is better remembered when associated with past learning.

The unit outcome provides an overview of the complete intention for student learning. It connects all elements in ways that show how they are contiguous and mutually necessary. Components align with the overview unit outcome and are designed to ensure learning over time with a full understanding of the unit outcome's goals. Once components are learned, the students will be assessed formatively over the entire unit outcome.

Components:
- Identify and list types of background and contextual information useful in scholarly inquiry.
- Explain and demonstrate how someone uses such information to create a theory.
- Define *hypothesis* as something coming from a theory and give an example.
- Demonstrate how a hypothesis can be tested using a simple scientific experiment.

- Demonstrate how background knowledge, theory development, and hypothesis testing can be used in the study of any subject.
- Explain how that activity stimulates better retention of new learning using one or more examples.

After completing this exercise, our professors arranged an opportunity for us to work with teachers and classrooms in the local school district. I was assigned to a seventh-grade science classroom for an orientation conference. The teacher, Celia Johnson, and I discussed our collaboration.

Insights from Celia Johnson

Celia previously worked with my professors and knew what to expect when I arrived. We discussed my university professional development courses, how they are different than most teacher education processes in the past. She understood the New Learning Infrastructure strategies and why they are important for the future of education.

Celia asked, "How do you feel about the process so far?"

"It was interesting but a bit perplexing. The logic behind setting up mastery statements made sense but sometimes seemed overdone. Also, coming up with a curriculum aligned with every nuance and possible dimension of a topic or subject seemed excessive. I wish the whole thing could be more straightforward."

"I understand. I've experienced that challenge myself. That kind of activity is not like our day-to-day lives and how we communicate."

Both of us were familiar with tweets, texting, emotionally charged entertainment, jargon-filled conversation, the flood of acronyms, and media that offered simple answers to complex questions. The real world constitutes a barrage on the senses, little of it meant to stimulate contemplation, reflection, or an exploration of meaning. Neither Celia nor I place a moralistic or religious mantle on twenty-first-century life, but we accept the idea that human beings deserve more and can become more.

Devising unit outcomes and components that have depth and meet criteria given us by Bloom's taxonomy felt like an exhaustive process. Just writing Unit Outcome Number One took two hours with subsequent rewrites. The same was true with preparing its components.

Celia laughed. "I've been there!"

Both of us felt queasy. Our mastery statements seemed too abstract—too full of big words and run-on sentences for middle school kids to understand. I wanted to tone down the course mastery statement, unit outcome, and components to simpler and more direct language, but my professor would not allow it.

Celia understood. How in the world could seventh-grade students, traversing from childhood to adulthood, get their heads around a word like *hypothesis*?

We reminisced about our own middle school days. Bored with official seventh- and eighth-grade material, back them we mastered big words and complex ideas while immersed in the Harry Potter books. Classroom activities seemed more like repetitive indoctrination into basic stuff, a rehash of topics already covered in kindergarten through sixth grade.

Maybe the New Learning Infrastructure made sense for improving twenty-first-century living. Celia had come to believe it, and I was starting to get the message.

Teacher Accountability: A Function of Academic Conviction, Depth, and Purpose

Mary Chapman felt both fascinated and frustrated with the New Learning Infrastructure's teacher preparation—too many moving parts and complexities, both seemingly unnecessary in the technology-infused world of the twenty-first century.

Mary remembered watching 1930s biopics that depicted early-day inventors, scientists, change-agent politicians, intrepid explorers, and other societal mavericks. These rogues worked against the grain yet ultimately came out on top. They thought deeply, experimented regularly, and risked much, usually for the betterment of society. Mary wondered where those people came from and how they became the way they were.

They possibly despaired about human suffering—disease, war, economic collapse, ignorance, hunger, social injustices, and a myriad of other problems. All of them seemed curious with an intellectual itch that needed scratching. Superficial or trivial thinking was not part of their persona.

Do people like that exist today? Occasionally television producers create a story about a man or woman making unbelievable contributions to humanity. Most of the time their stories are in the "life well lived" category, people who made remarkable contributions yet received no universal recognition until they died.

During the pandemic journalists acknowledged the sacrifices of health workers and others behind the scenes. But the difference between health care workers and teachers was striking. For the most part, health care workers executed their usual jobs but in a more intense and demanding way.

Teachers had to come up with all kinds of strategies to fit every imaginable platform for conducting instruction. Most teachers had to "wing it" with virtual instruction, primarily because they were not prepared to work outside the system's boundaries. Forced almost overnight to become semi-independent agents, they figured out how to work with students in a different reality.

Today's students possess the potential for absorbing and mulling over powerful ideas, connecting them to their perceptions of the world's challenges and opportunities and emerging as adults with insight and a sense of purpose. Teachers must be held fundamentally accountable for these goals. Yet the pandemic and low "trivial pursuit" learning expectations turned school into an uninspiring kind of drudgery for both students and teachers.

Conviction, depth, and purpose are the touchstones of accountability.

Mary learned how accountability to her students and academic discipline was not just doing what someone else expected. She learned to be a scholastic leader more than a transmitter of isolated facts. Her role emerged as someone who inspired and led through an honest conviction that what she taught had intellectual depth and behavioral purpose.

Mary continues with her story:

Celia told me that writing and implementing mastery statements, as well as unit outcomes and components, became easier over time. She felt her brain become more active every time she did the work as these tasks were not just "one-offs."

Once written, their active descriptors remained for years. Even better, they were available for others to see online, tweaked or radically changed whenever necessary. Colleagues, administrators, parents, and patrons saw them. Parents knew what was expected of their students, especially if teachers posted their instructional calendars or pacing guides. Teachers and parents partnered in the education of young people, whether taught in standard classrooms or virtually, and these descriptors could be debated to serve sources of accountability.

I felt bothered by all that openness. Could I trust parents to understand mastery statements, unit outcomes, and components? Some parents might find the language and structure mystifying.

"Celia, debating mastery statements, outcomes, and components is not something I want to do with some parents, then use them to hold me accountable. I don't think so."

Celia understood. "For twenty years we've been told accountability is determined by how well our students perform on standardized, high-stakes tests, a check for quality at various points on the academic assembly line to see if we employees are doing the job correctly.

"At first I accepted that idea of accountability, because it seemed logical, straightforward, and clear, a good way to compare the effectiveness of teachers, schools, districts, and even states. It was theoretically objective and therefore devoid of bias.

"But it came with an underlying suspicion that two other motives were in play. The first was that standards and tests could be developed by, or under the supervision of, political leaders suspicious of academic motives."

"Yikes! And the second motive?"

"That using test-generated data to compare schools and districts is an effective way to keep costs under control. Educational entities that do not meet expectations as reflected in data may be financially penalized."

Celia sighed. "Rigid micromanagement of education hamstrings the academic potential of both teachers and students. As much as experts in psychometrics claim otherwise, no written test can be one hundred percent valid *and* reliable. Nor can such tests measure the subtleties of the human brain as it evolves day after day.

"Competition between and among educational institutions is flawed, Mary, because no school or district controls the communities they serve. As our nation becomes increasingly diverse, poverty, the educational level of families, and other variables become harder to control. And it is ridiculous to financially penalize schools and districts that serve lower socioeconomic populations, unable to raise scores on high-stakes tests no matter what they do."

"Agreed."

The New Learning Infrastructure is based on mutual goals and ongoing dialogue, no matter how uncomfortable. Celia told me it works in her classroom, primarily because openness sparks and maintains trust while deepening scholastic inquiry and exploration.

Celia became convinced that the university's professors taught us well by instructing us to create our mastery statements, unit outcomes, and components. They forced us to present and defend them to others who needed convincing, those who questioned our motives, investigated the depth of our thinking, and tried to destroy our logic.

That gut-wrenching experience was a mild precursor to what might happen in an open house with parents, individually or collectively. Some parents and patrons might come with a bias I do not understand or cannot accept. If I become arbitrarily defensive, everything I want to achieve with my students might blow up in my face.

My job is to listen and respond the best way I know how and offer others an opportunity to express opinions. Compromise is not always the best solution, but when I draw the line, I do it with evidence, conviction, and with the obvious best interests of my students. If that is unacceptable, those who disagree approach other avenues of redress.

Does that sound volatile? Maybe, but Celia learned that everyone respects a teacher who demonstrates true concern and is articulate enough to express beliefs and convictions with respect and courtesy. Not everyone demonstrates those characteristics in the early years of his or her professional service. But if arduously prepared, we learn to find or develop a solid rationale for every point we make. I will certainly try!

· · · ● · · ·

Over seventy percent of teachers are young women. While attending public schools, they tended to be attentive and compliant, appreciative of their teachers and well-behaved. They grew up in middle-class homes with loving families. They love children and learning. Confrontation is rarely something they accept or live with. Conflict makes them feel vulnerable and unsettled, and they avoid engaging in that type of behavior.

But they learn and act on that learning. The New Learning Infrastructure asks us to do something alien to our nature, to what we thought teaching was. We do not merely write and use mastery statements, design down and deliver up, use effective unit outcomes and components.

We accept the challenge of becoming more professionally assertive than we believed possible. We overcome feelings of inadequacy and vulnerability in the face of change. We become a professional somebody, not "just" a teacher who performs mechanistically and compliantly.

6

Quality Learning Requires a Different Kind of Teaching Environment

The National Parent Teacher Association still exists as a viable organization. It has historically played a significant role in American schools. A similar group, the National Parent Teacher Organization, operates with a slightly different agenda. Both groups advocate partnerships that advance the *quality* of education. Most parents are supportive of elementary schools although that enthusiastic support dwindles in grades seven and eight. It diminishes even more at the high school level, but partnership and engagement are still needed. These groups exemplify the "bridge" metaphor. Infrastructure connections between teachers and families may weaken and need significant repair.

School reform efforts related to No Child Left Behind changed the partnership dynamic. Accountability shifted away from local interactions. Instead, they became a fulfillment of expectations set out by state and national governments or their proxies, appointed to create standards and high-stakes tests, one more reason the New Learning Infrastructure cannot be governmentally micromanaged. Partnerships at the local level remain critical, currently superseded by policies and regulations emanating from powerful agencies and state and federal decision-makers.

An even bigger problem exists as American teachers are ground down by overbearing bureaucracies, reduced to being pawns in the political and regulatory system, assembly line employees asked to promote mass mediocrity instead of learning quality. We must assist American teachers in overcoming feelings of inadequacy and vulnerability. Those feelings, already prevalent in our culture, have been exacerbated over the past twenty years by No Child Left Behind and dictates emanating from that era.

Consider a study of the Curriculum Leadership Institute's resource titled *The Teacher as Somebody: Skills that Make Teaching a True Profession.* This issue remains so fundamental that anything else done in the New Learning Infrastructure depends on how quickly we address and correct the problem.

Quality learning in an improved teaching environment.

Quality is difficult to define in exact terms. We know it when we see it. Quality things look good, do not break, and last a long time. Quality people are given that designation based on what the culture values. Quality learning endures in meaningful ways that upgrade human thinking and ways of behaving. Mary recognized that too many American students fail to achieve quality learning. They achieve certain skills and understandings that lead to little more than mediocrity. How to change that condition is becoming more important to this young teacher.

Let's join Mary again:

I graduated from the university in 2016 at age twenty-two after completing my unique preparation for teaching. The significance of its uniqueness became clear when I talked with my supervisor in the professional development school where I completed my field internship.

The No Child Left Behind mandate was instituted when I was a first-grader, so my indoctrination to NCLB thinking began before I knew anything different. Obviously, I knew little about how teachers complied with the new regulations, nor did I have any feelings about it. School was just school.

My parents recognized something new was going on with school improvement but did not question its effectiveness. Occasionally I heard them talking about incompetent teachers, how holding poor teachers accountable was a good thing. When I graduated from high school in 2012, I cared nothing about school reform and school accountability. I studied what I was told, took the required tests, and threw my mortarboard into the air at graduation.

My first two years of college seemed typical—okay classes, making friends, and participating in activities. I decided to pursue a teaching career in spite of the emphasis on women entering technical fields. Many girls in my sorority and classes were tempted, especially those demonstrating an aptitude for math. University officials told us jobs for women who entered engineering and other technical pursuits were ours for the asking, a carryover from the affirmative action days but much more than mere compliance with regulations. The idea of including women in jobs previously dominated by men seeped into the culture.

My purpose in life underscored how to help others in both academic and emotional realms with the crossover point of leadership. But I knew twenty-two-year-old female college graduates would not be hired to fill managerial roles, with one exception—the military.

The army encouraged young college women to participate in ROTC, with the promise of a commission as officers upon graduation. But the military way of life did not appeal to me. While a good career move, its fundamental purpose for existence bothered me. To serve and defend my country through violence? Not my forte!

The Peace Corps represented the flip side of time in the military, so I investigated that option. The service aspect appealed to me, but as with missionary work, only negligible long-term career benefits.

The mother of one of my classmates worked as an industrial trainer. Active in what was then known as the American Society for Training and Development, Beverly was also an accomplished speaker and workshop leader in the electronics industry. But I wanted to work with young people, not adults. As I listened to the story about Beverly's work, however, I gained a few insights. Prior to becoming an industrial trainer, Beverly worked as a specialist in the information technology (IT) field as an expert in website development. Her college background in math and electrical engineering proved invaluable in digital hardware and software work.

Over time, employers moved Beverly into training positions so she could offer others the benefit of her education and training. Unlike other "techies," Beverly turned out to be a gifted speaker and writer. Extremely well organized, she encouraged student involvement and effectively worked either on-site or virtually. Beverly's clients described her as a "personality with smarts." Follow-up evaluations of her work proved that she made a discernable difference in the effectiveness of her trainees. They applied her teachings in their own work with new applications showing up in terms of product quality.

When Beverly entered the field, American industry was still in the throes of Total Quality Management (TQM). As a spin-off movement, TQM was initiated by William Edwards Deming and operationalized in Japan after World War II. "The Deming Management Method" revolutionized industry by a powerful emphasis on methods to achieve quality.

Prior to Deming, American industry let itself slip into a kind of competitive hubris, which allowed mass production and marketing to become more important than quality of product and service. When that fallacy resulted in loss of profits, American industrialists started paying more attention to achieving quality constantly and profitably.

Beverly believed in Deming's philosophy. She convinced the profit-focused clients and employees she trained that nothing was more important than quality. Over the decades Deming's "quality" principles were vindicated. They seemed simple on the surface but offered considerable depth.

The New Learning Infrastructure parallels with the Deming Model. Substitute "quality of product and service" with "mastery learning" and the similarities are striking.

The similarities are seen in *how* mastery and quality of product and service are attained:

- Deming's "constancy of purpose" aligns with ongoing ways to govern an academic program.
- Deming's call to "cease dependence on external inspection and depend on making constant evaluations" aligns with the need to drop high-stakes tests and continually check for learning mastery.
- Deming's advocacy of "building employee leadership" aligns with giving teachers greater professional responsibility and authority.

What I learned about Beverly's work segued into my teacher education program. It opened my eyes to what I really wanted to be as a teacher—not someone who just goes through the motions with students but rather a leader who engages and inspires them to become more than simply what others expect in the way of minimal proficiency.

· · · ● · · ·

Overcoming Feelings of Inadequacy through the Pursuit of Quality Learning

Just as industry generates quality products and services, so quality and mastery learning result from mastery workmanship, not the result of assembly-line employees who routinely perform tasks as expected by supervisors, employees held accountable to meet a supervisor's expectations and penalized when the product fails to meet inspection criteria at a checkpoint. Functionaries, automatons, or human-like robots do only what they are programmed to do.

Nonhuman robots perform precise functions the way they are programmed, and some industries use them for that purpose. However, the best products are built by human experts using their hands and brains. The quality of a handmade Lamborghini far exceeds anything assembled on a typical automotive assembly line. The hands that built the Lamborghini from the wheels up belong to exceptional engineers and technicians who know what they are doing. They are committed to perfection of even the smallest detail.

Deming attempted to find a middle ground by devising an organizational model, creating teams of workers committed to quality and demanding the best of each other, who discussed quality and how it could be improved each day, who gave allegiance to quality because they hated to disappoint the team—or themselves.

Building quality children and young people is infinitely more complex than assembling a car or washing machine. It involves interpersonal and interactive connections so convoluted they defy ordinary logic. Good technicians intuitively solve problems, but nowhere nearly as intuitively as a good teacher. The technician solves a problem by using a different part, creating a better software program, or rethinking an entire mechanical system. The intuition that teachers use to solve a student's learning problem involves psychologically intricate and emotionally sensitive connections.

An instantaneous "aha" moment of clarity rarely happens. Building quality students takes time and patience, fits and starts, success and disappointments. Each victory is gained over time, filled with temporary failures and confusion. Measuring quality learning in a student never happens as a one-time thing established by a single test score. Quality is the result of an intermingling of mind and emotion from the teacher and the student.

The affective domain:

Mary is smart and insightful. Like many females, she knows that learning is not limited to factual knowledge or tangible abilities. As with all humans, not just women, feelings of inadequacy hinder motivation and effective behaviors. Bloom's cognitive domain does not use or imply the word "inspiration," but Mary discusses how a workshop leader revealed its importance in teaching and learning.

Mary continues to benefit from this insight:

One of the workshops in which I participated examined a frequently ignored piece of Bloom's taxonomy. When it comes to quality and mastery, Bloom's cognitive domain dominates as remembering, understanding, applying, analyzing, evaluating, and creating.

Two domains other than *cognitive* are *affective* and *psychomotor*, mostly ignored by educators. They classify learning differences attitudinally and physically, but their regular inclusion offers analysis overload.

The workshop leader, Evelyn, said the affective domain is important for student motivation. Attitudes play a huge role in how we receive and respond to phenomena, how we listen to and genuinely engage with others. We modify our viewpoints through deep interactions with individuals and groups. We allow ourselves to be positively motivated by diverse viewpoints. The affective domain includes how students feel about problem-solving, a skill most schools limit to tangibles such as math and science, using cognitive domain categories such as applying and analyzing.

But Evelyn said, "Problem-solving is as much emotional as rational."

The same is true of the ability called organization. We think of an organized person as being smart in the cognitive sense. But our priorities about organization bubble up from how we feel about managing our personal environment.

Problem-solving and organization are related abilities. They merge with cognitive skills such as applying, analyzing, evaluating, and creating. In some ways they resemble a reflective underlying catalyst introduced into a situation that changes its appearance or character. What is caused by the interaction of the emotive catalyst and logical thought operates in mysterious ways, manifested differently in different people.

Anything in the affective domain is an unpredictable variable that drives some people crazy. Derogatory terms like "touchy, feely" depict a behavior that depends too much on emotion or intuition. Some consider this behavior a weakness that debilitates and hinders a person's problem-solving and organizational skills. Conversely, "strong" individuals seem more straightforward, decisive, and clear-headed, with a kind of commanding presence. The word "analytical" connotes their response.

Human society crosses into a dangerous fallacy with the notion that only hard-as-nails personalities can be accurately decisive, making judgments using data-based and crystal-clear problem-solving and organizational skills. That thinking opens the door to opportunistic military, political, and business leaders revered by their followers for their toughness and self-assuredness—even when they prove to be blatantly wrong or demented.

Evelyn elaborated further on the importance of the affective domain. "It is the power of introspection and reflective thinking, not unbending dictates, that produces proposals for consideration and action—the willingness and ability to offer ideas suitable for molding that bring other people into the decision-making and action-taking orbit."

Evelyn served in the military and was also a historian. She used two World War II American generals as examples: Douglas MacArthur and Dwight Eisenhower. "MacArthur was egocentric and was convinced he could do no wrong. He considered his subordinates as members of his fiefdom, and those superior to him in constitutional rank as weaklings or lightweights. Any mistakes he made were never of his making but rather the result of subordinates or political leaders who made bad decisions.

"During World War II in his Australia-based headquarters, MacArthur spent more time devising winning strategies for West Point's football team than how armed forces in the Pacific campaign could avoid being slaughtered by the Japanese. Only his personal priorities mattered.

"Eisenhower was promoted to the rank of Supreme Commander of the Allied Forces in Europe because he sought and used the ideas of others in shaping strategy. He valued his subordinates and their opinions, not only for their cognitive knowledge but also because of their values and deep insights. Ike listened to all the members of his staff, which included military leaders from many nations. He considered their comments valuable. He accepted responsibility for making final decisions and followed through. Ike held to his own values with commitment, but he modified them as circumstances required."

Evelyn flipped through her papers. "Let's compare General Eisenhower with Bloom's taxonomy. In Bloom's affective domain, Eisenhower compared, related, and synthesized values, which allowed him to create a value system unique to the challenges ahead. He also created ethical standards to serve as guideposts for himself and others. Eisenhower led by example.

"The essence of accountability is not simply meeting the expectations of someone else. Accountability includes an external set of guidelines to be followed when and where feasible and appropriate but superseded by other proven values as conditions merit. Those values become visible when people demonstrate their commitment to discernably successful actions and beliefs, or to accept responsibility if those actions and beliefs somehow fail. Then they learn from those failures and do things differently. They make adjustments in the context of persistence—as in the adage 'If at first you don't succeed, try, try again.' That should be the measure of accountability for both teachers and students."

Evelyn shook her head. "Sadly, that is not the case in American education today. Fixed standards, high-stakes assessments, and other kinds of expectations prevail, thereby short-circuiting a real accountability for learning and becoming. Quality learning, in the context of mastery, involves the whole package from both the cognitive and affective domains, as with the teacher or student who continually says, 'Failure is not an option.'"

Evelyn smiled. "That's my favorite line from *Apollo 13*." Several in the workshop agreed. Failure indeed is not an option.

Evelyn concluded, "With few exceptions, most human beings begin life feeling inadequate. The culture in which we grow up either reinforces that view of ourselves or helps us overcome it. As a young woman, I wondered what it would be like to grow up and live in Saudi Arabia or in societies with similar value systems based on gender, race, personal preferences, religious beliefs, and other kinds of diversity.

"Even here in America during the twenty-first century, diversity continues to be a problem. While we women are better accepted in domains now more inclusive, microinequities still exist. Microinequities gnaw on us around the edges like an insidious, almost-transparent gas that hangs in the social atmosphere and seeps into our pores.

"The corporate world, governmental agencies—even churches—study and discuss microinequities. But they persist as odd prejudices that hang on and pervade attitudes, policies, regulations, laws, and day-to-day interactions. Microinequities bolster feelings of inadequacy, and those feelings degrade the possibility of achieving quality in learning and becoming—among both teachers and students."

• • • • • • • •

Mary reported what she learned in a workshop but believed it should regularly be addressed in all teacher education programs. Most teachers are women. Too many men in positions of authority disregard the importance of attitude about teaching and learning. In their opinion, subordinates, like civil servant teachers, do what they are told. They are held accountable for tangible learning results in their students. Such oversimplistic thinking degrades quality teaching and learning in our schools.

Can we finally recognize the problem and summon the courage to work against it?

7

Knowledge and Beliefs Translated into Real Public School Settings and Actions

ortunately, Mary received her preparation for teaching in a progressive
university program with high admissions requirements, and she
exceeded the standards. Her stable background and strong principles
associated with integrity made her a perfect candidate for acquiring
professional discipline. She devoted her life to service, building on the
youthful idealism of her students.

Mary believed learning should influence a student's lifetime as learning
happens in many settings, not just in school. She eagerly accepted the
idea that teaching is more than subjects and methods. It incorporates
belief systems as well. She also absorbed the notion that teaching was
more than conveying information gained from an outside source. Student
growth depended on *her* ongoing growth, academically and personally.

Intrigued with brain-based learning and all its ramifications, Mary saw
how these two offshoots needed professional discipline on her part. The
New Learning Infrastructure sounded vague until Mary was forced to
define what "mastery" means for a human being. She learned that mastery
is not a one-time thing measured by pencil-and-paper tests. Mastery
means a student fundamentally changes as evidenced by differences in
perspective and behavior. It requires soak time and reflection, discerned

by teachers only through evidence and intuitive observations over time—a formative or ongoing assessment.

Mary realized that she was taking a chance. Many school districts fail to structure learning by aligning their academic programs with mastery practices. "Design down and deliver up" needs to be executed carefully and precisely through well-written curricula and focused instructional formats. Words and wordsmithing in the New Learning Infrastructure are as important as any mathematical formula for ensuring precision and sought-for learning outcomes. Every word and phrase must imply meaning as the impetus for everything that happens in the academic program.

Mary understood how accountability was relevant to who and what teachers are. The word *quality* gave deeper meaning in that its achievement required hard work and the drive to constantly get better. Mary embraced the challenge of finding a school district compatible with her ideas and practices. She needed to locate a district with evidence that it used a collaborative academic governance system. The district also needed to prove to her its commitment to maintain an enlightened managerial policy, a clearly articulated long-range plan, and a full understanding of the mastery learning concept.

Mary also sought additional information about how the district created, implemented, maintained, and evaluated curriculum. She examined ways teachers designed planning documents and how well they aligned with curricular formats and content. Criteria for allowing a school district to benefit from her expertise remained stringent.

Compatible viewpoints and vision for teachers and the employing district.

Mary's search for a compatible district is critical. She has no intention of becoming a compliant civil servant dominated by regulations and administrative oversight. While not a maverick who resents authority, she understands the need for order and teamwork. But teamwork in Mary's world must be collaborative in order to draw upon the strengths of everyone involved, even "newbies." Mary's quest lies in programmatic quality, and she will not allow it to be short-circuited.

Her ideals were important to her and her continuing story.

A few months before graduation, I met Brad Miller on a blind date arranged by one of my friends. He was a young army officer raised in another state. We clicked, and the relationship grew, resulting in our marriage. Brad planned to teach after completing his army service, so we shared that goal.

But planning my search for a suitable school district became more complicated, because we both needed to find employment in the same area. After his discharge, Brad decided to work on a master's degree full time, so that helped us look for a good university in the area. That search increased my options for a teaching position.

People who specialize in job-finding often say we should interview our prospective employer. That practice gives a different mindset, because obtaining a teaching position is not simply an opportunity to make money and gain financial security. The school district operating under good motives and aspirations strives to do everything possible to make our professional goals possible.

I needed to find the personal and professional strength to be properly assertive, to find the answers to my questions. Would this district be a good "fit" for me, and would I be a good "fit" for the district? Some of my red flags included—

- Personnel officers who dominated the interview, thereby representing the district as a temple of correctness.
- Descriptions of certainty and strength, thereby expecting my compliance with that organizational culture. They might even talk about higher salaries, better working conditions, and benefits offered by their community.
- The importance of being a good "team" player, which can have both sinister and positive meanings—a "team player who complies with the rules" or conversely, "a team player who helps the team become stronger and more effective."
- Interviewers who lauded the magnificence of the institution mostly peddling "window dressing."

I looked for a personnel officer or administrator who responded to *my* questions, courteously interjecting questions about my ability and willingness to work within the district's culture. My task was to be polite, attentive, and professionally correct. That kind of dynamic interaction led to helpful conclusions on both sides of the table.

• • • • • • • •

School District Organization, Leadership, and New Teacher Professionalism

All job applicants research prospective employers ahead of time, and today the Internet reveals important information. Web pages and social media outlets reveal much about a district and its employees, both overtly and subliminally. How web pages are designed and what they include describes what the district considers important and where its priorities lie.

In her preliminary research into web pages, Mary looks for how well teachers are represented. What are their relationships with both the academic program and the students? How are decisions made in the district, and which policy documents outline processes for getting things done? Do they include links to policies, long-range plans, and definitions of student mastery? Are curriculum documents available on the website?

Does a link help parents substantively understand what students should know or do? In this age of COVID-19 and virtual instruction, connections with families remain as critical as efforts to upgrade hardware and software. What information does the district's website offer about those concerns?

Finally, what kind of response indicates an interview appointment? Will there be opportunities for the applicant to speak with teachers and other administrators? Will the applicant be allowed to inspect curriculum documents and other materials used to support teaching and learning?

New or seasoned teachers are professionals with beliefs and convictions.

Within Mary's thorough job search, she looks for more than money and benefits. She wants an educational organization that respects her talents and accepts her into their professionally viable team, a team dedicated to quality student learning emanating from engaged instructional settings.

During my last semester at the university, I participated in an intense job-hunting workshop. Most of us did not understand so much emphasis on finding teaching positions. Finding physical education and secondary social studies teaching jobs was a challenge, but special education and fields like physics remained competitive. My field was kind of in the middle.

The imbalance in those years came from too many or too few teacher education students majoring in particular fields. Working with special education students was known to be difficult, while those who majored in fields like physics found better-paying jobs in industry and government. Rural jobs were easier to find than those in suburbs or comfortable cities. Securing teaching jobs in areas with much cultural diversity prevailed over those in culturally homogeneous communities.

Compared to the difficulties brought about by a pandemic and nationwide cultural and political disruptions, the challenges of years ago seem almost quaint. But some still apply because past fault lines existing in the schools have now become chasms. Those chasms opened because most schools are still supported by a fragile infrastructure.

One of my professors told us that hierarchically structured organizations, even the military, become too dependent on charismatic or dogmatic leaders who are physically or emotionally distant from the people they lead. This professor served as an army officer. He said the best way to test the strength of any organization is to evaluate what happens when subordinates become separated from the larger unit—as when teachers are treated as subordinates who work behind classroom doors, or as during the pandemic, teachers are expected to guide learning via computer screens at home. In either case, they are as separated as anyone can get.

Therein lies the fault line or the chasm: the divide between people who view themselves as decision-makers and those seen as subordinates. My professor taught scenarios from his experience in the army in which lack of communication occured or operational unity was disrupted. That meant creating leadership deep into the organization, a leadership that continued to support the overall objective in the best possible ways.

I felt lucky to have received a state-of-the-art preparation for teaching, but I also wanted to locate a school district with forward-looking leadership who recognized the hazards of fault lines and chasms, who worked to close those separations through use of the New Learning Infrastructure, a model that enlarged the concept of leadership and the kind of unity brought about through a common cause.

Brad and I surfed through the Internet. We talked to key residents of the metropolitan area in which we lived. I followed suggestions offered at the university and screened out districts not meeting the appropriate criteria, dropping ninety percent of those we reviewed.

The remaining districts seemed to meet our criteria, but one stood out, with a link to every teacher in the district with pictures and information. Each included written comments on their goals for student learning and how they planned to meet them. Some talked about how they enjoyed working with teacher and administrative colleagues and ways they tried to maintain strong connections to each student's home.

That inclusionary feature alone seemed amazing! Even more amazing were the comments made by the superintendent, curriculum coordinator, and principals. Threaded throughout was the underscoring of commitments to collaborative decision-making, including links to academic program policies, long-range curriculum plans, and the district's philosophy as to what constitutes a well-rounded student.

Specific curriculum documents were password protected, accessed by the professional staff and parents/guardians. The prelude was written above the access point to express the district's strong dedication to working closely with every student's home, as well as the community at large. Woven through the statement was a beautifully written phrase defining the district's understanding of accountability. Was this too good to be true?

I applied immediately and secured a preliminary interview with the district's personnel director. During the interview they reviewed my baseline credentials and provided basic employment information. I spent three hours talking with others in the district, explaining my goals and expectations.

After arriving home, I received a schedule for the follow-up interview. It included teachers, administrators, a board member, the curriculum coordinator, and a couple of parents. While if felt overwhelming at first, Brad and I worked through my questions and created a possible scenario for what I might encounter.

• • • • • • •

The Welcoming Organization and the Novice Professional Teacher

Mary Chapman-Miller rejected ninety percent of the districts reviewed via web pages. Some emphasized only basic organizational structures. They gave lip service to their mission using a sentence or two. Others presented board members and an administrative staff with celebratory pictures of students involved in athletics. Test score rankings occupied center stage in some web pages, while others featured buildings. Links provided for academics usually focused on subjects and grade levels. Sometimes teachers' names or pictures appeared along with email addresses, but no substance.

Mary told Brad, "Most districts don't seem to have a soul. They're dehumanized agencies going through bureaucratic processes."

A school district's soul was important to Mary. She defined *soul* as an animated principle. The soul of the school district reveals who its people are, what they earnestly believe, and how they work together to achieve quality student learning.

Finally, Mary found a unique school district. Her interview experience included her search for the school district's soul.

An organization's "soul" reveals its ongoing belief systems, similar to a constitutionally run government.

Mary learned that many districts veered from one perspective to another based on their leadership. She also learned that overcoming the problem proved difficult because of governmental intervention, such as NCLB or state regulations.

Brad and I conducted a practice inquiry to ensure that my knowledge was thorough. We developed a set of incisive and probing questions with the focus on student learning: what student learning involves, how to stimulate it, and what the result should be.

Most of all, we were interested in how the district's policy remained stable over the years, thereby avoiding what my professors called TYNT: "this year's new thing."

An initial meeting was set up with the district's personnel director. During three hours of the second day, I met with other district employees, parents, students, and patrons. It was exhausting as well as exhilarating. The tenor of the two-part interview surprised me most as I felt my opinions mattered. My questions were not considered rude. Everyone eagerly responded and asked why I so vigorously pursued certain points.

They listened intently, and my answers often elicited lengthy discussions.

One startling aspect was how much everyone already knew about me. True, I wrote extensively about my beliefs and background as part of the application process. But these people had actually read and reflected on my words. I surprised them by knowing so much about the district, because its web page was complete and informative.

It was clear that my membership on their team would not be characterized by compliance but rather by a dynamic give-and-take. In this district, intellectual engagement mattered. These people were not just playing linguistic games. They immersed me in an inclusive interchange of ideas and possibilities.

When I told Brad about the experience, he said, "It sounds like my IT work with more creative thinking. The important outcome needs to be convergence."

Convergence in my husband's company represents a type of thinking outside each person's cubicle. Convergence in this district felt similar. Each teacher thought outside the walls of the classroom and subject matter to see the big picture in terms of student growth and becoming.

One of my older professors talked about the mid-twentieth century with a blossoming of "integrated curriculum." While many experiments occurred in elementary school self-contained class-rooms, middle and high schools also tried interdisciplinary team teaching. The movement picked up steam, especially in middle schools, until states began their push toward developing standards and high-stakes tests. But the final nail in the coffin was the imposition of No Child Left Behind in 2001.

Integrated curriculum was not designed to focus intensely on subject disciplines, the kind of knowledge students needed to pass high-stakes tests in specific subjects only. Scholastic rigor became the new mantra, discounting the importance of graduates connecting the dots between and among disciplines. A subject such as math, except for story problems, was treated in its purist application by any type of summative assessment—classroom-based or standardized. The only major iteration of that interdisciplinary approach today is found in STEM (science, technology, engineering, math) but limited to vocational/career applications, not broad-based integrated knowledge.

The word *convergence* does not refer to integrated curriculum or interdisciplinary instruction. Its meaning seems to be associated with two conditions: (1) the recognition that skills in one discipline can overlap another, such as math and economics, history and literature, science, and sociological changes; and (2) careful spiraling of curricular content from grade to grade.

An important sidebar definition of *convergence* is the relational side—how all stakeholders in the district think collaboratively. This convergence includes professional educators but also relationships with parents and guardians in student homes.

My perceptions and feelings about all those convergent topics were drawn out in depth. So my unique interview greatly influenced my thinking about the district, the programs, and its people.

· · · ● · · ·

Convergent Thinking and Solidarity in the New Learning Infrastructure

Mary's interview exceeded her expectations with professionally substantive topics and how she felt during the interview—not an emotional milieu but an overwhelming feeling of acceptance and oneness.

She remembered her father's enjoyment of the old TV series *A Band of Brothers*, the story of an army unit during World War II. The dynamics of the story paralleled the camaraderie he felt in the military. Mary studied camaraderie and found its synonyms to include *team spirit, fellowship,* and *companionship.*

But her emotion during the interview felt more like solidarity—not a solidarity as whimsy or "all for one and one for all." Convergence means more than agreement. Solidarity involves more than closely working together. Mutual effort, even in an interview process, will focus on one mission—quality student learning.

How can quality student learning defy easy definition? Because every student is different, an evolving human being—not something static or measurable at any given moment.

As Mary explained to Brad, "The interview made me feel like we were converged around a multi-part mission. Together we would accomplish the task by achieving a sense of solidarity."

Mary's reflection on solidarity through teaming flows back through history.

Experimentation with teaching teams is not new.

Mary learned that the one-time popular teaming of teachers was dropped soon after the implementation of NCLB. The intended outcomes of middle school interdisciplinary teams failed to align with standards and high-stakes tests. Intradisciplinary teaming at the high school level was also lost, because of locally established teaching/learning outcomes. Elementary self-contained schools may still use systemic collaboration with those who advocate professional learning communities—often effective at that grade level and beyond if their organization and purposes remain clear.

A friend of my family taught middle school language arts during the time when the middle school movement thrived in the 1980s. She served as part of an interdisciplinary team made up of other eighth-grade teachers and sometimes a counselor or parents.

The team met weekly. They talked about the progress being made by each student. While the primary focus was on academics, they also shared observations about behavior, emotional health, and other aspects of development. This weekly review underscored professional convergence and solidarity.

But by the end of the 1990s the middle school movement fell victim to the new national way of thinking: an emphasis on subject area standards, high-stakes testing, objective data collection, accountability processes based on those data, and comparative analyses of schools and districts. School districts could not revert to the old junior high configuration fast enough. Advocates of the middle school movement looked like misguided souls who had turned education into touchy-feely nonsense.

But clearly it was *not* nonsense. Its holistic emphasis evaluated the growth of the whole child. It addressed many factors ignored or disapproved of over the last twenty years by NCLB and later iterations of those philosophical underpinnings, the antithesis of what became micromanagement of schools by external bureaucracies and governmental agencies.

Sometimes called "Camelot days," teachers guided student development and formatively evaluated their progress. Interdisciplinary teams moved students toward fact-based decision-making, based on evidence and problem-solving skills. They used an understanding of science and math, an appreciation of the written word, and principles of democratic reasoning and application.

A partial remnant of the "Camelot days" is the modern-day professional learning community (PLC), a popular movement found in many districts, including the one in which I interviewed. PLCs do not all function the same way, as in the interdisciplinary movement. But if they are organized properly, the effort to stimulate professional dialogue proves beneficial when the PLC's purpose and operating agendas remain strong and accepted by its stakeholders.

The district in which I interviewed used PLC strategies to precisely develop and employ policy development. It systemically created and implemented long-range plans using a PLC called the "curriculum council," processes for writing curriculum, and making sure it was used as intended. The curriculum coordinator and other teachers showed me how the process worked in development and use.

Since I had applied for a seventh-grade science position, they showed me the curriculum for that subject and grade level based on the district's science mastery statement and a mastery (purpose) statement for the grade level. I showed them my work in the university simulation. The teachers liked my examples. They suggested that we discuss the differences and come up with something even better.

The day after my interview I received a call from the superintendent. "Congratulations for doing so well in the interview process. I will recommend your employment at the next meeting of the Board of Education. Please attend the meeting, prepared to answer questions members might ask."

The following day I signed the contract, pleased to join a high-quality district that shared the principles I believed in. I hoped the opportunity to work with my colleagues would make the system even better for meeting student learning and growth—the beginning of an exciting professional adventure.

• • • • • • •

Teaching Begins within the New Learning Infrastructure

New teachers always feel overwhelmed. They attend many orientation meetings and meet new colleagues. Policies and procedures seem difficult to absorb and comply with. Getting a classroom ready involves another challenge.

With Mary's university-based preparation and compatible systems in place, her first days as a seventh-grade science teacher felt focused and clear. She began her teaching career with expertise in systematic and systemic academic planning, design, and implementation within a classroom and institutional framework long acknowledged as being what school should be physically and structurally.

But five years later, when the worldwide coronavirus pandemic hit, that carefully honed idea of what constitutes a place of learning was dramatically transformed. Neither Mary nor her associates knew they were laying the foundation for a different kind of educational universe, one that worked effectively either within a brick-and-mortar structure or virtually in an electronic milieu.

Five years ago the New Learning Infrastructure made sense regardless of institutional configuration. The laser-like focus on quality student learning and conditions made it happen. The New Learning Infrastructure depended on solid intentions for student growth. Teachers created powerful curricula and established instructional processes aligned with it. They evaluated student learning quality and personal development.

The New Learning Infrastructure allowed a smooth transition from the traditional to the unimaginable world of COVID-19. This new scenario involved computers, the Internet, virtual interactions with students, and closer involvement with parents who became guides in their living rooms.

Hitting the ground running is a possibility.

Mary felt prepared in two ways. She was a curriculum developer as well as an instructional specialist. Her skills in developing a results-based curriculum made her formative assessment skills outstanding. She knew how to act and react in any instructional setting. Still nervous, she needed to conquer feelings of inadequacy typical of any novice. But she had a good head start.

Mary describes her first days on the job:

As with most new teachers, my first week on the job became a blur—survival training until things smoothed out and each day would hopefully become routine. Teaching is challenging because it involves the constant barrage of decision-making responsibilities.

Analyses of a teaching day often reveal dozens of decisions a teacher makes every minute.

Perhaps people in other vocations and professions do not understand the significance of this phenomenon. Occasionally a lawyer, executive, business owner, salesperson, or other non-teacher will assume a teaching role for a few days, just to see what it feels like. Sometimes those people are board members or laypeople simply interested in getting more insight into the work of teachers. Temporary teachers often find their experience exhausting and frustrating.

A barrage of decisions needs to be made while possessing a tolerance for ambiguity. The result of multiple micro-decisions seems ambiguous in terms of the impact on students without any certainty as to whether an answer or the issuance of instructions brings a positive outcome. The lack of time or opportunity to reflect on the possible result of decisions is frustrating. Something said in an offhand way to a student could be damaging in unknown ways.

As a new teacher, I wanted to be sensitive in how I responded to the many demands of my students. Would I pick up on their clues as to what my responses meant?

My new colleagues encouraged me. "It will get better in time."

But during the first week my poor husband became the sounding board to salve my emotions. How do teachers without a live-in partner survive that first week? Maybe social media helps. A lack of emotional debriefing can be psychologically devasting, especially for a new teacher not yet bonded with colleagues.

My district offered a debriefing team of counselors and seasoned teachers to help new teachers get their emotional and psychological feet on the ground. It was voluntary, and I opted out. But some of my new associates participated and found the service helpful.

One university class I took, "Classroom Management and Discipline," taught me what to do the first few days of a school year. As with all human beings, students individually and collectively size up the person in charge. The suggestion that a teacher should not smile until Christmas holds a modicum of truth.

But I was not interested in being seen as a martinet or severe disciplinarian. I wanted to be accepted as a competent young adult leader with a clear plan for helping my students achieve goals and objectives and to prove that intention through my first days on the other side of the desk.

The world in which seventh-grade students live is different than mine. Many adults shut away those memories of an era in which they were grateful to survive. But teachers do not have the luxury of just shrugging off a difficult experience. We must come across as purposeful, as leaders focused on the attainment of understandable and meaningful learning goals.

The mechanics of being a teacher in the first week breed stress. Classrooms need to be prepared, resources organized and ready for distribution, and lessons readied. My outstanding preparation, combined with compatible systems used by my district, made the mechanics manageable enough to help me succeed. My students and I got off to a good start.

Mary effectively handled *all* aspects of the New Learning Infrastructure, including the two most important: curriculum and formative assessment. Difficult schedules, classroom management, and other procedural difficulties such as adding virtual teaching/learning could be mastered quickly, and that was Mary's goal.

8

Performance Competence in the New Learning Infrastructure

As with all new teachers, Mary finds the first year of teaching stressful. It takes time to understand and work with an alien culture. Her emotional and psychological preparation mitigated some of the shock, but even good preparation cannot overcome all the questions.

How will Mary avoid looking or acting like an unprepared teacher? In what ways does she avoid making mistakes that will impact her students?

Performance competence is key to overcoming feelings of inadequacy, dependent on two factors: (1) the preparation before accepting the new responsibility and (2) how much support leaders of the organization give. Preparation and support—a truism understood everywhere. Both the quality of preparation and the level of support align with the responsibilities given neophytes. Two key words underscore success: *alignment* and *quality*.

In the mid-twentieth century neither quality nor alignment prepared teachers for initiation into a school culture. Teacher education programs focused primarily on lesson planning and instructional strategies. New teachers attended a brief orientation and used the resources given them. In larger districts, supervisors supported new teachers for the first year or two. Smaller districts depended on principals as the instructional leaders.

Neophytes rarely exhibit a self-actualized or transcendent personality.

Mary studied enough psychology to know what Abraham Maslow and his associates meant. Self-assuredness based on reality and mature introspection was rare in young adults. Brashness or timidity within young leaders undermines competence, so preparation programs must vigorously address the challenge with simulations, role play, and meeting sociological and academic challenges with reason and demonstrated confidence.

Mary describes the meaning of performance competence in the New Learning Infrastructure:

My new students needed to know I taught with purpose, with performance competence, a pleasant and earnest demeanor filled with a quiet yet persistent resolve, a resolve that conveyed direction and the route we took to arrive at our destination.

People of all ages respond well to assertive foresight when outlined and explained in ways that make sense and seem worthwhile. Nothing irritates more than a professor who mumbles his or her way into directionless lectures. Seventh-graders would eat that teacher for lunch before the end of the week. I did not want my students to respond that way. Unlike compliant college students, seventh-graders feel a newfound sense of dubiousness. They test limits as never before. Neither children nor adults, they realize the importance of peers and begin to question expectations in ways sometimes irreverent.

My seventh-grade teaching presented a good litmus test for the New Learning Infrastructure, a sociological lab in which my vulnerable and annoyingly forthright students grew as engines of insight.

My students often asked, "Why do we have to learn this stuff?"

If I were trying to assert my authority, I might respond with "Because I say so."

But that indoctrination fails as a guise of teaching and learning to force students into acknowledging the worth of what they must study. That type of response quiets fifth-graders, maybe even high school sophomores. But it motivates seventh-graders to become more negatively intent. Eventually it creates a me-versus-them climate that only grows worse.

Barbara, my new friend on the faculty, told me something profound: "Seventh-graders are different only in that they can be openly confrontational. Students in all grades ask the relevance question one way or another. But seventh-graders don't fear putting the issue on the table—sometimes vehemently."

My district's curriculum council and subject area committees grappled with the meaning of mastery in the context of relevance. Some teachers believed it was fruitless to discuss the relevance topic with students who struggled to understand how a skill could be useful in the adult world. Some skills were prerequisites to later skills as students progressed through the grades—not a sufficient rationale, dismissing the importance of relevance as an entrée into an evolving human brain. This relevance issue challenged the district's curriculum council and all the subject area committees, including science.

The teachers' perspective provided the first barrier as many teachers experienced the relevance issue themselves. Some of us shrugged our shoulders and accepted the arguments of our instructors. We studied harder because we trusted what our teachers said. Our learning that day was important for later grades and for life itself.

Barbara represented one of those compliant public school students, as did I. As students we tended to be insensitive to kids who needed more context for what they were being taught. The margins of our inner circle could be ignored, but now that we were teachers, these students could *not* be ignored. In the New Learning Infrastructure, mastery dominates. Students once dropped through the cracks using a bell-shaped-curve mentality now appear omnipresent. For teachers to smugly give those students Ds and Fs no longer works.

As Barbara said, "The district decided the first step in correcting the problem was to review the wording of mastery statements. Then check how curriculum outcomes and components are worded, to simultaneously give teachers in-service training on how to modify their thinking and responses to students."

· · · ● · · ·

Mastery and Relevance in the New Learning Infrastructure

Mary's conversation with Barbara opened her eyes to something rarely discussed at the university. Because of their background and academic successes, teachers fail to understand rebellious students. Dangerous assumptions based on macro-statistics or culturally based conclusions are drawn.

Seventy-seven percent of American teachers are women. No definitive research has been conducted about the social class in which most of them grew up. However, evidence suggests they came from middle-class families that valued education. They gravitated toward teaching partially because it was compatible with family life aspirations. They succeeded in higher education for the same reasons they succeeded in public school.

Women accept the values of a traditional American education and the systems that make them work. Women are expected to be compliant. Women like Barbara and Mary never socialized with students on the fringes, because they did not share their scholastic and personal values. In college Barbara and Mary aligned themselves with others like themselves. Staying on the straight-and-narrow felt safe for those who enjoyed working with children.

During the 1960s into the early 1980s, the federal government under the Great Society program of 1965 sponsored projects such as Teacher Corps, Competency-Based Teacher Education, and Cooperative Urban Teacher Education. These programs attempted to attract young people from diverse cultural backgrounds into teaching. The idea was that young adults from different segments of society might better engage recalcitrant public school students from different cultures, those students with different perspectives on the value of school. Those programs slowly died, and the standards movement began soon after issuance of the Nation at Risk Report in 1983.

Real-world challenges in American education involve community-based deliberations and a variety of opinions.

From conversations with her new friend Barbara and others in the district, Mary soon realizes that the issue of academic relevance is a problem with both her students and members of the adult community. Sometimes *relevance* morphs into *appropriateness,* which makes curriculum design and content even more challenging. Those issues never reach a final resolution. Wordsmithing a transparent and pliable curriculum focused on both student and societal needs remains an ongoing challenge.

Mary, Barbara, and other teachers in the district are now rethinking their attitudes toward students they once dismissed, modifying their responses to the challenges they present. This change represents hard work with curriculum design and implementation. More difficult are the acceptance and nurturing of young people who need convincing, as Mary soon discovered:

Barbara had taught eighth-grade language arts for two years when I joined the faculty of Sheridan Middle School. Barbara and her husband have two small children and live in a neighborhood a mile from the school. Unlike with my teacher education experience, Barbara's preparation was a more traditional program out of state. When she joined the Sheridan faculty, the district overhauled its entire academic program. While exciting for Barbara, the new experience made her head spin. A young superintendent brought an innovative school improvement model, a new kind of decision-making and action-taking system for developing and managing an academic program.

Barbara heard older faculty members express how wary they were of this new idea. Other whiz-kid administrators with bright ideas had come and gone. Those roller-coaster experiences caused jaded veterans on the faculty to call the phenomenon "TYNT"—this year's new thing.

Most of the board members were also new and intrigued by what the new superintendent called "academic program governance." With many components in the model, the central elements included a policy, long-range plan, and descriptions of what students completing district programs would know and do.

The most convincing argument in favor of the proposed model were its two fundamental characteristics: (1) it was written like a permanent constitution that could not be changed arbitrarily by just one person, and (2) it required a supporting set of practices and documents that guided curriculum management, instructional practice, and descriptions of student proficiency.

While the board seemed interested and supportive of this more stable form of academic management, one member presented his own agenda. As a businessman in his 40s, Vernon enrolled his three children in district schools. He also served as a civic leader on the board of the local chamber of commerce. Because he had run for public office, his biography was well-known, and he held nothing back. Vernon used his skills to build a successful real estate firm. Seven years later he joined the executive staff of a large property management company.

But Vernon had an unusual early background that he expounded on often in his campaigns and everywhere else. During his public school years he was frequently suspended. He graduated near the bottom of his high school class. After three years in the Marine Corps, his life had more focus and he left with an honorable discharge. Then he attended a vocational-technical school. During his first year in the school, Vernon became intrigued with housing construction. He took every course on the building and repair of houses, studied courses in real estate, and made straight As.

After graduation Vernon worked three years in real estate and succeeded financially. He and his partner started a company, which did well. He enrolled in a few business courses at a local college. Always the aggressive entrepreneur, Vernon took chances that landed him in court a few times, never criminal infractions but behaviors that led to civil lawsuits. He never lost a case.

By the time Vernon reached his late 20s, he had amassed over three million dollars. He sold his part of the company and entered law school. A born problem-solver, he sailed through the law school admissions test and graduated near the top of his class. While in law school he met his future wife, Amy, who also enrolled in the school. Vernon's studies concentrated on corporate law. Amy, much more the idealist, focused her attention on constitutional law. Together they started another successful real estate firm and raised three children, now enrolled in district schools.

The topic of relevance appeared high on Vernon's priority list, and he was adamant about presenting his point of view or questions about anything new the district attempted. That made board meetings interesting, especially when the new superintendent introduced this new kind of academic program.

. . . ● . . .

Birthing the New Learning Infrastructure

Vernon's extreme story exemplifies the quote by Mark Twain, "I have never let schooling interfere with my education."

Most teachers encounter smart yet disinterested boys and girls, students like Vernon, who hit middle school wondering what the fuss is all about. They look and act bored. Sometimes those students, like Twain or Thomas Edison, are passionately engrossed with aspects of the world outside the classroom. They cannot care less about the value of academic credentialing. Intelligent but bored students like Vernon sometimes land on their feet. But those distracted because of abuse, addiction, poverty, illness, or another kind of dark influence on their psyche face a much harder road. Mary discovered how seventh-graders struggle with who they are and what they should be from one minute to the next, even in the best of families and circumstances.

In the 1980s researchers believed catering to individual learning styles might reach students like Vernon and those alienated from school. They believed teaching and learning must be individualized. It did not last. In addition to its logistical complexity, learning styles were abandoned when the standards and testing movement began.

Politicians loved to denigrate what they called misguided pedagogy. They dismissed efforts to individualize learning as ridiculous because it was complicated and expensive. Policymakers thought mass education worked, symbolic of real-world circumstances and relevant to real-life challenges—a way to educationally support people who persevered in a bell-shaped world of winners, losers, and all those in between.

Vernon blossomed as an adult in a dog-eat-dog atmosphere, but he failed to respond to a manufactured school environment. Simulations did not interest him as they seemed like academic trivial pursuits. Now an elected member of the school board, Vernon was a hard sell for the new superintendent. His history with school and penchant for legalistic problem-solving made him confrontational.

Citizen involvement in school management is an American tradition with valuable but challenging overtones.

As parents and citizens, Mary and Barbara recognize the importance of lay involvement in managing schools and districts. Elected local boards include challenging members. However, even those with controversial personal agendas may be helpful to the district's programs. The diminishment of local board prerogatives because of the growth of legislative authority due to equity and funding policies proves detrimental to quality local education.

Mary paid attention to Vernon's involvement on the school board:
Barbara related how the district became part of the New Learning Infrastructure when NCLB was in force. It evolved during the external imposition of standards and high-stakes tests and launched despite ongoing confrontations with Vernon.

My father is a lawyer with a specialty like Vernon's, but not as ambitious or aggressive. So I understand a lawyer's mindset and penchant for making strong assertions to prove a point. Vernon's aggressive arguments continued. He reviled the curriculum as meaningless trivia. As a student he disliked sublimating his intelligence to allow mediocre students to be properly served. Yet as a parent and board member, he feared a worse alternative.

"How do we create a meaningful curriculum?" Vernon asked. "How do we challenge all students to learn in ways that match their abilities without overcomplicating the instructional process?"

Vernon prided himself on being a legal and commercial problem-solver with logical, fact-based, and straightforward thinking. He admitted to lacking the creativity to create his own answers, yet he remained suspicious of projects touted as panaceas.

Board meetings attracted members of the community, including teachers. Deliberations seemed civil enough, but people grew tired of the continuous impasse, similar to an evenly matched tennis game, between an articulate superintendent and a vociferous lawyer.

One day Vernon's wife, Amy, showed up. She surprised Vernon by sitting on the front row of the audience. Her presence rattled Vernon and led to consternation among the community members. Amy, a stay-at-home mother trained as a lawyer, was known to be as outspoken as her husband. She stood and told everyone, "My background is constitutional law. Vernon and I discuss topics on the board's public agenda. I agree that meaningful curriculum and individualization of instruction are valid, but I do *not* agree with Vernon in how the district should answer them."

Vernon looked stunned, but Amy continued: "Vernon seems to be looking for executive solutions, as would any corporate lawyer." Then she turned to the superintendent. "Is your proposal closer to executive decision-making or participatory program-building?"

"Participatory program-building," the superintendent replied. After the superintendent briefly explained the new school model, Amy smiled at Vernon. Then she addressed the audience. "Let me assure you that our marriage is intact. These are the family dynamics when two lawyers live together." Amy got to the heart of the matter. "In the absence of a constitution-like document, everything depends on the intricacies of evidentiary law. With Vernon's approach, the board is trying to deliberate a convoluted mess."

All eyes turned to Vernon. With a sheepish grin, he held up his arms in surrender and said, "My wife is correct." Then he turned to the superintendent, who looked shellshocked. Vernon said, "I'm ready to vote in favor of the proposed new model."

But Vernon and the other board members wanted to be involved with the development and implementation of written policies for the academic program.

That moment in time changed everything. It brought about focus and an understanding that the district's academic program would be built and implemented on solid procedural and philosophical ground.

* * * * * * * *

Mary's experience with her lawyer father gave her unusual insights into the local board. Still, Mary could not understand the extent to which state government wrestled away the authority of community school boards. As problematic as a local Vernon, someone else with the same background and opinions might serve in a legislature. Because of court-imposed equity and funding laws, states now assume the greatest expense for education. State lawmakers express concern about use of the taxpayer's dollar. To economize, they dictate policies and procedures to school districts. Elected legislators promote their opinions and succeed in passing laws that hobble the effectiveness of local boards and the districts they oversee.

Because they are elected officials, legislators believe their actions as representatives of the people are valid. Parents and school patrons often agree. But state legislators, governors, and members of the US Congress sometimes move democracy toward a remote and politically partisan hinterland that demotes local board members and professional educators to the level of underlings. That process now begins to weaken with evidence that it destroys the viability of teaching and learning at the local level—a step in the right direction for implementing the New Learning Infrastructure.

9

Foundation-Laying in the New Learning Infrastructure

S ome Americans struggle to accept The New Learning Infrastructure. Ironically, many citizens believe free enterprise supersedes constitutional law. Whatever makes sense at the moment seems more viable than following well-crafted rules. This philosophy proves disastrous for building bridges and detrimental to our nation's schools. Unfettered enterprise and democracy are not mutually supportive. They coexist in both positive and negative ways, a delicate balance.

Free enterprise has been the hallmark of American growth and power in the world. Constitutional provisions place guardrails on our system to uphold the rights of everyone, not just those who amass property and acquire power. The marriage of assertive enterprise and constitutional law *can* work together in the management of a school district's academic program, but only with a few caveats.

Board members often affiliate with the corporate world. They believe a district superintendent owns executive decision-making power. They want someone with enterprising leadership skills. That approach works with managing finance, personnel, property, legal matters, facility planning/ development, compliance with general regulation, and relationships with external service providers.

It does not work well in the development and management of academic programs. Most board members fail to realize the intricacies of curriculum, instruction, and assessment while most certified administrators are not well trained in these domains.

Professional inclusion takes time to absorb and longer to become a contributor.

Barbara's story is somewhat different than Mary's because she did not share the same quality teacher education preparation. The understanding of curriculum design was new when introduced to the district. At first Barbara did not feel qualified, but now she understands the collaborative principles and tools used to build a state-of-the-art academic program.

Barbara enters as a main character in the story. She provides different insights as a teacher of eighth-grade language arts. Her observations follow:

Unlike Mary's experience, most of my courses focused on teaching methods and lesson planning. Publishers of educational materials used their resources to prepare and develop lessons. I enrolled in a university program designed to prepare elementary teachers, with language arts as my area of concentration, giving me certification as a middle-level language arts teacher.

The New Learning Infrastructure process used in my district began when I joined the Sheridan Middle School faculty. Because of his wife's intercession at the famous board meeting, board member Vernon Preston supported the effort, but he remained dubious. Vernon became part of the ad hoc steering committee assigned the task of creating an action plan. That plan centered on just one thing: creating the academic program policy.

The board and superintendent decided to include representatives from teaching and administrative staffs on the steering committee. In addition, they included representative parents and patrons. Surprisingly, they also appointed me to the committee. Consultants from the Curriculum Leadership Institute (CLI) helped launch the steering committee's work. Vernon's wife, Amy, expressed her pleasure when she learned the steering committee was equated with a kind of constitutional convention.

Creating our bylaws for governing the academic program felt tedious, but essential for the long-term management of curriculum and instruction. Without such guidelines, program governance would be ineffectual. CLI shared helpful templates, as well as examples from other districts. With CLI's help we completed a draft of the bylaws in two days. After deciding to name the primary governing body the "Curriculum Council," we completed these sections:

- Curriculum Council definition and description
- Council functions
- Council meeting procedures
- Amendments to the bylaws
- Personnel serving on the council
- Council leadership
- Selection of council members
- Membership terms and duties
- Record-keeping
- Appointment and oversight of subject area committees

During those early weeks of the first year, I found it hard to explain how I felt—both professionally and emotionally. I expected a year to become acquainted with students and organize my lesson plans, trying to stay ahead of routine challenges associated with subject matter knowledge and classroom management. My self-perception in August described myself as a young and inexperienced teacher looking forward to years of gaining the maturity and experience needed to become a true educator. Those feelings persisted, but with the unexpected caveat of sitting at a large table in the board office as a full member of an important decision-making group. Our committee included key administrators, board members, and other people from the staff and community.

Rebecca Johnson, the committee chair, served as assistant superintendent for curriculum and instruction. In her 40s, she had already earned a doctorate. She was self-assured and conducted the meeting cordially yet purposefully.

Later that day I told my husband, "Participation in those few hours changed me."

"How so?"

"It broadened my outlook. It authenticated my place as part of a team commissioned to validate the importance of education. Today I had a voice, and other young teachers in the district also had a voice. We established a system in which we were heard. Do you know how rare that is? This system will deliver on our promises to enlighten children and young people. This isn't just impacting my career. It's going to enrich the lives of the students we teach. What an amazing opportunity—and responsibility!"

• • • ● • • •

Accountability and Attention to Detail in the New Learning Infrastructure

Barbara Morgan's training and teacher preparation were adequate—but traditional. Her professors and field supervisors competently taught her *how* to conduct instruction and manage a classroom, but they failed to delve into the *what* and *why* of teaching and learning.

Traditionally, the *what* includes curriculum created by someone else. Traditionally, the *why* ensures that certain skills and knowledge areas are covered with little or no mention of relevant mastery. Those descriptors of *what* and *why* become unacceptable in a district using the New Learning Infrastructure model. Teachers create and implement the curriculum. Skills and knowledge areas are never just *covered* but rather are taught to mastery.

Barbara felt like a neophyte in a familiar setting, but from the other side of the desk. She quickly admitted the driving influence behind her work as a teacher revolved around her experience as a public school student, not her professional teacher preparation. Barbara felt inadequate to be selected as part of a groundbreaking endeavor. But ready or not, she enjoyed meeting new challenges, new ways of making a difference with her life.

Young teachers are almost always motivated by altruism, an underlying motive for helping professions such as medicine, social work, counseling, and the ministry, but with a slight yet important difference. Other helping professions hold at their core a definable skill set usually associated with a discipline: doctors and nurses thoroughly trained to diagnose symptoms and treat them, social workers and counselors trained in the application of procedural or legal protocols designed to help clients heal themselves, religious leaders and support persons trained to listen, comfort, and convey meaning to underlying beliefs associated with their doctrines.

Those who teach, at any level, hold a responsibility divided into two parts: the enlightenment of their students and the ability to motivate them toward a change of thinking or behavior. This sharp dividing line causes some pundits to ask, "Are you a teacher of students or the teacher of a subject?"

The answer is both. Therein lies the problem of teacher accountability. The emphasis on standards, high-stakes tests, and measurable student competency concentrates on a certain kind of enlightenment, associated with a knowledge base that can be tested at any given moment. Ordinarily those tests operate at the knowledge, understanding, and application levels with easy-to-measure skills. Analyzing and evaluating skills can be measured but require more time and sophistication. With its many facets, the skill of creating defies instant measurement and classification according to competence levels.

Accountability is an inbred characteristic, not an accepted expectation.

Barbara begins to realize the importance of acting accountably—not because she is supposed to but because she is that kind of person *and* a professional educator. While some may believe accountability is old fashioned, Barbara serves as a model for her colleagues and students.

To what is a student to be held accountable? And to what extent is the student's teacher held accountable for ensuring an acceptable level of achievement? Barbara strives to answer:

Even though I was a new teacher, my peers chose me to represent middle-grade teachers on the steering committee in accordance with the bylaws' provisions prepared for the newly formed curriculum council. Working with key decision-makers in the district invigorated me, but I feared my inexperience was evident. My opinions did not always correspond with those of others. I tried to be courteous and considered my observations carefully before speaking. Listening was an important part of the process, so I often took notes on the points others made.

While serving on other committees, I learned the "yes—and" principle to entertain reasons someone else's ideas held merit. But could ideas be made even better with a little tweaking? My contributions confused some people at first, especially those who enjoyed confrontation. In time, the conversational dynamics seemed to change. Even Vernon settled down a bit.

The policy-building activity was akin to forming a club. But Dr. Johnson, who insisted on being called "Rebecca," made certain the underpinnings of the process were understood as more significant. She said, "We should never take our eyes off the reason for creating a policy."

This reasoning remained a stabilizing element in our ongoing decision-making and action-taking processes. The presence of the policy was a declaration of accountability, a commitment to clear and systematic governance of the academic program. No one board member or administrator possessed authority to unilaterally modify the academic program and its day-to-day execution.

In the past some building principals independently made programmatic decisions. Under the new bylaws, the district or the building administrators could make only slight adjustments without the council's permission, but any changes needed to be reported at the monthly meetings. Accountability under this system was not a chain-of-command function for the academic program but rather a pervasive design associated with agreed-upon principles and procedures starting with the bylaws and filtering down to subject area committees and individual teachers. Accountability in the district's academic program management prevented sloppy thinking or whimsical actions. Attention to detail underscored the goal as a mandate in the context of making certain everyone gave full allegiance to previously agreed-upon practices and beliefs.

Working from the bottom up, students now knew what we expected of them. Teachers knew what they must do to guarantee students met those expectations. Administrators knew what we required of them in creating an organizationally possible environment. The curriculum council maintained or adjusted policies to facilitate everything, under the auspices of the board of education. The New Learning Infrastructure required accountability and attention to detail.

Still, I needed to learn more about both my roles—as a classroom teacher and participant in the governance of academic programs.

• • • • ● • • •

Teacher Accountability Is Both Essential and Multi-Layered

Accountability to what? In schools the answer is student learning. The next questions include— "What is student learning?" and "How is it accomplished and measured?"

In American business and legal structure two processes define account-ability: (1) the person in charge is accountable for making sure everyone in the organization meets specified goals, or (2) leaders in the organization's staff are held accountable for ensuring subordinates fulfill expectations.

Neither of those definitions work in educational institutions because *genuine* student learning cannot be measured the same way as profit and loss. NCLB and subsequent systems of standards and use of high-stakes tests tried to make it work through use of numerical goals and compari-sons, but *quality* learning cannot be measured that way. Quality learning is not associated with right and wrong answers on a simplistic test based on information recalled from a classroom or other instructional setting. Quality learning is *formational* in that students become more introspective, intuitive, and creative. Accountable teachers represent good models of that kind of becoming.

Heaping disdain and criticism on teachers whose students do poorly on simplistic high-stakes tests is a travesty, especially when the system itself remains unable or unwilling to provide enough collateral support. Top-down fault-finding never works as an incentive for teachers to improve. Accountability is not solidified and verified through a single test score or even through the opinion of a principal or supervisor.

Real accountability is measured in terms of how well one teacher or teaching team succeeds in bringing students to some level of genuine, formational, and relational mastery—the kind of mastery that transforms students in meaningful and productive ways. Strong guide-on-the-side assistance works for teacher accountability because peer reinforcement calls for interactive and personal contemplation and upgrades in purpose-ful beliefs. This is especially true when the curriculum is locally developed and targeted to specific learning objectives. Teachers need the support of other teachers to help them improve everything from classroom man-agement/discipline, to enlightening students academically, to stimulating their intellectual and emotional growth.

Barbara Morgan and Mary Chapman-Miller were both idealistic and smart neophytes ready to serve future students. Differences existed in how they were prepared, college graduation dates, subject area concentra-tions, and when they were hired by the district. Barbara joined the district in a watershed year and was included in the founding of its New Learning Infrastructure. Mary joined later and brought with her skills that made the new model work. Like two people building a ship, one understood about the superstructure. The other was more expert in the machinery that made the vessel work. Both remained accountable for making sure the ship floated and moved through the waves.

Accountability for formational student learning comes from relational interactions within a professional teaching staff.

Fortunately, Mary found a district that valued the perspective of accountability. She also found an associate who understood the basics of the interactive academic program governance model being used.

Barbara continued her journey as teaching with the New Learning Infrastructure:

Mary and I became friends and professional colleagues at Sheridan Middle School. Our families are socially close and participate in many of the same community activities. We often discuss our pre-service and in-service preparation for how we teach. Undergraduate teacher education, even Mary's, fails to address a district's academic governance processes because they are not universally the same. However, creating and implementing an *inclusive* decision-making and action-taking governance system remains critical in our district. The importance of creating a governance model is essential to both the day-to-day and enduring success of any system. But the operational machinery—with its many moving parts—is just as important.

The district's academic program bylaws became the foundation for everything in terms of how, who, and why. The curriculum council answered the questions of what, when, and where through creation of a long-range plan (LRP). As the council discussed the long-range plan, we spent hours talking about its ramifications because the long-range plan was vital.

Making substantive changes to a curriculum requires time, especially when using collaborative techniques. The first step involves deciding on the "core" curriculum. If based on traditional configurations, it includes mathematics, language arts, science, and social studies. Some districts change that core through using interdisciplinary techniques, combining disciplines such as language arts and social studies. Other districts combine a traditional discipline considered tangential but important—science and technology.

As I told Mary, "Making these decisions will have a significant long-term impact and affect how a curriculum is written and used. While it's exciting to be innovative, the domino effect can be overwhelming. Changing the core curriculum to interdisciplinary arrangements affects resource selection, teacher skill sets, community expectations, and alignment with state standards."

Mary acknowledged the emphasis. "Understood. But how will the district weave its way through bureaucratic compliance issues? If the council already approves alignment with standards as an endpoint in curriculum development, they'll need to discard the previous practice of unpacking those standards."

"Yes," I said. "But we don't unpack them first, which is acceptable to the state since we have a validation system in place. High-stakes testing is losing its grip on the nation, but the practice is still being perpetuated. We decided to *eventually* accept a more interdisciplinary approach, because evidence shows that students coming out of that kind of preparation do as well or better on high-stakes tests than those coming from more traditional programs. But moving in an interdisciplinary direction takes time."

Mary and I often discussed these issues in the teachers' workroom while other teachers listened. The council wanted us to include these topics in departmental/grade-level meetings as well as sessions of the building leadership team. Those activities promoted variations on the professional learning community (PLC) culture that started many years ago.

Most teachers we talked with agreed the district should, for the time being, stay conservative (focus on individual disciplines) in setting up the five-to-seven-year long-range plan. As with the curriculum council, teachers appreciated the idea of attacking one core discipline a year, adding compatible noncore disciplines during those years.

Since language arts involves so many facets, it required two years for the learning of reading and writing skills in lower grades and the study of literature and composition in the upper grades. But which subject should we start with? Both mathematics and language arts seemed top choices, but language arts prevailed. I would chair what became the K-12 Language Arts Subject Area Committee.

Mary taught science. We were both trained in how to write a results-based curriculum and design compatible lesson plans. Mary learned the process in preservice teacher education while I learned how to do it in district workshops. Together we often reflected on what might happen in the years ahead. Mary would eventually be appointed chair of the K-12 Science Subject Area Committee.

Although we played different leadership roles in the New Learning Infrastructure, we both felt exhilaration and responsibility. We were part of creating a better kind of schooling, one in which we and our colleagues accepted the responsibility for years to come.

· · · ● · · ·

Long-Range Plan's Influence on
Subject Area Committee (SAC) Work

As a member of the curriculum council, Barbara and her associates completed the district's long-range plan, which answered these questions: What subjects constitute the district's curriculum? When are those subjects prepared as elements of a teachable and learnable curriculum? Where over time does each phase of curriculum development, implementation, validation, and assessment strategies occur?

The council chose language arts as the first subject area committee, and they created a timeline. With its overlapping characteristics and as the first chosen, the language arts subject was given four school years to complete. The council encapsulated the plan in table form.

LONG-RANGE PLAN									
	YEARS OF SUBJECT AREA COMMITTEE WORK								
SUBJECTS	1	2	3	4	5	6	7	8	9
Language Arts	C	VC	R/A	VA	C	VC	R/A	VA	
Mathematics		C	VC	R/A	VA		C	VC	R/A
Technology/21st Century Skills			VC	R/A	VA		C	VC	R/A
Fine Arts (Art, Music, Drama)			VC	R/A	VA		C	VC	R/A
Science				C	VC	R/A	VA		C
Foreign Languages				C	VC	R/A	VA		C
Wellness (PE, Health, Student Support Services, Social Skills)				C	VC	R/A	VA		C
Career & Technical Education (Business, FACS, Industrial)					C	VC	R/A	VA	C
Social Studies					C	VC	R/A	VA	C

Abbreviations:
- **C** Development of curriculum documents
- **VC** Implementation and validation of the new curriculum
- **R** Resource selection
- **A** Development of common outcome assessments
- **VA** Implementation and validation of the new assessments

The process to be repeated after each four-to-five-year cycle

With Barbara chosen as the language arts committee's chair, representatives from each grade level or cluster were added, as well as one building principal, special educator, and media specialist.

The council considered organizational variables. For example, What would be the availability of teachers? With so many subjects to teach, an elementary teacher of many subjects could not expect to serve on an SAC every year while some SACs benefitted from the presence of other subject areas, such as the media specialist for language arts. Every SAC included special educators and principals, and the council decided to combine some subjects into broader categories. Modifications to the plan might occur, so they established amendment provisions.

The council invited Mary to the language arts SAC meetings to learn how the process worked and to serve as a resource. Betty Wilson (math teacher), Don Baker (music teacher), and Jennifer Mitchell (district technology coordinator) also participated.

Collaborative decision-making and action-taking can be systematic and results-based with a lasting impact on the quality of curriculum, instruction, and student learning.

Mary and Barbara join Rebecca, a district administrator, in expanding the effort to upgrade the curriculum and enlarging the number of involved educators.

Barbara's story continues:

Rebecca met with Mary and me a few days after the curriculum council created the long-range plan. We needed to develop a system for launching the language arts subject area committee (SAC).

Rebecca said, "I wanted both of you present for two distinct reasons. As SAC chair, Barbara's job is to establish a project agenda. Mary's job, as an undergraduate prepared to write curriculum, is to serve as a resource person. A consultant from the Curriculum Leadership Institute will assist us on site or virtually, but a few ground rules must be established.

"The school board authorized two important incentives: off-contract time for the SAC to meet monthly during the school year, and salary stipends set between five and ten percent of your annual salary. The variations in stipend size depend on your levels of responsibility and involvement.

"Your SAC work involves more than attending meetings. You'll be asked to prepare materials individually, so the salary approach underscores your professional expertise over your hours on the job. As you can see, committing to this project involves a major attitude adjustment on many levels."

We realized under the New Learning Infrastructure that the first revolutionary idea of school improvement started with teachers. That perspective alone required trust, intense involvement, and recognition of the importance of teacher professionalism.

We were intrigued but still wondered what Rebecca meant in practical terms. On her laptop she clicked on a simple graphic and introduced us to the "walls."

	SEQUENCE OF SAC INFORMATION GATHERING AND DISCUSSION ACTIVITIES
TASK 1	SAC members gather information about the currently taught curriculum. This is the starting point, as teachers are considered experts in their own subjects.
TASK 2	SAC members indicate in short phrases what students will know or do at the end of the term (semester or year).
TASK 3	SAC members hang butcher block paper on the walls of the room. Phrases on strips are transferred to the wall by grade level and course.
TASK 4	SAC members examine information on the walls for (1) grade appropriateness, (2) scope, (3) sequence, and (4) relevance of content.
TASK 5	SAC members move, discard, or add new strips within and between grades to meet the four criteria.
TASK 6	SAC members review standards, modify content on walls, and transcribe information on documents to create new curricula.

The SAC used the interactive process of the "walls analysis" to show teachers that what they already do is an important starting point. What they *think* the curriculum should be is the first step. Why was this process so important to Mary and me? Because teachers intentionally validated as important decision-makers and academic leaders help SAC members interview other teachers. They systematically convey to other committee members what they do in the classroom.

Moving from left to right, kindergarten to grade twelve, everyone saw the curricular content—how it unfolded year to year, even with unintended overlaps and gaps. Deficiencies in grade level and student readiness considerations became apparent. Most of all, we saw the viability of a curriculum covered in terms of topics.

Rebecca turned from the computer to face us. "As time goes on, we must transform this 'walls' language to measurable verbs and substantive content fields. As leaders and resource persons, we recognize that our job is to help fellow committee members convert a passive curriculum into one that is focused, spiraled, teachable, and measurable."

To some this process seems excessively time-consuming, laborious, and expensive. Costs for outside consultant (nonprofit) assistance are reasonable but not insignificant, as are expenses to cover off-contract work for teachers in the district. On the other hand, money encumbered for staff development is better spent on this kind of intense activity than payment for speakers and nonproductive workshops.

10

Transformation— Who Teachers Become

The New Learning Infrastructure depends on our ability as a culture and nation to transform ourselves, to become different kinds of human beings, to consider teachers as more than automatons trained to do particular functions over and over again. Being sentient creatures allows us to do more than what nature programs us to robotically do. Nature gives us the ability to adapt and transform ourselves to become creative, assertive, and sensitive.

The SAC's procedure associated with the "walls analysis" involves much more than a step-by-step activity. It represents the first action that validates teachers as professional decision-makers. In the New Learning Infrastructure time and money must be allocated in sufficient amounts to do the job right—no unfunded demands for improvement, no threats of punishment if goals fail to meet arbitrary expectations.

America sometimes seeks the cheap yet popular quick fix. Many continue believing that economizing is more important than spending resources to improve the common good. School funding policies exemplify such frugality. Equitable funding remains difficult because of the inconsistent source of money. Wealthy districts or states utilize higher incomes from property taxes and other sources of revenue. Poor districts and states cannot compete. Available federal money constitutes less than ten percent of school budgets, which goes either up or down depending on national priorities.

Mary, Barbara, and Rebecca work in a district that utilizes a good tax base and in a state with resources and polices that support communities and infrastructure. The board and superintendent make good use of discretionary funds. They also seek grants to upgrade the quality of teaching and learning. But the "walls analysis" takes time, intense collaboration, and challenging forms of decision-making with subsequent actions substantively more important.

Barbara finds acceptance as a gifted young leader because she is organized, responsive, reflective, and full of initiative—a perfect choice as chair of the district's first subject area committee. The more mature and experienced Rebecca exemplifies an administrative leader in the realms of curriculum, instruction, and assessment. Together Rebecca and Barbara launch the SAC process. Both utilize their intelligence and general knowledge of what the next steps include. The challenging work of creating a new kind of curriculum begins.

Professionalism is characterized by ongoing transformations.

Mary exemplifies what new teachers should become through both preservice preparation and continuing growth in service. These facets of professionalism operate in tandem. It takes time, but Mary describes how schools benefit from such a transformation.

Although Mary is young and inexperienced, her training specifically prepared her for designing a curriculum meant to clearly enunciate the results inherent to the New Learning Infrastructure. Awed by the responsibility, Mary feels ready to proceed and shares more of her story:

Little did I know that I would become a key player in a school district's conversion to methods inherent to the New Learning Infrastructure.

The district's "walls analysis" validated the professionalism of seasoned teachers. It allowed them to collectively probe curricular elements not individually considered before. In my preservice classes we researched curricular content and made decisions based on logic. Experienced teachers do the same, with the added benefit of knowing their students' needs.

Rebecca and Barbara examined the work in my preservice training. Rebecca shared the mastery statement my fellow students and I developed with members of the council. Then she asked me to attend a council meeting to explain it in greater detail. Council members assertively peppered me with their questions:

"What is meant by 'deep understanding'?"

"Why should public schools be teaching 'entrepreneurship'?"

"What does 'mindfulness' mean in terms of a school curriculum?"

"Since when is it a school's responsibility to teach 'personal values'?"

"What exactly does 'intellectual passion' mean?"

The mastery statement developed in my undergraduate days survived well. We made some changes, as expected, but the council deemed the discussion itself as highly instructive. Barbara's language arts subject area committee needed the approved district mastery statement before creating the mastery statement for its subject.

My work in college focused on drawing from prior knowledge with wording. The district's language arts teachers used words and phrases implicit to language arts. My leadership tasks transformed me each day, making me more confident and self-assured, better able to engage with teachers much older and more experienced than me. But because of the process, they were also being transformed.

• • • • • • •

Transformation Requires Leaving a Comfort Zone and Exploring the Unknown

As Mary continues her work with the language arts subject area committee, she leaves a personal and professional comfort zone. While a few overlaps exist, a science curriculum is not the same as a language arts curriculum. As a necessary amalgam of skill sets, language arts uses a maddening array of topics and word configurations designed to stimulate and elicit emotion, a far cry from science as defined in traditional terms. Even Barbara finds leadership of the language arts SAC challenging.

Grades kindergarten through three teachers see language arts as a combination of skill-building (reading and writing), sparking the imagination of young people through storytelling and acting out. Upper elementary grade teachers further hone basic reading and writing skills. They also introduce students to more sophisticated forms of literature and composition. Middle and high school teachers use literature and composition as catalysts for deepening student interest and ability in reflection, creativity, and insight.

Members of the SAC become professional decision-makers through the "walls analysis" process. While they value this important process, they also know the new curriculum involves more than a matter of sorting and sifting the old curriculum with new sequences and extent of coverage. The language arts curriculum must accept key elements of the district mastery statement. It must acknowledge the role of the discipline in developing a well-rounded adult who contributes in a positive way, an adult who appreciates the wonders of the world through meaningful words and expressions.

Breaking big goals into actionable teaching/learning activities needs thorough and ongoing analysis, discussion, and committed follow-through.

The most challenging human endeavor is to act on the lofty goals set by organizational leaders and dedicated followers. Religious doctrine, constitutional provisions, mission statements, and other aspirational documents require constant review, analysis, and examples of how their principles should be applied.

Mary works with Barbara in guiding the creation of the subject area's mastery statement, thereby expanding the self-perception of teachers as academic leaders. Mary explains this part of their work:

Barbara gave me an assignment involving two parts while the language arts SAC members conducted the "walls analysis." To apply an old farm expression, we "primed the pump."

"Okay, Mary. Pull apart the district's mastery statement and find the portions that speak directly to the language arts discipline. Then locate language arts mastery statements being used by other districts or suggested by organizations—you know, advocates for better language arts teaching."

The ultimate purpose of my assignment was to help teachers accustomed to procedural skill development to overcome or modify old habits. Those old habits involved scope and sequence priorities, a cover-the-curriculum mentality, and hyper concern about meeting tested standards.

The tricky part was to help teachers *modify,* not dismiss old habits. Our work was evolutionary, not revolutionary—a distinction lost on some teachers. Many older teachers were accustomed to radical forms of school improvement, but the New Learning Infrastructure would not throw out the baby with the bathwater. It merged what we knew was good for student learning with what was even better.

Below are elements I found in the district's mastery statement that needed discussion and reflection. I decided to put everything in tabular form to do a side-by-side analysis of each point on the left and language arts interpretations on the right.

ELEMENTS OF DISTRICT MASTERY STATEMENT	INTERPRETATIONS AND RAMIFICATIONS FOR THE LANGUAGE ARTS CURRICULUM
expand an understanding of reality	Reading a wide variety of fiction and nonfiction books is the traditional way students expand reality. Today's information sources, including social media, can distort reality. Making intelligent judgments as to accuracy and validity are critical.
know themselves and how they fit into the world.	Reading or viewing all forms of literary media, classical and modern, are effective ways for children and young people to understand how human beings mature and identify cultural niches for themselves. Adding role play opportunities personalizes that new awareness.
solve complex problems	Success in life depends on an ability to solve different kinds of problems. Reading and discussing how fiction and nonfiction characters meet challenges and solve problems they create provide insight. Participating in role-play activities enhances that skill.
think and act creatively	Creativity is the highest shown of Bloom's taxonomy of educational objectives and the most difficult to teach and evaluate. Creativity in composition is a language arts domain, so the SAC needs to prepare mastery outcome statements accordingly.
manage their own needs responsibly	The one aspect of this element pertinent to language arts is plagiarism, which is not responsible behavior. The language arts SAC's mastery outcome statement on this topic will likely show up in all grades and needs to be written in as positive a way as possible.
use principles associated with entrepreneurship	Communication is critical for success in commerce, starting with preparing a business plan and possibly convincing others of the viability of the enterprise. Marketing challenges involve convincing customers and starting early with persuasive writing ability.

ELEMENTS OF DISTRICT MASTERY STATEMENT	INTERPRETATIONS AND RAMIFICATIONS FOR THE LANGUAGE ARTS CURRICULUM
become lifelong learners	Learning involves more than school. Learning how to learn over a lifetime should be the primary purpose of a formal education. Reading, writing, listening, and speaking allow stronger interactions with our world. Weave lifelong learning into the language arts curriculum.
know how to learn and become motivated to do so	The beauty of Bloom's taxonomy, if used intentionally, underscores how learning is more than remembering and understanding. Motivating students to apply, analyze, evaluate, and create is the foundation of a lifelong quest for becoming more effective adults and members of society.
exhibit curiosity regarding how to stretch boundaries into new and different realms	Curiosity is fundamental to quality human life, stimulated by a need to answer the question "What if?" Stories heard or read, then created, enshroud us with wonderment. They lead to richer lives in terms of invention, discovery, and an appreciation of the arts.
possess an inherent drive to learn continuously	How does a student develop an "inherent" anything? "Inherent" suggests an ongoing feeling that cannot be dismissed, like an ambition that never abates, a determination that never ceases.

The longer I worked to align the district's mastery statement with language arts, the more I realized how fundamental language arts is to virtually everything else in the district's curriculum. Similar to the piano of education, language arts is the basis for everything. Everything in human learning depends on communication. Science and math are no exception. Numbers, symbols, problem-solving equations, research strategies, construction, and virtually everything else depend on being able to understand others through language.

• • • ● • • •

Expanded Thinking and Beliefs

Because of her state-of-the-art teacher education program, Mary knows the difference between mere tweaking of an academic program and substantive improvements. Substantive improvements go to the heart of who teachers are and what they believe. Her "prime the pump" service is essential to the language arts subject area committee.

While it may seem ludicrous that a young woman new to teaching and professional education plays such a strong leadership role, this story is based on personal observation. Our culture today reveres the benefits of maturity and vast experience. But history also shows us the most dramatic improvements in human existence often come from people in their early adulthood or even late teens. Scientists, composers, political and military leaders, inventors, artists, writers, and educators are so young, the idea of failing or being wrong seems inconceivable. Many do fail, of course, but even that experience proves more instructive than demoralizing.

Mary and Barbara are smart, insightful, well-prepared, and female role-breakers. Filled with vision and resolve, they ambitiously take risks. Mary's story continues:

I took a deep breath. The district mastery statement seemed deeper and more comprehensive than I expected. Transcribing it to fit a language arts mastery statement felt challenging and time-consuming, but the effort markedly broadened my perspectives.

My task ahead was to help members of the language arts subject area committee experience what I experienced, to transform themselves into becoming students of pedagogy in its best application. This art or science of teaching functioned way beyond the mere coverage of subjects, skills, and knowledge areas. My analysis and interpretations follow:

ELEMENTS OF DISTRICT MASTERY STATEMENT	INTERPRETATIONS AND RAMIFICATIONS FOR THE LANGUAGE ARTS CURRICULUM
Ask good questions.	Too many teachers believe teaching and learning are about information-giving and skill-building, providing answers when students ask no questions. As learning theorists and researchers know, that belief is fruitless. Learning depends on curiosity and inquiry.
Accept diverse ideas in which feedback is vigorous and stimulating.	Diversity is more than cultural or racial. Freedom of speech calls for different opinions and interpretations, a willingness to enter a vigorous discourse that stimulates new perspectives, central to a quality language arts curriculum.
Gain self-confidence through experience with widening groups.	"Widening groups" involves student ability and willingness to engage others both orally and in writing. Interactions must be more than simulated, as confidence grows with real and challenging conversation.
Take meaningful initiatives (reach out).	While simulations and role play are effective, real opportunities to reach out to others in the school and adult community must be included in the language arts curriculum. "Reaching out" involves oral or written communication as interactive as possible.
Receive consistent encouragement from respected associates.	Positive reinforcement of learning is the best way to cause long-term retention. Younger students need encouragement from their teachers, but older students feel significant support from the recognition of peers and others in the school or community they respect.
Practice mindfulness in clarifying priorities and actions each day.	"Mindfulness" means sensitivity. Students learn how to habitually prioritize actions and responses, typically involving effective oral and written communication in ways that support their own learning and assist in the learning of others.
Be open to others from different backgrounds.	A strong acceptance of diversity's importance culturally and racially reveals ramifications in terms of age, gender, religious beliefs, political opinions, and socioeconomic standing. Stories, documentaries, historical works, and other projects play a significant role in language arts.
Understand and work to achieve self-discipline and personal values.	Families play a more significant role in guiding young people in terms of self-discipline and values development. But the language arts curriculum contributes through the study and discussion of literature and compositions about how people attain success in life.

ELEMENTS OF DISTRICT MASTERY STATEMENT	INTERPRETATIONS AND RAMIFICATIONS FOR THE LANGUAGE ARTS CURRICULUM
Create and maintain the convictions to pursue these values.	Can "conviction" be taught? Although our sense of conviction develops in different ways, it almost certainly starts with an eye-opening experience or the introduction of a convincing new way of thinking or acting. Literature underscores conviction, especially when powerfully written.
Speak and write effectively.	Speaking or writing effectively requires many opportunities to do both, in settings that promote feedback and intellectual interactions. Teachers must agree where those activities start and in what ways they evolve through the grade-to-grade spiraling process.
Know how to make all people feel at ease.	"Making people feel at ease" involves more than the exercise of charm. It reveals a genuineness of behavior characterized by listening and showing interest in another person's ideas and values. How to initiate interactions can be taught.
Enter conversations with others.	Social awkwardness in adult settings is common. While the formula for overcoming social awkwardness is not clear, studying what others do through literature and visual media can be instructive. Example: Eleanor Roosevelt and how she conquered extreme shyness.
Show genuine interest in the ideas and activities of others.	Listening to what others say and showing informed interest in their observations is an important skill. Emulating behaviors of characters found in literature or in visual media and having those behaviors critiqued remain important elements of a language arts curriculum.
Grasp that problem-solving is a complex and interactive system.	"Problem-solving" is frequently defined as dominated by mathematics and logic. However, problem-solving most often relates to untying social entanglements. Literature frequently explores those interactions, giving insights as to how they are resolved.
Problem-solve through collaboration of all disciplines.	Problem-solving in the four primary school subject areas is clearly interdisciplinary when applied to real-world settings. Examples involve law (social studies), research (science), engineering (math), and personal/family relationships (language arts).

ELEMENTS OF DISTRICT MASTERY STATEMENT	INTERPRETATIONS AND RAMIFICATIONS FOR THE LANGUAGE ARTS CURRICULUM
Define intellectual passion in terms of knowledge and its significance.	Individualized instruction remains challenging but more important than ever. NCLB destroyed the middle school movement, which featured exploratory curricula. Preteen and early teen students need curriculum to search for and identify their passionate endeavors.
Communicate expressively both orally and in writing.	Our free enterprise society depends on expressive writing and speech to persuade, convince, and encourage others commercially, politically, and academically. The language arts curriculum once required "expression" courses. They need to be reinstituted.
Accept that life is an assortment of valuable experiences.	A valuable experience underscores who a student is and will become. All of us can pinpoint a time in our lives that changed our thinking and aspirations. Through language arts, teachers can expand options for students' valuable experiences.

This analysis of achieving consensus is not perfect, nor will it lead to absolute agreement between and among those serving on the language arts SAC. But it begins to initiate reflectiveness about what professional teachers do. It lays the foundation for developing our own language arts mastery statement—the next step in the subject area committee's work.

11

Building a Meaningful Subject Area Mastery Statement

C urriculum revision in the New Learning Infrastructure involves more than just a shuffling of topics, subjects, courses, and other traditional ways to reorganize the status quo. Revising schedules, organizational configurations, subject or course nomenclature, grade-level patterns, and teaching staff realignment failed to result in significant improvements in student learning. Experiments focused on team teaching, interdisciplinary structures, elimination of grade-to-grade advancement, and other novel ideas rarely proved lasting success.

The heart of the New Learning Infrastructure is a curriculum designed to be substantive in terms of student mastery in the sense that children and young people prepare to be fully capable and successful adults in a twenty-first-century reality. The language arts subject area committee hammers out a mastery statement that reflects the more expansive way of thinking about what students *really* need to succeed in life. Gaps between "what we do now" and "what we should do" occur in two domains.

The first gap is associated with student skill/knowledge development compared to a way of how thoughtful students think and behave. The second gap exists in the use of Bloom's taxonomy. Specifically, the traditional view of learning emphasizes remembering and understanding, compared to the contemporary focus on applying, analyzing, evaluating, and creating. The first gap reveals the difference between being a trivial pursuit expert and effectiveness as a member of society. While factual knowledge is useful and important, being a societal contributor is much more significant.

As for the second gap, the two levels of the taxonomy used in most schools today are remembering and understanding. While the New Learning Infrastructure acknowledges those levels, the other four persist: applying, analyzing, evaluating, and creating.

Project-based learning (PBL), essentially a resurgence of John Dewey's concepts developed and widely implemented in the early part of the twentieth century, becomes popular in the district. The growth of PBL started when NCLB-driven dictates weakened. High-stakes tests became less important while states reworked and rephrased their standards. Project-based learning depends on local formative assessment.

The definition of teacher accountability moved in a different direction, minimizing the importance of student performance on summative assessments. The growth of PBL benefits the New Learning Infrastructure in terms of meeting Bloom's applying goal and also carries over into analyzing, evaluating, and creating. But much depends on the student's individual effort as opposed to collaborative or interactive initiatives. Not bad, but not enough.

Collegial experimentation, development, and application define important elements of the New Learning Infrastructure and how things work in real life. PBL may not emphasize that kind of interaction.

Barbara and Mary Work Together

Sophisticated forms of communication lie at the heart of language arts.

This sometimes complicates human relationships. To respond effectively, students need to recognize this challenge and growth opportunity. Barbara and Mary work well together because Barbara is a language arts specialist and Mary was trained to write intended learning outcomes. But they encounter the challenge involved in measuring nuanced language arts skills.

Some members of the language arts SAC disagree with us. They try to balance the current curriculum with outlining and formally writing a state-of-the-art precise mastery statement. We do not apologize for this challenge. But after dialoguing within the committee, we agree to modify the mastery statement to make it more acceptable and less confusing.

We scheduled discussions leading to development of the language arts mastery statement in two parts. The first: a general review of the district's mastery statement and the accuracy and appropriateness of the interpretations we created. The second: a focus on creating a draft of our language arts subject area mastery statement. To create our statement from scratch and initiate discussion, we prepare a working draft for critique and modification.

Students participating in and completing the district's language arts curriculum will master outcomes corresponding with written intentions for learning at grade level. Intentions for learning include the following:

● Defining reality in the context of decisions made valid through background knowledge and evidence.

- Gaining insight into human interactions and behaviors as depicted in literature that discusses cultural influences, thereby gaining an appreciation and respect for diversity.
- Interpreting problem-solving as the ability of human beings to consider challenges, weigh the accuracy of options found in all types of literature, conduct trial-and-error tests, and work in teams to create and evaluate possible or probable solutions.
- Establishing a working definition of creativity as being an authentic learning goal, characterized by the dynamic nurturance and acceptance of novel ideas, proposals, and behaviors that depict curiosity and devotion to some endeavor.
- Demonstrating responsible behaviors in the context of what is read as valuable in terms of good taste, logical reasoning, and being instructive to readers as guidelines for living and learning. Responsible behaviors also manifested in written works reflective of the writer's own creativity, ability to express ideas, opinions, and factual information offered through quality syntax.
- Developing through reading and writing an appreciation for competition based on valuable insight, examples of moral/cognitive/physical self-improvement, and willingness to take risks for reasons other than self-aggrandizement. Accepting persuasiveness based on conviction and improving the common good as the appropriate model for entrepreneurial enterprise.
- Accepting the idea that reading, writing, speaking, listening, and interacting through language are the basis of lifelong and worthwhile learning.
- Using literature and other media as catalysts essential for making learning a conscious, intentional, and ongoing part of life.
- Making curiosity a fundamental part of living and becoming, through reading or accessing diverse forms of media on a regular and ongoing basis.
- Inquiring by using questions posed appropriately and regularly.

- Participating in the interchange of vigorous and stimulating ideas in which feedback is welcomed.
- Recognizing the acquisition of self-confidence as the result of taking initiatives in widening groups. Using insights taken from literature and other media and applying skills in speaking, writing, and listening to the act of reaching out.
- Placing oneself where encouragement of others is given and received.
- Practicing the art of mindfulness by being sensitive to prioritize actions and responses, particularly through effective oral and written communication.
- Articulating the meaning and practice of self-discipline and development of personal values, reinforced by the reading of quality literature and the viewing of uplifting media.
- Interacting with others easily based on the art of conversation by maintaining the habit of staying engaged with the world and listening carefully.
- Pursuing knowledge and sharing that knowledge with humility and sincerity through both speaking and writing.

We knew this draft of our subject mission statement might be difficult to initially understand, even confusing. We imagined how it might upset some teachers who held traditional opinions, but we had no idea how much heated discussion it would cause.

· · · ● · · ·

Controversies about the Subject Area Mastery Statement

Barbara and Mary anticipated the intensity of any discussion about the proposed language arts mastery statement. Seasoned teachers argued that everything in the mastery statement was already being taught in their classes—in subliminal and nuanced ways. To pinpoint behaviors and responses in specific terms seemed both impossible and ludicrous. Experienced teachers believed that evaluating students formatively and individually, using some of the verbs found in the mastery statement, involved vague evidence and slippery teacher opinions. Both operated in the subjective realms of attitude, bias, and belief systems.

For decades American teaching and learning based their curriculum on a pedagogical discipline that glorified factual precision, both taught and assessed in concrete ways—more scientific and fact-based as well as more measurable and significant. The antithesis of such thinking untethers opinion emanating from emotion or supercilious conjecture, a belief grossly unfair to truly professional teachers who effectively plumb the depths of their intuition and inspired imagination.

The New Learning Infrastructure depends on the human gift of intuition and imagination, just as much as on measurable facts and statistically measured outcomes. Expanding on a traditional language arts curriculum remains a major challenge.

No one disputes the need for students to prove the extent of their knowledge (as in comprehension) or to perform in ways established as effective and proper (as in reading, writing, composition, and speaking). Those foundational and critical elements represent skills we use to interact with our world and each other. They are not in themselves symbolic of our intellect, creativity, and resourcefulness.

Curricular expansion incorporates behavioral outcomes rooted in reflection, deep background knowledge, and broad understandings of the human condition. The challenge faced by Barbara and Mary was to help their colleagues expand on traditional thinking to ensure that the final draft of the language arts mastery statement was not simply "same old, same old" written in outcome language. Despite some dissension in the traditional ranks, Barbara and Mary continued to work:

> We scheduled a subject area committee meeting for five contiguous hours. With twelve SAC members, not including ourselves, we broke the group into four teams of three each. We asked the teams their opinion of the proposed outcomes as an academic program that traditionally includes basic skills in reading, writing, speaking, and listening. In what way should those intentions for student learning be included and in what grade levels?

Then we gave the teams three outcomes within the proposed mastery statement to review and critique. We categorized the recommendations as follows:

1. Is this outcome appropriate for our K–12 language arts curricula? If not, should it be in the curriculum of another discipline? Should it be included in *any* district curriculum?
2. If it is appropriate, does it need to be modified? How should it be addressed at each grade level? In what grades should this outcome be introduced, reinforced, and mastered?
3. For an outcome considered appropriate, what does it mean? In what way does it fit conventional or virtual classroom settings, teaching/learning schedules, and dynamic student involvement?

The first intended outcome we addressed was defining reality in the context of decisions made valid through background knowledge and evidence. This definition of reality means life as we perceive it in our present world and in the future. We define reality by what real people do as they interact with each other in real-world settings. They succeed or fail in their personal endeavors as they accurately perceive the world through their own insight and acceptance of available evidence.

This intended outcome fits conventional or virtual classroom settings in terms of role play and use of scenarios, strategies that require considerable planning, and follow-up. Those instructional techniques have significant ramifications for the use of virtual teaching platforms. Teaching/learning schedules must be as contiguous as possible and not chopped into abbreviated segments. Dynamic student involvement includes both individual and group interactions.

We waited for arguments against the first outcome—arguments repeated in all the other outcomes shown in the proposed mastery statement. Experienced teachers accustomed to "covering" a curriculum said the operant verbs and content fields appeared too broad for all the outcomes in the mastery statement. Planning lessons for either on-site or virtual classrooms take considerable time. Implementing those lessons via use of role play and scenarios would be challenging and arduous for virtual instruction.

We offered no counterpoint to those perceptions because we knew them to be accurate. We discovered those challenges in our teaching or in our preparation for teaching. Big ideas need big time to convey, so the answer allowed *time* to be the variable—not a lesson's content. For this first outcome alone, planning and execution of the instructional program appeared massive, almost as challenging as the evaluation of student learning.

Barbara challenged the SAC with a definitive question: "How can teachers begin assessing the effectiveness of students in defining reality?"

Mary provided the answer: "Students will be asked to make distinctions between what is and is not 'real.' This seems ludicrous on the surface, but twenty-first-century technology and political discourse confuse everyone. What we choose as being valid may or may not have authentic underpinnings."

Unfortunately, the English language can be manipulated to justify almost anything by anyone adept at selling an idea or relating an opinion. Our ability to define reality is inherent to the survival of both capitalism and democracy. Both can be manipulated by people who wish to sway opinion in a direction advantageous to themselves. Some members of the language arts subject area committee dug in their heels, disputing even the first of the many outcomes in the proposed mastery statement.

We decided ahead of time what was worth debating. What must be accepted? What could be compromised or dropped?

Our curriculum director, Rebecca, joined our discussions. She helped us make *go/no go* decisions, basing her decisions on those made by the curriculum council and the board of education. The curriculum council made decisions based on the New Learning Infrastructure goals. The council then asked the board to confirm decisions that required major and even expensive modifications in curricular design.

Teaching and learning a more impactful and significant curriculum meant changes in priorities and the techniques needed to meet them. Teachers must have the opportunity to offer opinions and arguments, but final decisions about emphasis and expense must be made by those responsible for policy and the acquisition of financial support.

Now the real adventure begins! How will members of the language arts subject area committee discuss and debate the proposed mastery statement? And how will final decisions be made?

• • • • ● • • •

Causing Real Change Requires Difficult and Exacting Work

Self-proclaimed and popularly acclaimed change experts proliferate in many organizations. They speak, write books, conduct workshops, or coin pithy admonitions. Some morph into what we euphemistically call a "sage on the stage." Americans love these kinds of change experts, because they frequently entertain with humorous and dynamic stories, pearls of wisdom that capture the imagination and momentarily inspire new ways of thinking and acting. Some make fortunes by "blowing in, blowing off, and blowing out." Those who achieve celebrity status are welcomed effusively, perform magnificently, and depart triumphantly. No worries about whether their message changes anything. They leave it to local leaders to take care of managing the details. Once the prophet of change answers a few questions, walks off the stage, and collects the massive fee, the task is achieved. Our expert prepares for the next venue. This perspective about many American change agents sounds cynical—intentionally so.

While politicians scream for more accountability from schools and teachers, pied pipers of change skip down the lane toward big money without worrying about how much difference they made in curriculum design, student learning, or teacher performance. Who cares? Accountability relates to how popular they are, how many more gigs they gain, and how much income they generate.

They are not like Barbara, Mary, and Rebecca—three members of a team of local leaders working elbow to elbow every day, week, and month with colleagues and professional associates, facing the hard stuff and working through processes designed to make a difference.

The New Learning Infrastructure does not need or want change-agent pied pipers any more than replacing worn-out bridges needs visionary dreamers without on-site skills to build them. More than a simplistic difference of opinion is involved as divisions are cultural and historical, hard to resolve.

As Barbara and Mary work with the subject area committee, opposing arguments are based on five pervasively traditional viewpoints:

1. Causing students to think is not the mission of public schools. Public school curriculum must deal with basics and not delve into philosophical aspects of learning and behaving. In brief, public schools convey information but are not responsible for making students think deeply.

2. Schools are held accountable for curricular coverage. Public school teachers face accountability for teaching content breadth, not depth. The task of preparing and implementing lessons more than factual coverage is too complex and time-consuming.

3. Testing student knowledge must be objective for schools to meet measurable expectations. Assessment of student learning in the New Learning Infrastructure is subjective, formative, and difficult to record and track. Parents expect definitive progress reports using number or letter grades, because these reports seem more definitive than teacher judgments based on observations alone. Student progress reports and transcript notations remain part of the standard database for academic records and official transcripts. Summative assessment scores remain sacrosanct in the minds of many teachers, parents, and school patrons.

4. Students in the lower grades are not ready for abstract reasoning. Most public school students through the first years of high school are incapable of the abstract reasoning required to meet analytical and scholarly outcomes.

5. Teacher preparation programs fail to prepare novices for such advanced ways of teaching and learning. University coursework

and instructional methods programs rarely if ever guide prospective teachers toward development and application of
sophisticated learning behaviors in their students.

These vignettes are meant to be more than just stories.

They depict the essence of the New Learning Infrastructure.
Professional educators in all categories interact to build program
structures and content, to design ways to continue that intense
interaction over time.

Barbara and Mary continue:

Rebecca was well acquainted with the obstacles we encountered
in discussions with the subject area committee. We started our
committee's work with the "walls analysis" to authentically involve
significant teacher input from the beginning. From the beginning
we told teachers they were a critical part of the process and we
meant it. But we believe that what the district now utilizes is not
enough, and moderate tinkering with curriculum-mapping strategies will not help.

Rebecca made that point clear to the committee, an action
that eased our follow-up work. "Analysis of the current situation
was a good start, a baseline, like analyzing an old bridge for what
was good about it in terms of location, foundational and subsoil
support systems, and compatibility with the surroundings. But
the replacement bridge needs to accommodate different kinds of
traffic volume and patterns. Vehicle weight and speed are serious
considerations.

"In other words, keep what is good, but plan for the future with
structural innovations."

Rebecca forthrightly told SAC members that she already knew
their concerns when they paired the existing curriculum with the

new language arts mastery statement. She gave each SAC member six index cards. The top card was light blue with the phrase

> **INNOVATION USING THE NEW LEARNING INFRASTRUCTURE**

The other five cards were white with the following questions:

> Is real learning remembering facts and demonstrating skills? Or is it how students *think*? What is the reason for your answer?

> Is curricular depth (deep study) more important than curricular breadth (coverage)? What is the reason for your answer?

> Which is the most important kind of assessment to ensure quality student learning: formative or summative? What is the reason for your answer?

> What is abstract reasoning? Are K-12 students capable of abstract reasoning? What is the reason for your answer?

> Do university-based teacher education programs prepare candidates to think and help their students think? What is the reason for your answer?

We told Rebecca we anticipated a problem interpreting the mastery statement, which led us to develop a scenario around the first outcome: defining reality in the context of decisions made valid through background knowledge and evidence. That outcome clearly involves student thinking and reflection.

We interpreted the outcome as focusing on the use of language in real-life settings. Using such an interpretation meant extensive use of role play and scenarios, even in virtual instructional platforms. Role play and scenarios necessitate more planning and instructional time, paired with the need for ongoing formative assessment and intense student interactions. Our concerns paralleled Rebecca's points on the index cards.

"It's better to use the generic questions on the index cards," Rebecca said. "They create a first layer of reflection among SAC members. Once basic principles are discussed and agreed upon, it's easier to establish common ground in dealing with the mastery statement itself."

We agreed with Rebecca. Without a baseline agreement about essential principles, we might drive ourselves into the ground with minutiae as we parsed each element of the proposed mastery statement.

Ideally, everyone on the subject area committee would come around to the perspective of John Dewey: schools are for preparing students for the real world—not the simplistic saying so often attributed to Dewey, "Students learn by doing." What Dewey really said was that students learn by *thinking about* what they are doing. For students to think deeply in applied circumstances, the curriculum in which they participate must give them time and opportunity to do just that. And the ramifications are enormous!

12

Subject Area Mastery Statement Structure for Discussion

Since the beginning of our nation, Americans have argued. Yet that ongoing rancor often results in unexpected unity—like the married couple who constantly battles with each other yet resents anyone else telling them how to behave or what to believe. Their relationship depends on bickering. What is the psychology behind that phenomenon?

Stubbornness is clearly at play and culturally rooted convictions often involved. Our history describes how differences of opinion result in open combat—struggles for political or social dominance, a social dance we perform with each other until something unexpected intercedes or insight and reflection give us a different perspective. We authentically change our outlook and behavior because something in our brain is internally triggered, not because another person or authority figure *forces* us to think differently.

As a consultant to schools, I listen as much as advocate—the intellectual engagement process. The person with whom I work realizes we share a common responsibility—meeting the needs of those depending on us—the school's students. Meeting the needs of students makes "being personally right" back-burner stuff. How we fulfill our larger and more important mission transcends isolated opinions, especially true with those in a profession dedicated to serving others.

I have worked with hundreds of subject area committees and curriculum councils. Some will listen to me when they do not listen to each other—a phenomenon based on the myth that expert consultants live fifty or more miles away. My job as a change agent is easier than what local leaders face, but clearly, the only difference is my experience in other districts with similar or identical challenges. Because of that experience, I have insight into what works and what does not work.

An exploration of meaning in any piece of writing is challenging but important.

It must be ongoing for reinforcement to occur and to help those not originally involved in preparing a document. The kind of intense labor expended in preparing and using these curriculum documents is new to most educators accustomed to being given easy-to-use guidelines prepared by publishers. But we enhance professionalism by the effort.

As members of the local staff, Barbara and Mary need to build credibility at the local level. Navigating that challenge requires a procedural structure as Barbara and Mary work together:

With Rebecca's help, we initiated discussion by analyzing the work draft of the language arts mastery statement. To help clarify thinking and responses, we took key elements from four of the five points Rebecca provided. Stated in positive terms, they follow:

- Public education should stimulate and enhance the ability to think and reflect.
- The ability of students to think and reflect comes from experiences that emphasize systematic analysis over time.
- The ability to think and reflect are regularly evaluated, consistently demonstrated, so creative behaviors can and should be the result.

- The ability to think and reflect comes from an encouragement to use data, researched findings to explore nuances, and the abstract "what ifs" of our world.

For purposes of discussing merits of the work draft, we condensed each of the four points to one-word identifiers, similar to those found in Bloom's taxonomy: reflecting, analyzing, evaluating, creating.

Assuming members of the subject area committee accepted the importance of curricular depth over breadth, review of the work draft concentrated on the following:

- The extent to which it stimulates those four behaviors in students (significant/partial/none).
- The time required to meet intended student learning outcomes (excessive/considerable/some).
- The teaching methods required to teach outcomes (highly interactive/dynamic/creative).
- The power of the process to advance personal and academic growth through acquiring evidence and applying creative thinking (considerable/significant/some).

To facilitate discussion, we set up the work draft in tabular form, consisting of the draft itself and an adjacent column to record comments. We presented the table on a computer projection, thereby allowing us to record group conclusions during the discussion.

WORK DRAFT	SAC MEMBER COMMENTS
Students participating in and completing the district's language arts curriculum will master outcomes corresponding with written intentions for learning at grade level. Among those intentions for learning are the following: • Defining reality in the context of decisions made valid through background knowledge and evidence. • Gaining insight into human interactions and behaviors as depicted in literature that discusses cultural influences, thereby gaining an appreciation and respect for diversity. • Interpreting problem-solving as the ability of human beings to consider challenges, weigh the accuracy of options found in all types of literature, conduct trial-and-error tests, and work in teams to create and evaluate possible or probable solutions. • Establishing a working definition of creativity as being an authentic learning goal, characterized by the dynamic nurturance and acceptance of novel ideas, proposals, and behaviors that depict curiosity and devotion to some endeavor. • Demonstrating responsible behaviors in the context of what is read as valuable in terms of good taste and logical reasoning, and instructive to readers as guidelines for living and learning. Responsible behaviors manifested in written works reflective of the writer's own creativity, ability to express ideas, opinions, and factual information offered through quality syntax. • Developing through reading and writing an appreciation for competition based on valuable insight, examples of moral/cognitive/physical self-improvement, and willingness to take risks for reasons other than self-aggrandizement. • Accepting persuasiveness based on conviction and improving the common good as the appropriate model for entrepreneurial enterprise. • Accepting the idea that reading, writing, speaking, listening, and interacting through language are the basis of lifelong and worthwhile learning. • Using literature and other media as catalysts essential for making learning a conscious, intentional, and ongoing part of life. • Making curiosity a fundamental part of living and becoming through reading or accessing diverse forms of media on a regular and ongoing basis.	

WORK DRAFT	SAC MEMBER COMMENTS
• Inquiring by using questions posed appropriately and regularly.	
• Participating in the interchange of vigorous and stimulating ideas in which feedback is welcomed.	
• Recognizing the acquisition of self-confidence as the result of taking initiatives in widening groups.	
• Using insights taken from literature and other media, and applying skills in speaking, writing, and listening to the act of reaching out.	
• Placing oneself where encouragement of others is given and received.	
• Practicing the art of mindfulness by being sensitive to prioritize actions and responses, particularly through effective oral and written communication.	
• Articulating the meaning and practice of self-discipline and the development of personal values, reinforced by the reading of quality literature and the viewing of uplifting media.	
• Interacting with others easily based on the art of conversation by maintaining the habit of staying engaged with the world and listening carefully.	
• Pursuing knowledge and sharing that knowledge with humility and sincerity through both speaking and writing.	

We knew even more groundwork needed to be laid before opening discussion with the SAC members.

• • • • • • •

Impact of the Subject Area Mastery in Language Arts

The New Learning Infrastructure is not a patch job but a complete overhaul, coming from a different way of thinking about what twenty-first-century American education should and must be. Its philosophical underpinnings surfaced a century ago, central to the progressive movement in the early twentieth century. Educational philosopher John Dewey led that movement, designed to be compatible with helping all Americans be more democratically engaged. Dewey believed democratic involvement required a thinking citizenry, people who knew how to reflect, analyze, evaluate, and create, and who did so on a regular basis.

Schools requiring students to gain those abilities support and use curricular depth while never ignoring foundational skills and knowledge areas. Neither do they overemphasize such basic skills as was the case with No Child Left Behind.

These schools recognize that how to read, write, and mathematically compute remains critical to everything else in the curriculum. These skills are essential to communicate and create. The ability to read, write, and calculate helps us become better citizens, family members, and workers.

The No Child Left Behind initiative used that rationale, but NCLB bureaucratized and emphasized it to the point that curricular depth was hindered in the name of measurable accountability. NCLB did not attack progressive principles head on, but it succeeded in narrowing curricular imperatives by focusing on baseline skills in reading and mathematics through the use of standards, high-stakes tests, and constricted application of ESEA funding. NCLB also redefined accountability through use of data based primarily on student performance on those high-stakes standardized tests. The data made it possible to classify and compare teachers, schools, districts, and states, a number-based accountability— simple, measurable, and seemingly precise and accurate but superficial and meaningless in human terms.

The New Learning Infrastructure vigorously accepts accountability but in different ways than numerically driven data and comparative inferences. The difference is qualitative more than quantitative. It recognizes human diversity. It accepts intelligence as something found in different packages. Qualitative data are descriptive narrations that paint a picture in which each human being becomes *more* within many dimensions:

- More curious and effective
- More involved with life
- More creative and responsive to new ideas
- More effective as leaders or active participants in a dynamic and worthy culture

Many policy-makers and administrators dislike qualitative data. They believe that type of measurement is not precise enough—too open to interpretation, human foibles, and behavioral nuances. Conversely, precision is too robotic. Accountants, technical workers, and others responsible for exacting accuracy consider robotic behavior valuable.

Innovative thinking and acting are always questioned by some individuals and groups, especially true in education for centuries.

The debate will not disappear, nor should it. Open discussion is imperative; however, diminishing the teaching profession to the status of civil servant compliance is unacceptable in any culture, because stagnation is the result. Rebecca, Barbara, and Mary are aware of the chances they take as they lead the development of mastery statements and a resultant curriculum. But they are convinced quality student learning depends on what they and their colleagues create and execute.

But the twenty-first century contains a plethora of machines programmed to be precise via programs developed by people creative enough to design and build them. In deliberations conducted by the subject area committee, these points of disparity are laid bare. Teacher participants may not see it that way. But Rebecca does, and Barbara and Mary must as they continue their teamwork:

Rebecca provided a structure for SAC discussion about the language arts mastery statement. We wrote a work draft of the statement itself. The work draft came from principles and syntax associated with a more progressive and universal view as to what public education should accomplish. For that reason alone, some SAC members view it as blatantly biased in the current political climate.

The same is true among some members of the curriculum council and school board. They know the language arts curriculum greatly impacts the work of subsequent subject area committees. It also influences district and school policies. For that reason alone, we take this risk.

If language arts SAC members accept our rationale and create a curriculum characterized by depth, other elements of the curriculum need to be structured that way. Social studies would move from a historical overview and governmental basics to an examination of the impact of past events and decisions of leaders. Math and science, already deeply affected by the STEM movement, could be even more influenced by practical applications that require considerable classroom time.

Our preliminary discussions with Rebecca and Superintendent Ken Towers involved conversations designed to identify conflicting principles in simple terms and to attempt to sort them out. The positive result of those discussions meant that both administrators were willing to take the risk, even while knowing they would be on the hot seat with the board, parents, and patrons if the new approach became a political issue.

Ken and Rebecca knew that money and school purposes were prevalent in the minds of some constituents—those who believed curricular breadth a product of efficiency, that public schools are meant to produce a competent workforce for a dynamic free enterprise system. With that administrative go-ahead supporting us, we talked through how to approach the language arts SAC.

The commonly accepted perspective of a K-12 language arts curriculum looks like an inverted pyramid. It begins with children as young as five or six learning the basics. It terminates with young adults of seventeen or eighteen using those basics to expand their literary horizons. The early grades teach basic skills in reading and writing. Those skills are gradually applied to communicate ideas and information via writing, speaking, reading, and listening. The usual debate involves transition strategies used in moving from basic skill development to transmission of sophisticated ideas and information—two interdependent realms.

Reading recognition and comprehension, combined with writing and oral expression, listening, and understanding are essential tools for human communication. But tools are important only when they are used skillfully and creatively, which creates a challenge in curriculum design and teaching methods.

We felt ready to guide the language arts subject area committee toward the possibility of spearheading a district-wide movement. It required a careful approach and patience, but we felt ready for the challenge.

· · · ● · · ·

Subject Area Mastery Statement and Foundational Discussions

Transforming the district's existing curriculum into a succinct mastery statement presented a challenge. With its patchwork approach to school improvement, the standards movement of the last three decades made it difficult to succinctly identify a purpose for American public schools. Because of that piecemeal influence, eight grade levels of the current curriculum were broken into isolated competencies, meant to be measured both formatively and summatively, a carryover from the Common Core scope and sequence created in 2012. Its design, while based on the philosophical rationale behind NCLB, was meant to be more flexible and controlled by the states. The Common Core curriculum in language arts was limited to grades one through eight, broken into measurable competencies associated with categories such as literary reading, informational reading, writing, speaking, listening, and language usage. While those grade and topical divisions made sense, the piece-by-piece manner of teaching and assessing student proficiencies was mind-boggling. For example, second-grade reading literature included the following competencies:

Reading Standards for Literature: Ask and answer such questions as *Who? What? Where? When? Why?* and *How?* Demonstrate understanding of key details in a text.

- Recount stories, including fables and folktales from diverse cultures. Determine their central messages, lessons, or morals.
- Describe how characters in a story respond to major events and challenges.
- Describe how words and phrases supply rhythm and meaning in a story, poem, or song.
- Describe the overall structure of a story. Describe how the beginning introduces the story and the ending concludes the action.
- Acknowledge differences in the points of view of characters. Speak in a different voice for each character when reading dialogue aloud.
- Use information gained from the illustrations and words in a print or digital text. Demonstrate understanding of its characters, setting, or plot.
- Compare and contrast two or more versions of the same story by different authors or from different cultures.
- Read and comprehend literature, including stories and poetry, in grade-appropriate text complexity, with scaffolding as needed at the high end of the range.

All these competencies for second-grade language arts were for literary reading with more competencies listed for informational reading, writing, speaking, listening, and language usage. The problem clearly exemplified excessive minutiae, presented to be regularly assessed. Each portion of every competency was meant to be tested in some fashion, thereby assuring that students received high percentages on standardized tests containing similar challenges. Good teachers always felt accountable for ensuring student proficiency, especially when following their own processes for meeting that goal. But these standards dictated teaching methods and types of interactions with students.

Consider the last competency in the list. The first operant verb is merely an activity ("read"). Another is vague ("comprehend"). Then it mixes two literary forms (stories and poetry). It refers to "grade -appropriate text complexity" as if an established standard unto itself. Then it refers to "scaffolding" as a kind of grade-to-grade building block to achieve an optimum level within a range of complexity.

This is as with training and testing a prospective bridge engineer and worker to perform every conceivable function, regardless of how different the challenge or size of the task may be, reflected in the following language: "Examine all bridge designs, understand their functions over both creeks and major rivers, explain how they are different in complexity, and incorporate maximum safety features in bridges of all types."

People trained to work with bridges are admitted to preparation programs because they are bright and demonstrate acute problem-solving skills, not automatons who require behavioral programming to meet challenges associated with every future contingency. In like fashion, teachers are not meant to be automatons. Like other professionals such as engineers, teachers recognize the uniqueness of each situation and make appropriate decisions. They solve problems, no matter how unique.

Training and public school education involve human beings with the potential to exercise insight and common sense. Trying to micromanage their professional work is both insulting and fruitless. Adult trainees solidify learning through on-the-job training. Second-graders do the same with immersive classroom experiences in contextual interactions between and among teacher and classmates, in strategies often referred to as project learning.

Teachers and instructors consider the objectives found in a standard, but they should not be held accountable for ensuring that every student responds well to standardized summative tests.

Other reasons for not using standards and high-stakes tests to micromanage schools include the following:

- Inadequate contact time between students and their teachers. There is not enough time per school year in on-site classrooms. Time and opportunity are also inadequate in online or hybrid programs.
- Reinforcing individual learning through grade-to-grade articulation is difficult. While curricular articulation remains essential, grade-to-grade knowledge and skill-building require tracking via individual progress charts—an intricate, time-consuming, and expensive process.

Barbara and Mary continue their story:

We designed the first meeting of the K-12 language arts subject area committee to be as straightforward as possible. Rebecca gave a brief orientation to teacher members selected by the curriculum council. "You were chosen because of your classroom competence, intelligence, and interest in improving the district's curriculum. The initial process will be an intensive two-year commitment.

"The New Learning Infrastructure model is different because external standards and high-stakes tests are not used as starting points. Instead, there's an emphasis on what you teachers believe, know, and do in your classrooms with an acceptance that beliefs, knowledge, and methods will become more sophisticated over time. Intentions for student learning must align philosophically, structurally, and contextually with the district's mastery statement."

In the first SAC meeting Rebecca struggled to help teachers born and raised in the external standards and high-stakes tests era to accept her suggestions. It was like turning everything upside down. Teachers entering the profession within the last twenty-five years might be shellshocked by the New Learning Infrastructure or amazed that the work for which they had long been held accountable now featured *who they were* as much as *what they did*.

Rebecca helped lay the foundation for this new way of thinking and becoming in discussions prior to examining the nuts and bolts of curriculum content and design. She included meaningful interactions about what learning really is. "Learning is acceptance of how we as human beings get better, how we become more effective in terms of proficiency, how we build societies that are inclusive, innovative, and purposeful."

• • • • • • •

Subject Area Mastery and Modifying Mindsets

Helping younger teachers understand who they are as professional educators remains a serious challenge. Are they conveyors of information? Agents of a society that enculturates children and young people in prescribed ways? Automatons who teach elements of a curriculum designed by someone in political, institutional, or economic power? Facilitators of thought and nurturers of innovation?

Rebecca headed toward the answers to those questions, and she wanted teacher members of the SAC to follow her lead. Although the board and superintendent agreed to implement the New Learning Infrastructure, the current political climate made the task especially challenging.

Micromanaging schools and curricula remains a goal for Americans who believe in maintaining a certain perspective about the nation's history and values. Giving public school educators latitude to make decisions about curricular content and implementation is a tough sell. Teachers must have—

- Intellectual and emotional depth
- The ability to interact positively and effectively with patrons and parents
- Courage of their convictions regarding the purpose of education

Rebecca, Barbara, and Mary met several times to align their thoughts before discussing these points with SAC members in terms of *who* they were as professionals: (1) demonstrating personal depth, (2) interacting positively and effectively with others, and (3) displaying courage in advocating educational purpose.

All three characteristics were associated with leadership. Their challenge involved how to create academic leaders accustomed to being compliant followers. The discussion proved interesting as Barbara and Mary continue the story:

The new Language Arts SAC met for three days during a scheduled staff development break in the fall semester. We created an agenda for those days, making sure we gave enough time to become acquainted with each other, review the leadership idea, and analyze the district's mastery statement as a foundation for the curriculum we would create.

Those chosen to serve on the district language arts committee included the following:

- Ken Towers, superintendent (ex officio)
- Rebecca Johnson, assistant superintendent for curriculum and instruction (ex officio)
- Bryon Garrett, representative member, board of education
- Barbara Morgan, middle school language arts teacher and committee chair
- Billie Yost, first-grade teacher
- Jackie Smyth, third-grade teacher
- Bob Snyder, fifth-grade teacher
- Mike Hall, high school language arts teacher
- Joan Bell, special education coordinator
- Myra Jackson, elementary school principal
- Jack Dodd, high school principal

Liaison members:

- Mary Chapman-Miller, middle school science teacher, science SAC chair designee
- Betty Wilson, high school math teacher, math SAC chair designee
- Don Baker, K-8 music teacher, fine arts SAC chair designee
- Jennifer Mitchell, district technology coordinator/media specialist

With some exceptions, the fifteen people chosen to serve were not well acquainted. Their roles in the school district's operation varied widely. As administrative and decision-making leaders, the superintendent, assistant superintendent, and representative board member needed to open the door to new possibilities. Ken, Rebecca, and Bryon prepared their remarks.

As committee chair, Barbara believed it was important for traditional district leaders to explain the New Learning Infrastructure, particularly the need for changing how teachers think of themselves as professional educators. Ken began by telling how schools must stimulate and enhance students' ability to think and reflect. Rebecca discussed the importance of helping students analyze systematically.

Bryon, as a board member, noted, "Teacher accountability indices are shifting toward ongoing student growth in terms of reflection and creativity."

Ken wrapped up the presentation by emphasizing the importance of students drawing conclusions based on data used to explore nuances and the abstract "what ifs" of our world.

Barbara wrote the words *reflecting, analyzing, evaluating,* and *creating* on posterboards hung around the room. She initiated the discussion by asking each committee member to "define one key word in terms of how that activity would be approached in your language arts teaching."

Billie and Jackie, teachers of grades one and three, answered in similar ways. They chose the word *analyzing* and defined it in ways they believed appropriate for their students. Billie explained, "The curiosity of young students is almost limitless. The challenge is to help them use observation and language to explore their expanding world, draw accurate conclusions, and describe what they learn. We're already emphasizing that approach to teaching and learning. We believe in helping students think and act creatively."

Bob said, "Analyzing is also important in my fifth-grade class, but reflection helps students connect world events to their lives. Personalization of learning is the way students grow academically and emotionally. My strategy asks students to write, critique, and debate."

Mike, high school teacher, and Jack, high school principal, saw value in continuing the analyzing and reflection elements in secondary school. "Those two behaviors stimulate creativity. We encourage that ability, but high school students should be evaluating ideas and perspectives, given opportunities to weigh products and actions according to data and stated criteria."

Joan said, "I believe the district's special educators need access to the regular curriculum as well as interpretations. While IEPs (individual education plans) are essential, just as important are expectations for student growth found in the district's mission statement."

Liaison members of the committee participated in follow-up discussions and took careful notes. Designated chairs of other subject area committees realized their members would be involved in the same exercise in the context of their fields of study.

This first interaction of our language arts subject area committee consumed an entire workday. Notes would be reviewed at the next meeting.

What teachers currently do in their classrooms is an important beginning point from a logistical perspective. But opening the door to the more philosophical aspects of the New Learning Infrastructure is even more essential.

· · · ● · · ·

Subject Area Mastery: Reasoning as Well as Performing

We recognize what is happening in the district's first SAC meeting. The change factor, while dramatic, must not ignore the positive aspects of traditional American education. Although the pandemic deeply affected the organizational structure of today's schools, they nevertheless have a solid foundation and historical significance. The New Learning Infrastructure is not meant to replace schools as we know them. It is to help them become more effective, more capable of preparing students for twenty-first-century challenges. In brief, the differences follow:

- Professional collaboration—not line-and-staff, top-down decision-making
- Curriculum designed to produce a thoughtful, creative, and real-istically productive citizenry—not one meant to prepare societal and economic minions
- Curriculum developed by sensitive and accountable professional educators—not issued by those in political and economic power or authority
- Assessment of student learning that is ongoing, intense, and multi-faceted—not limited to summative methods for measuring outcomes that generate accountability data

The story moves beyond Barbara and Mary, but they remain central figures, symbolic of a movement that requires different kinds of teachers—teachers who are "somebodies," collaborating with each other in the educational community, creating powerful curricula and effective instructional programs, serving as responsive yet assertively accountable educational leaders.

Superintendent Ken Towers and assistant superintendent Rebecca Johnson act as colleagues with everyone else, transformative roles with both executives and equals, collaborative decision-makers on the curriculum council and subject area committees.

Bryon Garrett's role as a board member is also transformative. He represents both the opinions of his peers and the perspectives of educators on the SAC. He serves as a conduit between and among professional educators, school patrons, and parents of students enrolled in the district.

Ken, Rebecca, and Bryon serve as important role models for everyone else on the language arts subject area committee. They convey personas that represent two worlds, one in which leaders have the authority to issue directives, another in which they are "first among equals."

"First among equals" comes from the Latin *primus inter pares,* an honorary title for a person who holds an official title in an organization yet is recognized by the organization's members as being one of them. It is similar to a prime minister who implements the will of a political party, an executive director who serves a professional organization, or a church pastor who both guides and is responsive to the will of the congregation—an academic analogy akin to a university administrator introducing herself as "professor of biology currently serving as dean of the college."

A big challenge to the New Learning Infrastructure is that the profession of teaching has so many divisions: different subjects, grade levels, leadership roles, and support units.

Other professions also have divisions but are somewhat more capable of coalescing around central themes. For educators to make collaborative decision-making work, they must enhance their levels of understanding and trust in each other. That is the challenge in the following scenario.

Key to the effectiveness of the language arts SAC is development of the "first among equals" way of thinking and acting. Reaching that goal requires considerable dialogue and a slowly shifting mindset, so Barbara guides the growth of the collaborative decision-making conversation:

I started the next meeting of the language arts subject area committee. We reviewed Mary's notes from the previous meeting. Mary surprised me. She put her notes down and asked the liaison members to offer their impressions. These were designees of future SACs like her, as well as Jennifer, Betty, and Don.

Mary began: "In our previous discussion our liaison members were not given an opportunity to participate. But they listened carefully because they are responsible for continuing the New Learning Infrastructure model in their own SACs. Betty, as chair of the upcoming math subject area committee, what was your takeaway from yesterday's meeting?"

Betty shifted a little in her chair and almost whispered, "I felt kind of conflicted about some of the ideas. Math is my teaching field but also my favorite discipline, because it requires focused and logical thinking and acting, a tool for managing or understanding our world systematically, whether in economics, engineering, science, or any other aspect of human life. It cuts across everything we do and are." Betty then looked at Ken and said, "Dr. Towers—"

"Call me Ken."

She did a doubletake and smiled. "Okay, Ken—you offered two perspectives you may believe are compatible with the application of both language arts *and* mathematics. You said students need the power to reflect and draw conclusions based on data. I agree with those points. Then you said something about exploring nuances and abstractions in our world."

Betty cleared her throat. "Maybe language allows for the exploration of subtleties and innovative ideas, but math is only a tool to explain or verify. It appears creativity is being pushed to the forefront of our district's mastery statement. While I do not dispute the importance of creativity in both the academic and real world, I'm not sure how my upcoming math SAC should handle that objective."

Ken sat quietly a moment before attempting an answer. Looking at the ceiling, he then said, "Language is also a tool our brains use to interact with the world. Words and phrases describe and explain, perhaps in a more subjective way than numbers, formulas, and computations. But numbers and words are both just tools to help us navigate challenges and make our lives better.

"Our district already pushes project learning as a central teaching method. It both simulates real life and engages with it, and real life amalgamates learning, ignoring education's tendency to separate everything into subjects.

"My son is close to completing his degree in mechanical engineering. He and other students built a special device to help quadriplegics. Except for statistics describing muscular behaviors, cognitive impairments, and physical limitations, numbers were not enough for the team to solve the problem. Both linguistic and numerical descriptors were needed to interchangeably epitomize the problem—to invent a solution that worked mechanically, cognitively, and emotionally.

"Creativity used a mixture of methods to problem-solve. My son's professor said good engineering is like that, using language and numbers interactively to imagine possible answers, then build devices that work for the benefit of humankind."

Mary nodded. "Jennifer, as our technology specialist, I wonder what you think."

Jennifer sat on the edge of her chair, ready to make a serious contribution.

"Emphasize the twenty-first century's dependence on technology."

"Yes," said Mary. "Jennifer makes a good point. Technology is more than mathematics alone. Real life has always been more than mathematics or any other one skill or knowledge area. In fact, real life includes many behaviors and understandings not even found in a school curriculum."

The New Learning Infrastructure's challenge is to make schools more like everyday life. Everyday life cannot break five or six hours into reading, then mathematics, then science, and so on. Even our workdays are an amalgam of skills we use both interchangeably and productively.

Elementary teachers in self-contained classrooms often accept interdisciplinary configurations if resources and textbooks are written that way—typically *not* true for those teaching in middle school or high school. Teaching their favorite subject is now a pleasure.

Some SAC members find it difficult to coalesce around a broad curricular theme, a theme not limited to their own narrow discipline. Betty recognizes that problem, and Ken's response confused her. To Betty, society elevates mathematics to premier status. Genius is often equated with proficiency in math. Why should schools let math be absorbed by other intellectual pursuits?

Ken's remarks about engineers using language and numbers interactively to imagine possible answers clearly struck a chord for Jennifer.

"Technology is really nothing new," Jennifer said. "Human beings have been discovering ways to make life healthier and more convenient for centuries. The definition to focus on in this district is the knowledge of how our universe works and how that is put to practical use. Too many people believe technology is something electronic, magical, and mysterious.

"But that way of thinking minimizes technology's real importance to us, both historically and sociologically. Does this sound strange coming from your district's twenty-first-century technology specialist? We need to paint technology with a much broader brush. Let me explain by sharing this definition I found in an Internet search."

Jennifer flipped through her yellow legal pad. "This is a quote from *WordLift:* 'The word *technology* refers to the making, modification, usage, and knowledge of tools, machines, techniques, crafts, systems, and methods of organization—in order to solve a problem, improve a preexisting solution to a problem, achieve a goal, handle an applied input/output relation or perform a specific function. It can also refer to the collection of such tools, including machinery, modifications, arrangements, and procedures.'

"See—that definition does not say anything about computers, electronics, robotics, or any other gee-whiz stuff. If we break that broad definition down, the key idea has to do with using our brains and resources to invent tools. These tools help us solve problems, improve something, meet goals, and improve functions. Period."

Jennifer looked at Ken. "I was only partially aware of the district's strong interest in project teaching and learning. Technology curricula have long been based on that approach. But some of our teachers feel academically inferior to those teaching in the subject disciplines, perhaps because of the traditional definitions of accountability—how student learning is measured using high-stakes tests. Not long ago I talked with a retired professor who once taught a course titled 'Foundations of Education.'

"The professor told me his course was philosophical. Various theories were studied and discussed, including theories about learning and how teaching should be conducted to make it happen. He and his students dove into the beliefs of educational leaders of the late nineteenth and early twentieth centuries."

Jennifer looked around at the group. "That retired professor was discouraged by what happened after World War II. He was convinced that war changed our nation's priorities. Americans became more focused on practicalities and making money. Technical, economic, and social progress was good in many ways, but it also promoted cause-and-effect thinking as being more important than reflection on the meaning of life."

Myra and Joan looked at each other and smiled. Both were members of the same church, clearly ready to jump into the conversation about cause and effect versus the meaning of life.

Joan asked, "Are you suggesting that cause and effect, probably the basis on which we make most of our daily decisions, is a wrong way of thinking and acting? If so, where does that leave science? How does that influence the importance of data in managing our individual and corporate lives?"

Before Jennifer could respond, Myra said, "I think Jennifer is saying that reflection on anything, especially the meaning of life, depends on more than data analysis. And I'm not suggesting a converse situation related to ignorance, superstition, or religious belief systems—that they should somehow replace scientific knowledge or its acquisition.

"Reflection helps us put data and reality into a more human context, which includes emotions and subliminal perspectives. Rationality is more than developing and testing hypotheses. It has much to do with intuitive thought processes."

Mary could not resist a response. "Yes, Myra. What many people do not understand is that even building a hypothesis involves a powerful imagination. Many scientific effects we readily accept today originally came from conjuring up a string of 'what ifs,' notions that sounded looney to other scientists and researchers. In the context of their reality at the time, reinforced by each other's professional approval, such proposals were considered implausible or even silly."

Jennifer said, "Our world is more than right and wrong, black and white, and even cause and effect. At the root of technology is imagination, which makes past assumptions about calculations and operating principles only part of the picture. I am invigorated by the district's emphasis on project teaching and learning—not in just one discipline or subject but in all subjects and combinations of subjects."

We needed to take a lunch break, so I suggested our post-lunch conversation focus on the primary mission of our subject area committee—language arts, incorporating the additional points discussed. I summarized our discussion and created a lead-in for the next conversation. "Many ideas have been presented today. Let's see if we can carry away from this phase of our discussion a few points of general agreement in a multi-point proposal. The district is moving toward emphasizing project teaching and learning. That approach may require—

1. More instructional planning including multiple teaching methods and group interaction
2. Teacher imagination
3. Acceptance of interdisciplinary considerations
4. Real-life applications
5. A mindset that accepts creative language as a medium for incorporating other disciplines
6. Skills associated with storytelling to frame complementary ideas and actions
7. Creating scenarios that teach probable outcomes as well as alternate possibilities

Was I on a suitable track? I felt encouraged when Betty commented, "I'm willing to enter this whimsical world because I want the best learning environment for my math students. But truthfully, I also want the best for myself as a professional educator."

I smiled and said, "Let's break for lunch and then see where the discussion takes us."

13

Creativity as a Companion to Cause and Effect

Rebecca earned her doctorate in curriculum and instruction. Her dissertation topic studied the effectiveness of Ted Sizer's Coalition of Essential Schools (CES). As an influential educational leader in the late twentieth century, Sizer detailed how to align America's high schools with principles originally advocated decades earlier by John Dewey.

CES high school proponents believed that—

- Learning means using one's mind well.
- Less is more (depth over coverage).
- School goals should apply to all students.
- Personalization should be emphasized, with teachers held responsible for individualized student progress.
- Students are held accountable for learning, with teachers serving as their coaches.
- Mastery of learning is determined through student performance of real tasks, using multiple forms of evidence, concluding with an "exhibition" of skills and knowledge areas.
- A school's "tone" should be one of decency and trust based on clear-cut expectations, not standards and penalties for failing to

meet them.

- Interdisciplinary thinking prevails among all teachers, not an emphasis on subject matter, thereby demonstrating commitment to the school's total mission.
- Budgets focus exclusively on teaching and learning in such areas as planning time, personalization of instruction, and staff salaries.
- School policies are inclusive, democratic, and based on equality.

With some external funding, many high schools across the nation accepted these ideas. Extra funding made it possible to keep schools comparatively small and allowed them to meet the ten principles. But by 2018 the standards and high-stakes testing requirements, as well as political acceptance of micromanaged accountability, destroyed the movement. Then the COVID pandemic hammered the last nail in the coffin.

Rebecca knows about Dewey's philosophy, the rise and fall of CES, and how close the language arts SAC is growing toward constructing these processes. But she remains silent.

Soon she will comment on the ideas bubbling up from Barbara and other SAC members.

They realize two truths: (1) in some ways, they overlap the philosophy of the CES, and (2) they differ as they push the idea of language arts and technology used as core media through which everything else is taught and learned.

Rebecca knows that discussing Dewey and Sizer is an esoteric exercise for a group of building educators and a hard sell for the district. But she wants to see how the idea plays out, because this approach might be at the core of a New Learning Infrastructure.

Barbara's Discussion and the Summary of Prior Ideas

Using my computer and projector, I displayed the summarized points. The district is moving toward emphasizing enriched project teaching and learning, which may require—

1. More instructional planning, including multiple teaching methods and group interactions
2. Teacher imagination
3. Acceptance of interdisciplinary considerations
4. Real-life applications
5. A mindset that accepts creative language as a medium for incorporating other disciplines
6. Skills associated with storytelling to frame complementary ideas and actions
7. Creating scenarios that teach probable outcomes as well as alternate possibilities

Instead of addressing each one in sequence, I asked for questions and comments about any or all seven of the points. Rebecca raised her hand and talked about Ted Sizer and John Dewey. But that kind of academic background information seemed too philosophical for SAC members to deal with. Most of the SAC members frowned.

Recognizing the issue, Rebecca said, "I'll revisit those philosophical ideas later. Let's go back to Barbara's list. What do you think about her points?"

Billie mumbled, "Did we really talk about those points? They only look vaguely familiar, and it's only been ninety minutes since the end of this morning's meeting."

Others laughed, but I realized their agreement with Billie. "Maybe I editorialized a little to synthesize the ideas we discussed. Did I misinterpret or inadvertently add something only I was thinking?"

Billie said, "No, they just seem a bit exotic when summarized. Let me see if I can put them into language first-graders might recognize. In my classroom students are involved in a variety of things and love to talk with each other about common projects. And, wow, do they ever have imagination!

"My first-graders don't see the world in categories. To them the world is fascination with anything they can see, touch, analyze, manipulate, examine, explore, and wonder about. They see it as an amazing story in which they are a part.

"I laugh when adults use words like *conjecture* and *hypothesis* in serious ways, as if they are formal and scientific. My students may not be able to define those words, but they live their meaning every minute of every day. They constantly speculate, wondering what would happen if . . ."

Jackie responded by pointing to her laptop, where she pulled up information about *All I Really Need to Know I Learned in Kindergarten*, the book written in 1989 by Robert Fulghum. She read a few passages: "'I believe imagination is stronger than knowledge. Myth is more potent than history. Dreams are more powerful than facts. Hope always triumphs over experience. Laughter is the only cure for grief. And I believe love is stronger than death.'"

Jackie said, "Maybe that sounds like a silly reaction, but as a third-grade teacher I see the flash of curiosity disappear from the eyes of some students. When I walk down the hall and see my past students, now in upper grades, most of them look dazed. They stare at cell phones or nothing at all. It's as if school is drudgery, except for social aspects found in friendship, sports, and relationship-building. What happened to those first-graders excited about life and learning? Where does that excitement go?"

Bob, feeling somewhat defensive, said, "I try to encourage my students to be excited and involved with life and learning. The way to keep my fifth-graders engaged with life is to put them in simulated or real scenarios. It's a little hard to explain, but I acknowledge the existence of social media and recognize much of what my students are reading and saying. I recognize it, though not necessarily accept it as being valuable. But even something that looks like nonsensical trivia is valuable in the context of the larger issues of their day."

Jack, the high school principal, looked annoyed. "Our job as educators is to help students understand that society requires self-discipline, hard work, and the determination to make good decisions and serious contributions to our communities. That's what maturity is about. Learning that life is not just whimsy and playing pretend. It is preparing adults to enter the real world of work, to make a living, and be responsible citizens. More than ever, our nation and our world need that approach to education."

After Jack's declaration, I waited silently. Many people think the way Jack does and with good reason. Responsible behavior is certainly associated with following rules and laws—meeting expectations, coloring within the lines. To those people the concept of creativity is chaotic, uncomfortable, and unpredictable.

It was almost time to end the meeting, so I told the group I would transcribe my notes and begin tomorrow's meeting with a discussion of the emerging two points of view. How can we best merge those two viewpoints to result in a new way of thinking about curriculum?

· · · ● · · ·

Making Creativity a Companion to Cause and Effect

Divergent points of view are common in American society, often oversimplified as political opinion in how we define freedom, as a right accorded everyone or an opportunity for those trained and working to achieve it.

Jack's opinion lies in the "opportunity" camp. To him all actions result in reactions. Life is challenging and schools must prepare students to react well through cause and effect. To Jack, reacting well uses effective techniques in a disciplined manner. Those who react well are trained thoroughly and possess the self-discipline to use their training effectively. As with football players, their cause is to win, so the effect means the team uses fundamentals well. Not staying true to fundamentals, allowing someone to forget or reject them, or getting too creative results in losing.

The "teacher as coach" principle was advocated by Ted Sizer in his model, but only in the context of ensuring that no student is allowed to fail. To Sizer, fundamentals are fluid and interactive—not sacrosanct truisms. They shift when new strategies are needed, created by both leaders and followers when circumstances require different ways of thinking and acting.

If following fundamentals causes a team to lose, let's think differently. Why not be creative and face a different challenge in a novel way? This is the essence of twenty-first-century living and the reason we need a New Learning Infrastructure. Creativity and following fundamentals are not opposing curricular principles. Constructing creative and fundamental curricula describes the challenge facing Barbara and those serving on the language arts subject area committee.

Barbara's Discussion toward a New Level of Discernment

Opinions drift based on various factors.

An opinion expressed one day might change the following day, sometimes dramatically. Collegial decision-making must recognize and work with this condition. The dialogue that follows shows the importance of steady and ongoing discussion, giving everyone latitude to reflect and reconsider over time.

Jack's comment at the end of yesterday's meeting lessened the enthusiasm. Before his remark, connecting technology to language arts sounded like a way to open the door to creativity via project learning. I asked Jack to elaborate on his position.

He looked apologetic. "I didn't mean to shut down discussion, because I do understand the importance of creativity in a curriculum. Many teachers in my school agree. They use project teaching and learning activities in their classrooms. My comment comes from a concern. Are we lowering the academic rigor our graduates need to compete in post-secondary programs and higher education?

"As important as creativity is, we still need competence in basic skills and knowledge areas. If the pandemic proved anything, it's that our society needs more technicians, carpenters, electricians, mechanics, plumbers, and Internet technicians."

As a technology specialist, Jennifer agreed: "But technology evolves in ways that require insight and an ability to communicate effectively. The real world of work is not a static thing. It probably never was. Workers do not robotically do the same thing every day in any vocation or profession. Upgrades in devices and processes are constant, making the need for education and training ongoing.

"What is true today may be different tomorrow. I'm excited about the possibility of more project teaching and learning, mixed with technology as a baseline for many subjects we teach. In fact, I think we should use technical reading and writing as a baseline for our language arts curriculum, which may require us to modify those terms."

Jennifer read from her notes: "The standard definition of technical writing offered online by *Your Dictionary* states, 'Technical writing is where the author writes about a particular subject that requires direction, instruction, or explanation. This style of writing has a very different purpose and different characteristics than other writing styles such as creative writing, academic writing, or business writing.'

"Based on that definition, what I suggest may sound crazy, but I think all communication is explanatory. Technical writing does indeed 'explain,' but the same is true of creative, academic, and business writing. Creative writing requires an ability to explain so readers can identify with the story line, a departure from reality. The writer must explain a new reality in ways readers can intellectually or emotionally grasp.

"In other words, creating never totally disconnects from human understanding. There must be a link someplace. Academic writing is typically founded in research activities or findings, influenced by both its findings and hypotheses that initiated scholarly investigation in the first place. Proving a hypothesis through rigorous investigation proves challenging if that hypothesis comes from an intellect stimulated by seemingly untethered curiosity.

"Business writing ranges from the preparation of tech manuals to memoranda. Believe me—I've read hundreds of them. The most effective are those that use stimulating verbiage, relevant examples, and a convincing writing style. In fact, much business writing is now found on social media and web pages that creatively inform through use of graphics, videos, and other entertaining visual effects.

"All effective writing, technical or not, directs and instructs readers. It guides them toward new ways of thinking and behaving.

How to use tools is a direction or instruction. But so is writing that tells us how to better appreciate ballet, paintings, music, government, philosophy, and other elements of human learning. Reading what is written is valuable only when it changes us."

We stared at Jennifer and considered her thought-provoking arguments. Board member Bryon looked at the ceiling. Jack doodled on a legal pad.

Finally Joan spoke up. "You know, what Jennifer said resonates with me as a special educator. Students who are categorized as special, whether gifted or cognitively challenged, need tangibility, something concrete to connect their learning to, an idea that makes sense, a piece of knowledge or skill that somehow gives them intellectual or emotional comfort.

"In fact, we all need to respond that way for the sake of retention. If learning is the impetus underlying changes in behavior, as John Dewey believed, our curriculum must be written and taught with that objective in mind."

I asked everyone on the SAC what they thought.

Don said, "My head hurts. If we move in the direction Jennifer suggests, my courses in music appreciation will be dropped in favor of developing playing and performance skills."

I asked SAC members to pursue that idea a bit further in music and all other subjects, with language arts at the core. Some of the committee members were obviously confused or overwhelmed.

* * * * * * *

Connecting Tangibility and Creativity

This typical language arts subject area committee tries to make learning a change in behavior or thought. They aim to be insightful and willing to grapple with more than the standard scope-and-sequence challenge. Attention to scope and sequence is a standard approach to curriculum development and implementation, a traditional aspect of the New Learning Infrastructure. In ordinary language, scope means finding a way to label curricular size, as in how much should be taught and learned at any given time. Sequence is the order to be followed, how it should spiral upward and gradually expand.

Coordinating that spiraling and expansion appears maddeningly difficult. Historically, textbook authors handled it. Novice teachers trusted the sequence found in textbooks, which allowed education policy-makers to focus their attention on the adequacy and appropriateness of resource materials like textbooks. But managing scope and sequence minimized the importance of teachers, making curriculum a game of Trivial Pursuit. This method of curricular scope and sequence only adds more information or skills to previously learned material. It is systematic and mechanistic.

Because of that concrete approach, many policy-makers believe that through their administrative actions they control learning through four principles:

- Concentrate on textbook selection.
- Label professional teacher education as worthless.
- Initiate the development of academic standards.
- Promote the use of high-stakes tests.

Those policies sacrifice real student learning on the altar of managerial control. Excessive managerial control in any endeavor diminishes human potential. The language arts subject area committee members in our story understand the problem. They know human potential is tapped only when students attach tangible meaning to what they are taught. They realize learning involves more than a game of Trivial Pursuit, more than a memory game associated with incidentals and small pieces of knowledge. It is also more than meeting societal expectations based on how well one jumps over hurdles with academic credentials that open doors to jobs and social acceptance.

Meaningful learning associates with what is perceived as authentic, deserving of tangible action and interesting enough to play around with intellectually. Students appreciate the opportunities to manipulate learning in real-world terms, to create new ways of thinking and acting, to sense a need to change the way they live day by day.

Barbara Guides the Discussion toward a New Level of Discernment

Our discussion gained traction. Language arts could be approached differently, thought of and used as a means through which we manage our world tangibly, productively, and creatively. We suggested that language arts are tools through which other disciplines become more relevant if approached in a real-world context through project teaching and learning.

Don seemed doubtful as he suggested that courses designed to stimulate appreciation did not fit the mold. On the other hand, music performance corresponded in many ways with our thinking about communication, creativity, tangibility, and project learning. "Performance is associated with skills like 'reading' music, singing, or playing an instrument, creativity in the realm of musicianship and tangibility in conveying reactions such as emotion or pleasure. Performance communicates in the same way good stories do, so I can accept the comparison to language arts."

Committee members understood Don's logic. But why did he express concern about his music appreciation course? "It isn't just about music appreciation," Don said. "It's about appreciation in general. I struggle with what appreciation means and how it fits the mission of any educational program."

Bryon nodded. "Like other members of the board, my children attend your schools. During the COVID pandemic this district used a hybrid teaching/learning model. We understood how difficult it was for teachers to use that process. As laypeople and elected representatives of district patrons, we wondered what effect the hybrid model had on our kids. To be frank, it seemed minimal, especially in the category of appreciation.

"My kids finished their assignments, but they seemed almost lifeless in terms of academic growth. And they were unable to tell me what, if anything, they were getting out of school. In other words, I don't think they appreciated *any* of it, on *any* level."

Superintendent Ken admitted, "That's scary—but probably true.

The pandemic caught our society off guard, and we educators were no exception. Joan used a word educators throw around all the time. *Retention* was seriously affected by the pandemic. I suspect there was little retention of anything taught during the COVID years.

"Joan's work with lower-functioning special education children makes the goal of retention especially hard to reach. Many times the goal is met through constant repetition and the recognition of varied learning styles. Dynamic and continuous follow-up uses a variety of venues. But retention is a companion of appreciation, and both are a companion to relevance. We remember what we appreciate, and we appreciate what is relevant to our lives.

"Don, I don't know how you approach the teaching of music appreciation. Frankly, my music appreciation course in high school seemed like torture. But one part of the course I do remember—the composers, their stories, and what motivated them. Oddly, I remember two words: *genre* and *culture.*

"For one interesting exercise we wrote a story about Mozart, as if he had been born in 1856 or 1956 instead of 1756. We organized into groups of three to discuss the challenge, conduct the research, and prepare to present our papers.

"The question we needed to answer was 'What kind of music would Mozart have written in the assigned time and place?' My assigned place was the United States in 1856, specifically the mountains of eastern Tennessee. I described the culture and the prevailing genre of music when my 'Mozart' was twenty years old.

"You can imagine how much I learned, especially about how our culture defines creativity, how different kinds of genres produce particular ways of believing and acting. Of special interest were the findings of those assigned the Mozart born in 1956 in Los Angeles. That research and our findings made me appreciate the idea of music fitting into an era and lifestyle—how much they overlap, how music is an extension of who we are and what we believe."

After Ken spoke, I asked, "Have we identified another way language arts and the broader definition of technology provides a foundation for attacking something as challenging as appreciation?

While the type of music located in Ken's research was critical, its description and storyline development had to be presented in words, sentences, paragraphs, essays, and evidentiary writing."

The language arts SAC needed to stop theorizing and begin putting legs on these ideas, but the way was not clear. With the help of Rebecca and others, we started moving in that direction.

● ● ● ● ● ● ●

A Philosophical Foundation

The language arts subject area committee unintentionally drifted. Only the curriculum council and board of education could act. They needed a philosophical direction, so Rebecca conferred with Barbara. In a word, the direction was *interdisciplinary.* Non-language-arts teachers began to see the logic of connecting language arts and technology, to let language be the thread that runs through all subjects in a project-based environment.

To make that adjustment work and ensure compatibility, Barbara and Rebecca examined both district and language arts mastery statements, written with broad philosophical strokes and no conflicts. But the building blocks of a discipline were not specifically mentioned—no mention of vocabulary development, sentence structure, word meaning, grammar, spelling, handwriting, composition, and other technical aspects of communication.

They must give considerable attention to the specifics of mathematics, science, social studies, music, physical education, visual arts, or any other subject in public school curriculum. The New Learning Infrastructure underscores attention to detail. Details are always important, but they emerge over time. Policy statements acknowledge only a need, as in making the case for new bridges. Those kinds of policies refer to what constitutes quality in general terms, but they never specify what kind of girders or bolts to use. Policies include no assumptions. They imply, even declare, that contractors and their chosen staff are highly competent and skilled. Policies provide external safety inspections—critical accreditation in project development.

Unlike the policy approach, the No Child Left Behind agenda microman-aged the nation's public education system way beyond policy changes. This practice destroyed confidence in teachers, both in themselves and among those who worked with them. Before NCLB, associations created subject area standards and strengthened accreditation processes. Standardized subject-focused tests were created and implemented. Efforts improved teacher education programs. A movement began to increase teacher involvement in the decision-making structure, but NCLB short-circuited all those efforts and the rationale behind them. If bridge-building used NCLB strategies, bureaucrats and politicians would tell contractors exactly what they expected in detail, such as the particular weld used on girder number five.

Changing that mindset and practice in American education, especially at the district level, remains a difficult task. It requires Barbara, Mary, Rebecca, Ken, and all others serving on both the curriculum council and language arts subject area committee to operate at a high level of intellectual engagement, to align the district and language arts mastery statements in their thinking and actions without getting sidelined with details best left to the discretion of knowledgeable and creative teachers.

They start the process by discussing and reflecting on the two mastery statements—how to create more specific curricular elements. Then the language arts subject area committee drafts a recommendation for the curriculum council to consider.

DISTRICT MASTERY STATEMENT	LANGUAGE ARTS MASTERY STATEMENT
Students completing the full program of studies at XYZ School District will have skills that expand their understanding of reality—a deeper understanding of themselves and how they fit into the world. They can solve complex problems, think and act creatively, and responsibly manage their own needs. Graduates understand and can act on principles associated with entrepreneurship, the ability to become lifelong learners through knowing how to learn and being motivated to do so. They are curious about ways they can stretch boundaries into new and different realms with an inherent drive to learn continuously, to ask good questions, and become part of diverse communities in which feedback is vigorous and stimulating. They will understand the importance of self-confidence, gained through experience with widening groups, taking meaningful initiatives (reaching out), receiving consistent encouragement from respected associates. Graduates will practice mindfulness in terms of clarifying priorities and actions each day. They are open to others from different backgrounds. They understand and work to achieve self-discipline and personal values, to create and maintain the convictions to pursue these values. Students completing the full program of studies at XYZ School District will speak and write effectively. They will know how to make people feel at ease, those from every walk of life. Graduates will enter conversations with others and show genuine interest in their ideas and activities.	Students participating in and completing the district's language arts curriculum will master outcomes corresponding with written intentions for learning at grade level, defining reality in the context of decisions made valid through background knowledge and evidence. Gaining insight into human interactions and behaviors as depicted in literature that discusses cultural influences, thereby gaining an appreciation and respect for diversity. Interpreting problem-solving as the ability of human beings to consider challenges, weigh the accuracy of options found in all types of literature, conduct trial-and-error tests, and work in teams to create and evaluate possible or probable solutions. Establishing a working definition of creativity as being an authentic learning goal, characterized by the dynamic nurturance and acceptance of novel ideas, proposals, and behaviors that depict curiosity and devotion to some endeavor. Demonstrating responsible behaviors in the context of what is read as valuable in terms of good taste, logical reasoning, and instructive to readers as guidelines for living and learning. Responsible behaviors are also manifested in written works reflective of the writer's own creativity, ability to express ideas, opinions, and factual information offered through quality syntax. Developing, through reading and writing, an appreciation for competition based on valuable insight, examples of moral/cognitive/physical self-improvement, and willingness to take risks for reasons other than self-aggrandizement. Accepting persuasiveness based on conviction and improving the common good as the appropriate model for entrepreneurial enterprise.

DISTRICT MASTERY STATEMENT	LANGUAGE ARTS MASTERY STATEMENT
While each academic discipline is important, graduates will grasp the idea that problem-solving is usually associated with a complex and interactive system. Solving problems requires collaborative skills that allow all disciplines to work in concert. Graduates will understand the meaning of intellectual passion, a passion for not only attaining more knowledge but also for comprehending its significance and value. The ability to communicate expressively both orally and in writing is vital. Life is more than a single dimension. It is an assortment of experiences that make it worth living.	Accepting the idea that reading, writing, speaking, listening, and interacting through language are the basis of lifelong and worthwhile learning. Using literature and other media as catalysts, essential for making learning a conscious, intentional, and ongoing part of life. Making curiosity a fundamental part of living and becoming, through reading or accessing diverse forms of media on a regular and ongoing basis. Inquiring through the use of questions posed appropriately and regularly. Participating in the interchange of vigorous and stimulating ideas in which feedback is welcomed. Recognizing the acquisition of self-confidence as the result of taking initiatives in widening groups. Using insights taken from literature and other media, and applying skills in speaking, writing, and listening to the act of reaching out. Placing oneself where encouragement of others is given and received. Practicing the art of mindfulness by being sensitive to prioritize actions and responses, particularly through effective oral and written communication. Articulating the meaning and practice of self-discipline and development of personal values, reinforced by the reading of quality literature and the viewing of uplifting media. Interacting with others based on the art of conversation by maintaining the habit of staying engaged with the world and listening carefully. Pursuing knowledge and sharing that knowledge with humility and sincerity through both speaking and writing.

While one document remained preeminent, the SAC members attempted to make the two documents compatible by comparing meanings of words and phrases. The best example of their challenge is found in our government when state constitutions are expected to be compatible with, yet subordinate to, the national document. The Constitution of the United States is written in a direct and straightforward manner with words and phrases relatively precise. Authors of the Constitution knew its simplicity as both a strength and a weakness, so the Supreme Court was created to sort out differences of opinion. The authors also knew that a document written in 1787 might cause semantic issues over time in the context of both law and state level interpretations.

We know the amazing outcome of the United States governmental experiment, the first in the world for a large nation. It works surprisingly well in a messy, convoluted, and time-consuming way. Its genius forces dynamic dialogue on a regular basis, which although sometimes frustrating, forces us to avoid complacency and mediocrity.

That is the idea behind the New Learning Infrastructure. A faculty of intellectually engaged educators are dynamically involved with curriculum and the best kind of student learning. They stimulate cognitive effectiveness and academic creativity in their students.

14

A Proposal Is Readied for the Curriculum Council

A t the next council meeting Rebecca and Barbara present the proposal from the language arts subject area committee. But first they discuss it with Ken and Bryon in a leadership strategy session. The proposal requests that the primary mission of the district be supported with a merger of (1) communications, (2) technology, and (3) project-based methods.

Such a merger requires the language arts and district mission statements to be compatible, with the same being true of all other subject area mission statements. Ken told Rebecca and Barbara to write the proposal in easy-to-understand language. "Use examples and analogies. Indicate what sells the idea to school patrons, students, and parents of students."

Ken also suggested that they redefine learning, characterized as "continuous and meaningful output" more than "tested input." The curriculum in all subject areas, while founded on building knowledge and skills, also focuses on engaging students in problem-solving. Enough knowledge and skills are provided to prompt students to research and solve problems on their own, which then expands the breadth and depth of their learning, while technology plays a serious role.

Ken said, "Right now we provide students answers for which they have no questions. The challenge is to create conditions that stimulate curiosity, resulting in lasting and meaningful learning."

Rebecca responded by using her deep knowledge of learning theory. "What we're suggesting is nothing new. It goes back to Socrates, John Dewey, and hundreds of other philosophers over centuries. its most common label being *constructivism*, sometimes linked to inductive rather than deductive reasoning."

Rebecca reminded the council that constructivism works only if the following elements are present:

- Public school patrons and taxpayers agree with and support this learning theory.
- Curriculum includes outcomes that incorporate all learning categories.
- Teachers use appropriate teaching strategies and assessments.
- Evidence is offered that students are prepared for post-secondary education.

Rebecca Leads the Curriculum Council Discussion

As assistant superintendent for curriculum and instruction, Rebecca chairs the district's curriculum council.

She is the leader with the best understanding of pedagogy, but she uses those skills to enhance the professionalism of everyone. Rebecca ensures full involvement of all other professionals and stakeholders serving as members. Those skills are used to promote interactive discussion and effective decision-making. In this scenario she meets with the other council leaders *before* the full meeting: the superintendent, a board member, and chair of the language arts subject area committee. Their purpose is to review strategies to reinforce explanations for teachers, parents, and patrons.

Before taking the proposal to the curriculum council, I discussed it further with Ken, Barbara, and Bryon. We reviewed the basics of the language arts proposal, and we agreed that a constructivist approach was needed to incorporate it. But that system required that we prepare parents and patrons, become serious about applying all learning categories found in Bloom's taxonomy, upgrade teaching and assessment methods, and create and establish accountability measures.

This New Learning Infrastructure is novel in twenty-first-century terms. We expect parent/patron reactions to be mixed. A clearly understood foundation must be laid, including ways to encourage public acceptance, prepare teachers, and assure accountability. I elaborated on those three points with additional explanation:

Public Acceptance: While concerned about school quality, political divisiveness remains high. People think they know what they *don't* like, but they are not unanimous about what they *do* like.

Teacher Preparation: Undergraduate teacher education often fails to offer constructivist teaching/learning techniques. The same is true of in-service training. Therefore, teachers are not well equipped in terms of instructional methods and ongoing assessment of learning.

Measure of Accountability: For years accountability was based on statistically produced data generated by test scores, graduation rates, and other measurable information. Qualitative (anecdotal) evidence was rarely studied or reported.

Ken, Bryon, and Barbara understand the challenges. Finding ways to make the New Learning Infrastructure work, based on constructivist theories, becomes a major hurdle. Ken understands better than anyone, and not just because of a new way of thinking about curriculum, teaching, and learning.

"As superintendent, my biggest concern about making a dramatic change is public acceptance. The pandemic and multiple social controversies ripped apart anything accepted as being American education. It is no longer a matter of making improvements to the status quo. The status quo itself has been destroyed or reshaped.

"Board meetings are rancorous over the topics of mask-wearing and vaccinations. Teacher retention and recruitment remain high on the list of major issues. Student attendance has dropped significantly. Instructional delivery systems jump between in-person, virtual, and hybrid. Administrator burnout is real.

"Parents are more aware of school strengths and weaknesses, because they supported their children with online teaching and learning. Legislatures dictate curricular content and teacher behavior. Given all these issues, doing something as different as the New Learning Infrastructure seems looney, especially when we're doing all we can to keep our educational ship from sinking. On the other hand, history tells us that new ideas often thrive during chaos, but I don't know how that happens."

"Maybe we can figure it out," Barbara said. "As both a teacher and student of literature, I know that magnificent human stories evolve out of conditions that seem unbelievably messy. It's a little like a literary chaos theory—how one small influence can solve a messy problem."

While Ken and Barbara spoke, Bryon jotted down key points in the "public acceptance" side of the equation. Then he read his notepad ideas. Rebecca wrote them on a white board and added some of her interpretations:

1. The pandemic opened social weaknesses. The pandemic upset widespread understandings of how societal institutions work. Many weaknesses and misperceptions were revealed.
2. The pandemic underscores a need to clarify what schools are for. For years the public accepted schools as everything from social service institutions to credentialing organizations, from tax-paid babysitting functions to a sifting process designed to prepare young people for adult roles.
3. American schools are slippery stepping stones to adulthood. Schools have been accepted as a fixed reality where students are guided into their adult social and vocational roles, but American education never established a formal tracking system

found in other parts of the world. The curriculum in American schools is confusingly eclectic.

4. Measurable student progress is based on shallow evidence. Grade-point averages, scores on local and standardized tests, participation in sponsored activities, high school graduation levels, and other quantitative indicators supersede qualitative data. Qualitative data are better predictors of success in adult endeavors.

5. Schools are responsible for nonacademic services to children. After the initiation of the Great Society programs in the 1960s, schools became a primary means to care for "special" people with mental, emotional, or physical disabilities. These services are essential, but do they belong primarily in schools?

6. Technology is only a sophisticated tool that morphed into being a central focus. In this twenty-first-century era of technology-driven concentrations, STEM and similar initiatives dominated the school reform agenda.

After taking a break, Ken, Barbara, Bryon, and I focused our attention on how to work with the public acceptance situation. We planned to attack the teacher preparation and accountability issues later.

Public Acceptance

The word *politics* has become a volatile trigger for societal disputes concerning almost everything. Many people avoid both the word and its issues, but the word *politics* merely relates to the process underlying governmental decision-making. It takes on a negative connotation when logical and fact-filled debate becomes an argument based on opinions fueled by fear, principles based on ingrained belief systems, methods to gain or perpetuate societal power.

Sometimes all three elements work in tandem. The situation becomes especially acute when an external force initiates the fear. COVID-19 was a significant fear-producing force with many beliefs about the pandemic's origins, impact, and ways to fight it. People convinced themselves that their understandings were correct. The goal was to gain power—to perpetuate and spread their way of believing.

Schools were caught in the middle of conflicting opinions about virus management. They attempted to meet the challenges. All strategies involved parents and the public—an internal management of curriculum, instruction, and assessment. Some parents and patrons liked their students working at home in online classes. Many did not. Those not impressed were appalled at trivial lessons and an overall lack of depth and relevance. They did not blame teachers as much as they indicted a school's curriculum. What were the overall intentions for student learning?

Bryon thinks those experiences opened and exposed a weakness in schools not previously seen or acknowledged. Did we know what our schools are or should be for?

Ken agrees. He thinks we lack debate about what should happen in the first few years of school in terms of academic and personal growth. Socialization and cultural development are considered important in those early years. The purpose of middle-level and secondary grades is less clear, especially if competitive sports are removed from the scenario.

The junior high school originated as a preparation for high school and high school as preparation for college. A traditional four-year college curriculum includes liberal arts and sciences. These subject areas influence both middle and high school curricula, acceptable if post-secondary education was offered tuition free—if it featured a well-coordinated and focused curriculum and if it attracted all high school graduates. But post-secondary education, whether community colleges or four-year public/private institutions, seldom carry those characteristics. Most require tuition and employ instructors who function as semi-independent agents. Course syllabi are rarely influenced by carefully constructed curricula.

A large percentage of high school graduates do not attend traditional post-secondary programs. Instead, they depend on vocational training provided by communities or employers. High school dropout rates vary, but now they are greater due to the pandemic. Some students who leave high school before graduation mention boredom or lack of relevance. Of high school graduates, about two thirds enter college, and many of those fail to complete their programs.

Ken believes the district's parents and patrons should acquaint themselves with the reality of current public schooling, but traditional thinking will be difficult to overcome. With that backdrop in mind, Rebecca discusses public acceptance with her small leadership team: Ken, Barbara, and Bryon.

After the break we concentrated our attention on how to gain acceptance of the New Learning Infrastructure, using a strategy anchored by an amalgam of skills in technology-supported communication taught by using an interdisciplinary project-based system.

"I don't like the idea of imposing this idea out of the blue," Ken remarked. "On the other hand, I'm not sure we should get into a wide-ranging discussion involving parents, patrons, teachers, and other interested parties. That can turn into a mess.

"And I am *not* enthusiastic about using a drip method in which multimedia slowly informs and educates all stakeholders. Seems too much like indoctrination of the type used by telemarketers."

"That doesn't leave us many options," Bryon said.

Barbara asked, "How about bringing in a convincing outside speaker or team of consultants?"

Both Ken and Bryon groaned. Bryon said, "Too many school board association conventions and conferences use the 'sage on the stage' approach. Most go nowhere when attendees bring the ideas back home."

Then I suggested another tactic, one that links the old with the new, connecting conservative and progressive points of view.

"Wow!" Bryon said. "I didn't know that was even possible."

I agreed. "It might not be possible, but gaining public support for our New Learning Infrastructure requires what makes sense from *any* angle, actions that align with human needs and cause them to seek something better."

Before the meeting I accessed a copy of an old report, now more relevant than ever: *A Nation at Risk: The Imperative for Educational Reform. A Report to the Nation and the Secretary of Education,* by the National Commission on Excellence in Education.

The report, still online, is dated April 1983. https://edreform.com/wp-content/uploads/2013/02/A_Nation_At_Risk_1983.pdf.

Although nearly forty years old, the document included many conclusions and suggestions still relevant today. My favorite section is titled "The Learning Society." It relates to what we're doing now. I shared the document with Ken, Barbara, and Bryon using a projector and large screen with highlighted key elements.

Barbara seemed intrigued. "Didn't the US follow up on that report in a variety of ways? My education instructors often mentioned the report, usually all the initiatives that came from it: subject standards, high-stakes tests, Goals 2000, No Child Left Behind, and the Common Core State Standards. Yet we still face many of the problems discussed in the 1983 report."

I agreed. "We do indeed have many of the same problems identified in 1983. Maybe the reason those problems still exist is that the measures taken to fix them were wrong. In what way is our proposal different? In what way will the result differ if we implement our New Learning Infrastructure?"

"You know," Ken said, "most of those so-called 'fixes' were top down. I remember Goals 2000, the only federal program that didn't try to micromanage everything from Washington. States and individual school districts were encouraged through federal grants to find their own solutions. Bottom up."

I suggested we examine the possibility of the old *A Nation at Risk* report as the catalyst for gaining public acceptance of our ideas. We decided to discuss that possibility at our next meeting.

• • • • • • •

Revisiting *A Nation at Risk*

In April 1983 the National Commission on Excellence in Education issued a report created by President Ronald Reagan on the recommendation of Secretary of Education Terrel Bell. The commission's membership included educators, businesspeople, and office-holders. Bell's reason for forming the commission was "the widespread public perception that something is seriously remiss in our educational system." He solicited the "support of all who care about our future." Bell created the commission based on "responsibility to provide leadership, constructive criticism, and effective assistance to schools and universities."

The study focused on specific concerns and remedies associated with the quality of teaching and learning in public schools and higher education. Concerns addressed the question of what schools should be for and how well they responded to that objective. The resultant *A Nation at Risk* report concluded that for our country to remain strong and competitive, mediocre schools must create clear learning goals and achieve excellence.

Mediocrity was determined to be the result of many factors, excessive expectations that diminished education's ability to prepare students to work intelligently and creatively in a competitive environment. More significantly, the report commented forcefully on the need for "the intellectual, moral, and spiritual strengths of our people, which knit together the very fabric of our society."

Especially poignant with today's divisiveness and rancor was the following sentence: "For our country to function, citizens must be able to reach some common understandings on complex issues, often on short notice and on the basis of conflicting or incomplete evidence."

Another prophetic observation stated, "All, regardless of race, class, or economic status, are entitled to a fair chance and to the tools for developing their individual powers of mind and spirit to the utmost."

The commission found American students prepared for neither the competitive workplace nor participation in a society that required "higher-order" intellectual skills. Students demonstrated inadequate technical proficiency and insights "relevant to the human condition." Excellence was defined as related to setting and meeting high expectations for all students "according to their aspirations and abilities" through lifelong learning.

The report's key designation, "The Learning Society," underscored education as a pervasive characteristic of day-to-day living not limited to schools alone. The commission found no such condition existed nor was there a public commitment for attaining one. Unlike today, the primary concern of the commission was eclecticism in school goals and curriculum. In an era of high school mini-courses, middle school exploratory programs, "whole" student development, and other curricular objectives, they focused on students' emotional, psychological, and physical development. Experimental programs involved interdisciplinary subjects, learning styles, and elevating student self-esteem.

The commission's criticisms aimed at those programs. Its solutions tightened expectations and ensured that students met high standards. Included were traditionally accepted strategies such as demanding curricula and textbooks, testing, homework, graduation requirements, time in class, and stringent college admission standards. Improving the quality of those entering the teaching profession was a frequently stated imperative. National or state subject area standards, high-stakes tests, data collection and use, and measures of teacher accountability appeared absent or undeveloped in 1983. However, many or most of those practices were later implemented and justified based on the commission's report.

A Pandemic-Induced Nation at Risk

While a few conditions remain, our school problems today differ from those mentioned in 1983. In fact, they are worse. COVID reporting explains the problem every day. Parents, school patrons, and students appear confused and often disheartened. Teachers, principals, superintendents, and board of education members are frustrated and dismayed. Solutions seem to be associated with "returning to normal," but that status quo no longer exists.

Although the 1983 report is dated, it offers points that define a new normal answering the question "What are schools for?" Sections of the report describe a society we should strive to create, to ready students for work and meet life's challenges:

- "Hope and Frustration"
- "Excellence in Education"
- "The Learning Society"
- "The Tools at Hand"
- "The Public's Commitment"

The crossover between 1983 and today is the need to define and measure mastery of student learning. Commission members in 1983 defined mastery using traditional assessments and indicators of accomplishment. They accepted the usual measurement tools and criteria. Content to be mastered appeared in approved curricula and textbooks, which morphed into standards and the use of summative high-stakes tests. Proof of student mastery was associated with high-stakes test results, and teachers were held accountable for student success on those tests. The pandemic exposed seven flaws in the 1983 way of achieving learning mastery:

1. Mastery is not defined within curricula used in classrooms.
2. Teachers are not participants in designing their curricula.
3. Instruction is not linked to specific learning intentions found in a curriculum.
4. Learning intentions in Bloom's hierarchy beyond remembering and understanding (applying, analyzing, evaluating, and creating) are not easily measured or recorded statistically.
5. Teachers are not prepared to teach to true mastery.
6. Teachers are not allowed to use formative assessments to verify mastery.
7. Time is insufficient to ensure that most if not all students master intended proficiencies.

Schools that gave prior attention to achieving student mastery through well-constructed local curricula, linked to compatible instructional processes, maintained student learning during the pandemic. Their teachers were thoroughly involved in all aspects of curricular content, instructional design, and assessment of student learning. Such involvement provided a solid instructional platform when they were forced to use online instruction.

Today's schools are at risk because governmental micromanagement marginalized local decision-making, diminished the role of professional teachers, and defined excellence in terms of standardized test scores.

The small group of leaders (Rebecca, Barbara, Ken, and Bryon) will discuss how to use the old 1983 report to address public acceptance of the proposed modifications initiated by the language arts subject area committee.

A Nation at Risk Updated

The small group of leaders will try to shape strategies for introducing the proposal from the language arts subject area committee to the curriculum council. But the council itself will need to sell the idea to the district's board, educators, parents of students, and patrons. Once those hurdles are surmounted, another challenge appears—to convince governmental and professional bodies charged with accrediting the district.

The team of leaders analyzes the 1983 *A Nation at Risk* report. They agree with its descriptions of the kind of nation we seek. They disagree with strategies that the report offers, centered on a return to traditional techniques for creating and supporting curriculum and instruction. They also reject the suggestion that student learning and other indicators of achievement can be discerned through measurable data-generating techniques such as standardized tests and other statistically compatible instruments and indices. The leaders see a disconnect between the 1983 aspirations for this nation and the report's means for reaching those goals. But they agree on student mastery as the primary goal—now and in the future. The future includes COVID-induced logistical, political, and emotionally charged issues. Mastery of subject matter is still the foundation of educational excellence. But what is the distinction between "learning" and "mastery"? Are they synonymous?

Learning the alphabet is a far cry from mastering language as a rich communicative medium. The same holds true for learning basic arithmetic and mastering mathematics as a sophisticated computational tool. Cognitive development results in learning. Mastery operates at a high level of cognition, depicted in complex human behaviors that exceed the mundane.

The *A Nation at Risk* report vigorously rejected minimum competency tests. The report's well-written narratives depicted a "learning society" far beyond minimal learning. It defined "learning society" as intellectual rigor, a kind of human interaction that transcends the ordinary.

The "ordinary" is classified and based on remembering and understanding, the two lowest levels in Bloom's taxonomy of cognitive development, outcomes most often applied in traditional schools, accepted by the public, and measured on pencil-and-paper tests. True/false, multiple choice, short answer, matching, and fill-in-the-blank tests are easy to create, evaluate, and score. They are designed to be valid (measuring what is intended) and reliable (consistent results over time). Scores are aggregated and used as a database to determine the levels of scholastic achievement. But how should we define scholastic achievement? Using tests that merely check for remembering and understanding only scratch the surface. Mastery is more akin to the four learning categories of applying, analyzing, evaluating, and creating.

Applying is the third level up in Bloom's taxonomy, "learning by doing"—scholastically, not simply another way to describe an apprenticeship or on-the-job training but how someone *thinks* about what is being done.

Analyzing is the fourth tier, given more gravitas than a mere examination of something. Systematically or scientifically analyzing a condition or occurrence requires a strong foundation of previously existing knowledge.

Evaluating, once preeminent, remains close to the top of the hierarchy, but it is significant only if the one who evaluates has the scholastic and cognitive credentials to precisely examine something and draw valid conclusions.

Creating sits at the top, once lower in the taxonomy but now rightly reclassified. Creative social leaders in politics, government, medicine, law, the arts, business, science, technology, architecture, and engineering were not always successful public school students. For them, "school was boring or irrelevant." Their creative abilities were ignored, as was their ability to transcend the ordinary through the power of insight and challenging intellectual engagement.

The ability to create incorporates the five categories lower in the taxonomy. Creativity does not operate independently from the other cognitive forms. New ideas are not generated in an intellectual vacuum.

As the work of our school district leaders continues, they conclude that mastery is the key selling point to gain acceptance of the New Learning Infrastructure among stakeholder groups.

But they must explain it in ways that make sense to those who hold diverse political and philosophical opinions.

Rebecca Reflects on What It Takes to Gain Public Acceptance

One disadvantage for a public school administrator with a doctorate is when colleagues believe the degree is symbolic with deep knowledge, wisdom, and insight. What it really means is that I chose to enter a domain in which I was expected to think based on evidence generated by systematic research. The most successful doctoral student associates were not always the best students in public school or undergraduate university programs. Some described themselves as genuine mavericks who hated being constrained within academic boxes.

Many exemplary public school students who enter doctoral programs never finish. The usual reason is "ABD—all but dissertation." They complete the coursework but fail to make the leap to independent or creative thinking and acting. They meet explicitly issued expectations but are unable to independently and vociferously develop or pursue an idea.

As an above-average public school and undergraduate university student, I applied for the graduate program—a good foundation for the master's degree, but the PhD program was a different challenge. Three characteristics seemed essential for my success: unmitigated determination, risk-taking, and a fascination with problem-solving. My family helped me develop all three, using oft-repeated phrases such as "Johnsons never give up," "Accomplishing the impossible takes a little longer," and "Eat the problem-solving elephant one bite at a time." My gender was no excuse. My parents wanted a happy family life for me, but they knew relationships were valuable only to the extent they supported who I aspired to be as an individual.

I prepared to participate in the next meeting with Ken, Barbara, and Bryon, ready to suggest that we do some "shark tank" thinking, to convince as many people as possible that our district was serious about student mastery and how to achieve it.

15

Gaining Support of Stakeholders

The Language Arts SAC proposal develops a curriculum that combines language arts, technology, and project-based programs. Other subject area committees will do the same, to prepare interdisciplinary approaches that connect traditional subjects such as mathematics, science, and social studies to technology and project-based learning.

Ken, Rebecca, Barbara, and Bryon address basic implementation issues such as stakeholder acceptance, teacher preparation, and accountability.

Rebecca Suggests a "Student Mastery Profile"

Most of America's public school districts use mission statements with lofty language to describe their program goals—what their students in a general sense should know or do when they complete requirements. Our current district mission statement is used primarily on our website and other media as a verbal flag to salute. Short mission statements are inspiring, sometimes valuable as tools for envisioning how graduates or those finishing programs will conduct themselves.

But mastery statements are different. We have worked on two of them, still somewhat tentative. We adopted a general statement (for the entire academic program) the language arts committee used to nail down mastery for its discipline:

Students completing the full program of studies at XYZ School District will develop skills that expand their understanding of reality, a deeper understanding of themselves and how they fit into the world, to solve complex problems, think and act creatively, and responsibly manage their own needs.

Graduates will understand and act on principles associated with entrepreneurship, the ability to become lifelong learners through knowing how to learn and being motivated to do so. They exhibit curiosity about ways they can stretch boundaries into new and different realms. With an inherent drive to learn continuously, they ask good questions and become part of diverse communities where feedback is vigorous and stimulating.

They will understand the importance of self-confidence, gained through experience with widening groups. They take meaningful initiatives (reaching out), receiving consistent encouragement from respected associates.

Graduates will practice mindfulness in clarifying priorities and actions each day. They remain open to others from different backgrounds. They understand and work to achieve self-discipline and personal values. They create and maintain the convictions to pursue these values.

Students completing the full program of studies at XYZ School District will also speak and write effectively. They know how to make people feel at ease, those from every walk of life, entering conversations with others and showing genuine interest in their ideas and activities.

While each academic discipline is important, graduates will grasp the idea that problem-solving is associated with a complex and interactive system. Solving problems requires collaborative skills, allowing all disciplines to work in concert. Graduates understand the meaning of intellectual passion, not simply a passion for attaining more knowledge but also comprehending its significance and value.

The tentative language arts statement reads as follows:

Language arts students will display the ability to communicate expressively both orally and in writing. Life is more than a single dimension. It is an assortment of experiences that make it worth living. Students participating in and completing the district's language arts curriculum will master outcomes corresponding with written intentions for learning at grade level. Among those intentions for learning are—

- Defining reality in the context of decisions made valid through background knowledge and evidence.
- Gaining insight into human interactions and behaviors as depicted in literature. Discussing cultural influences, thereby gaining an appreciation and respect for diversity.
- Interpreting problem-solving as the ability to consider challenges, weigh the accuracy of options found in literature, conduct trial-and-error tests, and work in teams to create and evaluate possible or probable solutions.
- Establish a working definition of creativity as being an authentic learning goal, characterized by the dynamic nurturance and acceptance of novel ideas, proposals, and behaviors that depict curiosity and devotion to some endeavor.
- Demonstrating responsible behaviors in the context of what is read as valuable—in good taste, employing logical reasoning, and instructive to readers as guidelines for living and learning, responsible behaviors manifested in written works reflective of the writer's own creativity with the ability to express ideas, opinions, and factual information offered through quality syntax.
- Developing through reading and writing an appreciation for competition based on valuable insight, examples of moral/cognitive/physical self-improvement, and a willingness to take risks for reasons other than self-aggrandizement. Accepting persuasiveness based on conviction. Improving the common good as the appropriate model for entrepreneurial enterprise.

- Accepting that reading, writing, speaking, listening, and interacting through language are the basis of lifelong and worthwhile learning.
- Using literature and other media as catalysts essential for making learning a conscious, intentional, and ongoing part of life.
- Making curiosity a fundamental part of living and becoming, through reading or accessing diverse forms of media on a regular and ongoing basis.
- Inquiring appropriately and regularly.
- Participating in the interchange of vigorous and stimulating ideas in which feedback is welcomed.
- Recognizing the acquisition of self-confidence, the result of taking initiatives in widening groups. Using insights taken from literature and other media. Applying skills in speaking, writing, and listening to the act of reaching out.
- Placing oneself where encouragement of others is given and received.
- Practicing the art of mindfulness. Being sensitive to prioritize actions and responses, particularly through effective oral and written communication.
- Articulating the meaning and practice of self-discipline. Developing personal values, reinforced by reading quality literature and viewing uplifting media.
- Interacting with others based on the art of conversation. Staying engaged with the world and listening carefully.
- Pursuing knowledge and sharing that knowledge with humility and sincerity through both speaking and writing.

This set of behavioral profiles describes what those leaving our program do in terms of intellectual and interactive capabilities. Though not subject- or topic-specific, it cuts across all disciplines, behaviorally driven within collaborative scenarios.

Conventional school mission statements resemble aspirations. They cannot be held accountable for results. They accept responsibility only for the instructional effort needed to make learning happen without accepting responsibility for student effort and ability. As the escape clause states, "We did all we could to teach the students, but they had neither the ability nor the desire to learn."

Mastery statements are performance declarations with no escape clause. Their impact cannot be assessed in a social or intellectual vacuum. All skills involve interactions and participatory situations. Our challenge is to convince the curriculum council, board members, and all other stakeholders in the district that these mastery statements, whether general or subject specific, are what we want and need.

To gain stakeholder support for a curriculum that merges language arts, technology, and project-based learning requires painting a picture depicting what students *will* know and do in the context of real-life settings. Measurable verbs and clearly articulated content fields underscore critical elements for describing a mastery profile that includes character descriptions within situational narratives.

All our work ties together with a written agreement between and among the key players involved in teaching and learning. Though developed and used years ago, and while time-consuming and seemingly daunting, this contract idea becomes the basis of what we call the New Learning Infrastructure.

* * * ● * * *

Begin with a Well-Designed and Well-Written Curriculum

Rebecca suggests a new way to define learning mastery: the use of profiles instead of individual competencies. In this case, the noun *profile* means a broad description of student characteristics as an educated person. The profile reveals a macro evaluation system that replaces excessive use of isolated or disassociated skills and knowledge areas: the kinds of skills and knowledge areas measured on true/false, multiple choice, and short-answer tests.

Rebecca came up with her ideas about the profile as they evolved over time, especially during the period in which she worked on her doctorate.

Stimulants for initiating that study came from analyzing (1) the ways professional contributions are best evaluated, (2) how real and long-lasting learning is achieved, and (3) the true measure of accountable behavior.

Together those descriptors create the profile of someone who is purposeful, intellectually in motion, and accountable to both personal and social principles. True competence and effectiveness in any endeavor are found in a compilation of those characteristics, never just one or two skills or knowledge areas. Professionalism, scholasticism, and accountability work jointly for those having mastered their work and other aspects associated with life's challenges.

Think about this profile from a contextual approach. A student functions within a multifaceted and practical scenario, a departure from the piecemeal kind of learning associated with meeting assorted and marginally related competencies and outcomes.

Another novel process involves the use of a contract system for managing the teaching and learning relationship, an approach that is the essence of the New Learning Infrastructure. Articulate language is used to convey expectations, settings in which teachers ask their students to perform in more effective ways. Formal schooling has always been a contract system. Teachers agree to teach. Students theoretically agree to learn what is taught, but that agreement falls short on specifics and levels of commitment for both teachers and students.

A second problem involves the parents or adult guardians in the margins who need a form and process to overcome the problems. Together they convert mystery learning into mastery learning, a succinct way of saying that good teachers never play the professorial role in which students must figure out what mystery lies in the instructor's mind.

Front-loading curriculum and intentions for student learning make it clear that mastery is the goal from the beginning, similar to how a leader plans a mission. Include all necessary elements to make the effort successful. Although the teacher is the leader, he or she also serves as the school's agent. Elements of the curriculum frontload each student's contract. Loaded into the contract are high achievement unit outcomes and their components, complete with measurable verbs and explicit content fields.

Rebecca devised the student mastery profile system by first meeting with Barbara and Mary. Mary's teacher preparation proved helpful, especially the lesson plan resource (LPR). This tool, invented by the Curriculum Leadership Institute (CLI), became a link for a curriculum written in outcome language, each day's guided instruction used by all districts assisted by CLI. LPR's creation helped to escape the limitations of the daily lesson plan. Over time, lesson plans fail to connect learning growth, especially insufficient when complex material is taught (requiring multiple class sessions to master) in courses taught online or in hybrid configurations.

Mary and Rebecca used a condensed template to create an LPR. The curriculum council or subject area committee preloaded the cells containing the subject mastery statement and outcomes for the course, unit, and component. Individual teachers completed evaluation criteria for the component. They described assessment formats and applications.

Page one categories were titled "Context," "Teacher Methods," "Student Activities," "Resources," and "Extensions" as the teacher's responsibility. The responsibility for page two categories pointed toward either the subject area committee or individual teachers, depending on policies established by the district's curriculum council. Completing LPRs was a massive undertaking; however, the process grew much easier with practice. They saved the LPR online for repeated use, thereby allowing frequent tweaking.

Examples of completed lesson plan resource documents are available from the Curriculum Leadership Institute. (Check out the Resources section.)

The Hard Sell

Rebecca knows that Ken wants to gain public acceptance of the district's techniques for developing and implementing a New Learning Infrastructure, but the plan involves more than tinkering and playing around the edges. The pandemic and the necessity of using online instruction put pressure on teachers to create a new normal, which often proved weak and ineffective. It also exposed parents to what they perceived as being much less than what they wanted for their children. Many believed they were not getting their money's worth.

The challenge transcended the politics. One side believed the status quo simply needed an inexpensive upgrade. The other side supported an infrastructure overhaul—the New Learning Infrastructure. Teacher preparation was part of the public acceptance equation. Because teachers live in the community with friends among their students' parents, opinions emanated from sources other than their profession. Teachers who believed that the mechanics of the New Learning Infrastructure were oppressive or misguided constructed serious roadblocks to public acceptance.

Ken, the board, and members of the curriculum council must ensure that teachers enthusiastically support the New Learning Infrastructure. Although it seems tangential, accountability remains the most prominent issue in the political realm. How will our characters change the definition from techniques associated with numerical data collection and use to reflecting on how professional contributions are best evaluated? They must determine how real and long-lasting learning is achieved.

Rebecca knows that converting the accountability measuring tool from numerical measurements to narrative descriptors of mastery profiles presents a major challenge. But she already drafted a tool for getting things started, a template she calls "The Teaching and Learning Contract."

Creating the Student Mastery Profile

New Learning Infrastructure curricula are written for each interdisciplinary subject. In this scenario we focus on how the traditional language arts subject area committee decided to open the door to an interdisciplinary approach. They added technology and strongly referenced project teaching and learning as the instructional method of choice. The committee needed to expand its classification to something more generic than language arts. They decided to use the term *communications.*

Communications, as with each interdisciplinary subject, begins with a mastery statement encompassing all grade levels. Under that general rubric lie three levels of outcome: course or grade level, unit, and component. Why three levels? Because mastering a course (or grade level) is like building a house.

An architect first prepares an artistic rendering of the final product. Then he or she develops a blueprint to show contractors necessary materials and skills to make the house become what is envisioned. The contractor then hires subcontractors and employees to put everything together. In this analogy the house is the course while blueprints are the units. Components are what workers do to make the house a reality.

Another example lies with sports or the military. Winning is the objective. Winning requires attention to organizational detail, honing the skills of those doing the work, effectively designing down so the organization's functions and people deliver up.

The course outcome is the house or the act of winning. It stipulates what students will know or do at the end of a program of study. Unit outcomes are the tangible framework or organizational structures needed to meet the course outcome. Component outcomes are the pieces or fundamental skills necessary to meet unit outcomes.

In the New Learning Infrastructure each course contains five to fifteen separate units. Each unit has up to ten components. The course (grade level) outcome, if written for a standard school year, typically allocates up to 165 hours, split into unit outcomes of varying complexity and length. The level of complexity dictates the number of component outcomes each unit needs. The teaching and learning contract is a direct offshoot of the lesson plan resource (LPR); then the LPR frontloads the teaching and learning contract.

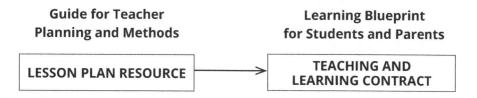

The overlap between the two documents is intentional. While there are necessary differences, all the key elements that influence student learning outcomes are the same. Both documents primarily address the component. However, the larger goals are also indicated as course (grade level) and unit outcomes. The abbreviated format for the contract reveals its contents:

TEACHING AND LEARNING CONTRACT

COURSE: Seventh-Grade Communications
STUDENT:
PARENT OR TUTOR:
RESOURCE CONSULTANT (optional):
COURSE OUTCOME (preloaded):
UNIT OUTCOME (preloaded):
COMPONENT (preloaded):
TEACHING STRATEGIES USED (Teacher preloads):
RESOURCES USED (Teacher preloads):
LEARNING STRATEGIES USED (student explains):
CRITERION (Teacher uses component verb and content field to convey learning expectation):
DESCRIPTION OF FORMATIVE ASSESSMENT (Teacher describes format and process):
CONTEXT (Also called "relevance." Student explains importance in the real world):
MASTERY PROFILE (Teacher inserts a sentence or more to convey the expected level of student mastery):

Rebecca knows this process will elicit astonishment and incredulous responses from her associates. But she presents it with enthusiasm and a strong recommendation that it be taken seriously.

Rebecca Prepares Her Case

Ken, Bryon, and Barbara probably wondered why I had produced such a complicated and bureaucratic system. The student mastery profile measures student progress, a complicated theory neither simple nor compatible with data-based accountability and program improvement. The bureaucratic concern relates to forms, development, and use of descriptive narratives. An enormous amount of teacher time is needed to create, input, and apply intentions for student learning, then for teaching/learning processes to follow.

Neither the current accreditation organizations nor governmental agencies easily compare schools and districts. Comparisons remain popular with everyone from politicians to real estate agents. The capitalistic notion believes competition encourages greater efforts to succeed, but this notion fails as a basis for school improvement.

Primarily, the model I advocate is based on the ineffectiveness of past quick fixes, similar to the physical infrastructure in this country: cheaply shoring up dangerous bridges, roads, water and energy systems, and other essential physical frameworks, like so-called school improvement initiatives related to standards, high-stakes tests, tinkering with grade-level configurations, and a myriad of other experimental approaches.

Circumstances related to pandemic-induced disruptions in the schools, societal controversies related to race, and disagreements about the purpose of American public schooling support my argument. Add the pressures on teachers and principals that cause the attrition rate to skyrocket, and admission rates to teacher education programs plummet. My vision of a New Learning Infrastructure cannot solve all of education's problems, but it could improve the following:

1. Curricular design and implementation in terms of content, alignment, measurability, scope, sequence, and transparency.
2. Instructional clarity and greater involvement of parents and other stakeholders interested in curricular content and efficacy.
3. Teacher ability to use multiple methods and media for conducting instruction and guiding student learning.

If the leadership team accepts my proposal fully or in part, I plan to create examples of how a lesson plan resource and teaching and learning contract would be completed. That challenging element of the process requires writing measurable intentions for student learning.

• • • • • • •

Replacing the Dominance of Standardization and Assembly Lines

A systems model for curriculum development is indeed a hard sell, like criticizing Henry Ford for producing cheap and poorly made automobiles after he created the automated assembly line to produce the Model T. Ford argued that standardization of parts and repetitive work were efficient, turning out millions of adequate machines to inexpensively transport the masses. He was right. While standardization of parts was not new, a large-scale assembly line was, and Ford's idea transformed America. Our ability to create adequate products quickly and inexpensively became the hallmark of American success, including the winning of World War II.

Twenty-first-century technology changes the look of manufacturing. Variability based on individual needs replaces standardization. Robotic uniqueness essentially meets the demands of a diverse marketplace. Ford's standardization and assembly line techniques influenced those responsible for creating public schools. Using that model, communities less expensively and more efficiently educated the masses to meet the needs of an industrial society. But standardization of academic content paralyzes creative learning, and the assembly line mentality reflected in grade-level configurations demonstrates archaic thinking.

Rebecca's Justification for the Teaching and Learning Contract

I expected pushback as the reaction to developing and using a teaching-and-learning contract system. It is complex, time consuming, and expensive—enough reasons to stop the effort in its tracks. But Americans are still enamored of the industrial processes created in the twentieth century, and that belief enters our political discourse. The reason is simple. Standardization and the assembly line mentality made us the greatest nation on earth. We are competitive in economic and military dominance.

In the latter part of the twentieth century we examined our nation's beliefs and actions because product quality and service were slipping. Too many people fell through the prosperity cracks.

Although our nation survived that slippage, we are now experiencing a slow transformation, partially because of the COVID pandemic.

Our schools must work differently. The pandemic and technological advancements caused us to recognize the need for quality intellectual engagement and an innovative mindset. Patterning schools on twentieth-century standardization and assembly line techniques no longer makes sense. We need to replace the old ways with the New Learning Infrastructure, incorporating the teaching/learning contract.

Two shortcomings for currently improving schools include (1) tinkering with a fundamentally flawed system and (2) basing school district organization on a standardization and assembly line mentality. Tinkering and quick fixes do not work, and imposed uniformity results in mediocrity. Some teachers, parents, and patrons need to be convinced of these failed past practices. They fear change and the unknown, so we need to prove the efficacy of the New Learning Infrastructure.

$$\cdot \ \cdot \ \cdot \ \bullet \ \cdot \ \cdot \ \cdot$$

Back to Bridges and Schools

The most frequently used analogy for the New Learning Infrastructure is the importance of bridges. In the physical infrastructure, bridges play an important role. New bridges provide more secure and safe connections, so we need better bridges between schools and the communities they serve. Current educational bridges are inadequate and falling apart. New bridges are necessary, built with upgraded technology that fits their unique uses, demographic applications, and geographic configurations.

The symbolic bridge in this case is the teaching and learning contract system that Ken, Bryon, and Barbara consider and critique before moving the idea farther up the line. The teaching and learning contract can be saved, completed, and used electronically by each student for every subject. A cover page describes general information while subsequent sections include the unit, the teaching and learning element that focuses on the component, the component's assessment element, and the component's achievement element.

TEACHING AND LEARNING CONTRACT

COURSE: Seventh-Grade Communications
STUDENT:
PARENT OR TUTOR:
RESOURCE CONSULTANT (optional):
COURSE OUTCOME (preloaded from curriculum):

UNIT OUTCOME (1) (preloaded from curriculum):

TEACHING AND LEARNING ELEMENT

COMPONENT (1) (preloaded from curriculum):
TEACHING STRATEGIES USED (Teacher preloads):
RESOURCES USED (Teacher preloads):
LEARNING STRATEGIES USED (Student responds):

ASSESSMENT ELEMENT

CRITERION (Teacher uses component verb and content field to convey learning expectation):
Formative Assessment (type[s]):   Oral (X):   Written (X):   Product (X):   Performance (X):
DESCRIPTION OF FORMATIVE ASSESSMENT (Teacher describes format and process):
CONTEXT (Also called "relevance." Student explains importance in the real world):

STUDENT ACHIEVEMENT ELEMENT

MASTERY PROFILE (Teacher inserts a sentence or more to convey the level of student mastery):

The Teaching and Learning Contract Created and Justified

Rebecca's form serves as a three-way contract involving the teacher, student, and the student's parents. This contract works best when an existing curriculum contains mastery statements for the subject and course/grade level with subordinate units and components. Most of the contract focuses on components that must align with the unit, and each unit must align with the course/grade level mastery statement—an exercise in wordsmithing, especially in terms of measurable verbs and clear content fields.

The biggest challenge? The contract system works only if the curriculum is well articulated, organized, and measurable.

Rebecca's Examples of a Contract's Contents and Use

To convince the team that the teaching and learning contract is valuable, I show them a completed contract and explain how I designed it. I know it will be a challenge to convince everyone that such a contract works. It requires a sophisticatedly created curriculum, instructional planning resources instead of daily lesson plans, and tons of time to complete and implement.

I need to convince them that the front-loaded documents and processes are plausible once we establish momentum and complete the basics. Other organizations such as the military and industry use such precise documents and methods. My example follows:

TEACHING AND LEARNING CONTRACT

COURSE: Fourth-Grade Communications
STUDENT: Sally Smith
PARENT OR TUTOR: John Q. Smith, father; and Mary M. Smith, mother
RESOURCE CONSULTANT (optional): Susan Ann Wayne, school media specialist

COURSE/GRADE LEVEL PURPOSE (preloaded from curriculum): At the end of fourth grade, students will use the writing process and incorporate six traits (voice, ideas, presentation, conventions, organization, word choice, and sentence fluency) to produce written narrative and expository texts; demonstrate standard writing conventions within their writing; read narrative, expository, persuasive, and technical text and identify examples of each; use key words/phrases to classify text characteristics; summarize text in their own words, providing necessary details and author's purpose; identify types of text structure; integrate phonetic principles and word recognition strategies while reading fluently on continuous text; apply knowledge gained from text features.

UNIT OUTCOME (1) (preloaded from curriculum): Students will define each of the six writing traits and produce accurate examples in published original essays incorporated into technological media.

TEACHING AND LEARNING ELEMENT

COMPONENT (1) (preloaded from curriculum): Students will define voice as a writing trait in terms of what makes different people unique, explain how uniqueness shows up in behavior depicted in stories, and explain how they are unique in their own personal stories. They will create one short story that depicts themselves as being unique and correctly upload it into an electronic medium.

TEACHING STRATEGIES USED (Teacher preloads): Students and I will read and view short stories in which strong characters exhibit discernable and unique traits, in terms of what makes human beings unique, drawing conclusions as to why those unique traits are important, how activities and hobbies make our own lives and the lives of others richer and more meaningful. Students will prepare an essay of at least 250 words that depicts their own unique character and voluntarily share it electronically in an online publication titled "Personalities." Students uncomfortable with digital sharing will work with their parents or resource consultant to do something similar.

RESOURCES USED (Teacher preloads): Books and video clips containing appropriate short stories and supplies essential for supporting the component's requirements.

LEARNING STRATEGIES USED (Student responds): I will read or view the stories provided and discuss those and other stories with my parents. I will discuss what makes people unique and fun to be around and explore ways I am unique. I will write a story about myself as a unique character. If I wish, I will contribute to the "Personalities" publication in class. I have the option of doing the same thing with my family or resource consultant.

ASSESSMENT ELEMENT

CRITERION (Teacher uses component verb and content field to convey learning expectation): Students contribute ideas in class by defining and explaining unique behaviors and creating a story that represents those behaviors in themselves.

Formative Assessment: Oral (X):   X   Written (X):   X   Product (X):   X   Performance (X):   X
DESCRIPTION OF FORMATIVE ASSESSMENT (Teacher describes format and process): Students will be evaluated by observation in terms of how they respond to the various assignments and are able to articulate the importance of individuality and uniqueness in life. Students unable to share their essay in class will do something similar with their families.

CONTEXT (Also called "relevance." Student explains importance in the real world): The relevance of this component is associated with understanding differences in people, why those differences matter in everyday life, and the importance of accepting diverse ways of being and behaving.

STUDENT ACHIEVEMENT ELEMENT

MASTERY PROFILE (Teacher inserts a sentence or more to convey the level of student mastery): The teacher and/or parent/guardian will draw qualitative conclusions as to how completely the student seems to understand the importance of uniqueness in self and others.

This teaching and learning contract looks complex. The same is true with the instructional planning resource from which it is derived. However, it seems complex only in terms of comparing past teaching preparation.

In the past, teachers prepared lessons that came from textbooks and other instructional materials already produced. They created daily lesson plans that incorporated resources and teaching strategies. A local curriculum guide proved valuable, but if an outcome-focused local curriculum was not available, the teacher organized instruction the best way possible from existing resources. This old process ended up being full of holes. Parents and other stakeholders failed to understand the teaching/learning loop. Sometimes teachers themselves were not vested enough in the process because they considered it either unimportant or counter to their own expertise or perspectives. This major problem continues today.

The teaching and learning contract explicitly ensures these important curricular intentions. More than one person is involved, decreeing that such intentions will be taught thoroughly in a cooperative setting. Anyone may disagree with the curricular focus but cannot unilaterally make changes. Parents and patrons who work in partnership with a teacher and entire professional body of educators in a school district continually review curricular content and instructional appropriateness. While not perfect, this process reduces misunderstandings or disagreements.

An important caveat: the teaching and learning contract dramatically changes the face of teacher accountability. Teacher accountability currently measures how well students perform on high-stakes tests, thought to be a straightforward input/output, data-rich measure, but flawed in terms of intended learning such as that shown in the example. Formative and qualitative assessments present better techniques to assure long-term retention of concepts and skills.

The most significant aspect of accountability found in the teaching and learning contract identifies to whom teachers are accountable. Under the current system, accountability involves the bureaucrats and assessment specialists who design and test standards—a political football. Taking parents and local patrons out of the picture as to what should be in a curriculum and how it must be taught and measured for effectiveness smacks of bureaucratic oppressiveness.

With a little trepidation, I present my case to Ken, Barbara, and Bryon.

16

Collaborative Decision-Making in a Change-Agent Environment

A "rubber meets the road" description follows.

What happens when innovative people who have thought about and acted on radical new ideas meet with those not previously involved or merely involved on the periphery? Rebecca is a major change agent with novel ideas. Ken, Barbara, and Mary engaged in the process but in different ways.

As a serious change agent, Rebecca designs exciting and creative ideas, moving many innovations to the forefront, which feels like organizational overload. People cannot process new ideas so fast, especially when new methods attack their comfort zone.

Mary knows the elements of the New Learning Infrastructure. Barbara seeks new ideas and practices to become part of her professional persona. Bryon is a layperson and patron of the district, intrigued with new ideas but essentially a product of tradition. He knows the system has pluses and minuses because he serves the community on the board of education. Bryon doubts the current system needs to be replaced, but he keeps an open mind.

As a district superintendent, Ken thinks and acts conservatively. He modifies processes *if* they can be justified to improve the quality of student learning. Ken remains "steady at the helm," effective in finding compromises, thus remaining in his position longer than most superintendents. He moves toward more prestigious leadership roles. He hired Rebecca as an assistant superintendent for curriculum and instruction because she impressed both Ken and the board with her intelligence, professional insight, credentials, and enthusiasm.

However, Rebecca is beginning to make Ken nervous. The decision-making and action-taking model makes sense as an inclusive model. Ken thinks it is time to spread out the source of ideas, to get more people involved in discussions.

Ken Calls for a Slow-Down

As superintendent, I (Ken) feel enthusiastic about the wealth of ideas pouring in and being reviewed. But I know from experience that we need to press the "pause" button to avoid getting carried away with too many ideas.

"Rebecca, this idea moves too far in front of the other stakeholders, even those on the Communication SAC. Your ingenuity, suggestions, and proposals impress me, because you clearly focus on how we can sell the key elements of the New Learning Infrastructure. Good job in examining teacher prep, how teachers can be held accountable. But let's take a deep breath. Review what has been accomplished. Determine how to spread the good news."

Rebecca said, "You're right. I've been a bit too aggressive and with a limited number of people. Let's ask Barbara to call a meeting of the Communications SAC. Start by reviewing their decisions. Introduce some of my newer ideas."

"Good idea, but first let's summarize. Think through where we stand. The Communications SAC is ready to design a curriculum meant to be mastered by all students yet leaving behind the emphasis on summative pencil-and-paper tests with traditional grading systems. And that will become a major problem among those who believe in the NCLB culture and the importance of standards and high-stakes tests.

"Accepting the value of formative assessment by individual teachers requires trusting teachers to draw conclusions about student progress using their own criteria and issuing accurate reports. Those reports must be accepted as valid by all concerned parties.

"The other dramatic shift moves away from the idea curriculum should remain separated into traditional subject areas. Our language arts morphs into something called communications and must regularly merge with practical technology. That's a big deal, Rebecca. If we tell our public we are not interested in aligning our curriculum with current language arts standards, that is enough to gain their attention."

"You're right," Rebecca responded. "By using the ideas of the New Learning Infrastructure, we move dramatically afield from the usual. Some people will question our sanity. They cannot understand the mechanics of the lesson plan resource or mastery statements."

"Yes. Your Teaching/Learning Mastery Profile is a work of art, but many teachers will have trouble creating and using it. Our district's stakeholders may not buy the idea as a replacement for high-stakes test scores."

Rebecca, a bit discouraged, shook her head. "What should I do?"

I convinced Rebecca that her efforts were valid. As a superintendent my emphasis focuses on collegial decision-making, but occasionally we reach a decision-making point when everything falls on my shoulders. It is either a "go" or "no go."

I assumed responsibility for helping move the process of the New Learning Infrastructure forward, which meant convincing parents, patrons, and other local stakeholders. But the difficult part was convincing state and accreditation officials, administrators of schools, and post-secondary and higher education administrators. I am worried but willing to see where it goes.

Barbara needs to call a meeting of the communications subject area committee to create a concrete proposal. Then Rebecca will schedule a meeting of the curriculum council to consider that proposal and hopefully act on it positively.

. . . ● . . .

The Communications Subject Area Committee Prepares the Proposal

The New Learning Infrastructure involves a different way of thinking about the following: teacher education, the role of teachers in decision-making, how districts are organized and led, the way curriculum is developed and implemented, methods for designing curriculum and instruction, the role of state and federal government, and the involvement of local stakeholders.

The nucleus of the New Learning Infrastructure presents a different kind of American teacher, no longer a mere functionary in the vast bureaucratic structure but rather a well-prepared professional with considerable skill and dedication.

At this point Ken tries to convince himself that Rebecca and the others are moving in a good direction. He sees obstacles ahead that make more planning an exercise in frustration—obstacles more associated with self-preservation than he is willing to admit. Nevertheless, he tries to stay the course and let Rebecca and Barbara move things forward.

Barbara Convenes a Meeting of the Communications SAC

In our last full SAC meeting I (Barbara) brought up the progress made by the subcommittee of Ken, Rebecca, Bryon, and me. Committee members seemed surprised and a little overwhelmed by Rebecca's proposal. Our last full committee conversation was generic and wide-ranging. To see everything coming from the subcommittee required soak time.

Ken agreed with the committee's conclusions and Rebecca's subsequent efforts to make mastery learning a verifiable reality, but the problem lay with differences in how it was defined by various interest groups.

Ken said, "The definition of mastery and how it is achieved in all students will be anything but unanimous. On the surface, many people may think we plan to achieve that goal by continuing to do what we do now—only better. They envision our continued allegiance to meeting state standards and assuring students do well on high-stakes tests. Also, they want high graduation rates, acceptance into the best colleges, scholarships, and academic successes accomplished more economically than ever. But that is not the direction we are headed, is it? To be frank, as much as I agree with the philosophical direction we are taking, our patrons' expectations worry me.

"I imagine walking out onto a stage with the audience ready to hear how we will upgrade curriculum"—Ken counted on his fingers—"to better meet standards, intensify staff development and supervision, ensure teachers do a better job in classrooms, extend opportunities for students to learn both onsite and online, and do it all under budget, exceeding expectations. But given our decisions so far, that is not the scenario I imagine.

"People's eyes will glaze over when they hear me say our new interdisciplinary curriculum does not precisely align with standards and high-stakes tests. What do I mean when I say curriculum will be taught as creatively written, with mastery learning verified qualitatively by teachers using formative assessment techniques? What happens when I tell them we are moving from curriculum and instruction that is less trivial pursuit, more focused on problem-solving and practical applications?"

Everyone looked at Ken. What was it with this guy? He seemed to like what we presented yet was concerned about the possibility of losing his job if things went too far. He fully supported the New Learning Infrastructure ideas early in the discussion. Was he getting cold feet about supporting the initiative?

A kind of stupor fell over the room. Finally, high school language arts teacher Mike Hall spoke up. "Am I right in thinking that everything we have discussed so far revolves around the meaning of *mastery*? That word describes a narrow kind of outcome in general usage. To master a language or some other discipline means to have command of certain specified skills, but I think we want the New Learning Infrastructure to go beyond that definition."

Puzzled, I asked Mike what he meant.

Mike cleared his throat. "As a guy who likes to play around with word meaning, I wonder if we're talking about adroitness that is a couple of notches above the demonstration of mastery. Ken told us about parents and patrons who think we should teach a curriculum that causes students to master state standards as measured on high-stakes tests. It's true that way of thinking has been inculcated into our society and accepted by many folks.

"The word *master* works in that context, but we're talking about human abilities that go way beyond that kind of measurement. I drew up a list of synonyms, such as *adroitness,* for *master.* However, they connotatively mean something more than a simple stimulus-response exercise.

"To master something can be nothing more than the ability to answer a question correctly, but we don't think of that skill as being adroit. What does it mean if someone functions ably, adeptly, artfully, capably, consummately, deftly, or expertly? Those words incorporate creative behaviors. They also reflect student ability to analyze and evaluate. If I correctly remember Bloom's taxonomy, the ability to analyze, evaluate, and create are at the top of the list of learning objectives—the crux of what differentiates education from mere training.

"We've allowed the assembly line mentality to dominate our essence as a culture, because people in economic and political power succeeded in equating efficiency with Americanism, yet efficiency is only a small part of what makes this country great. America's real strength comes from uncompromising ingenuity, something my father and grandmother constantly spoke about. To them, making life better was an ongoing invention. We invent because we see a need. Then we analyze it, conduct research and development, evaluate it through trial and error, and create something to better meet the need.

"I think Ken and all of us should use that argument to support the New Learning Infrastructure. The American way of life is in jeopardy because we allowed shackles to be put on our brains and academic enthusiasm. This forces us to do the same for students we teach, and it is killing our schools."

Ken looked at Mike with a slightly sardonic smile as if to say, *What universe do you live in?* Then he shrugged his shoulders. "American ingenuity as a theme might elicit a more positive response. Let's take the SAC's original proposal to the curriculum council and see how it flies under the rubric depicting a needed national priority."

* * * * * * *

Discussion of the Communications SAC's Proposal

The district's curriculum council instituted the organizational bylaws prepared by the steering committee, wrote the long-range plan, and appointed what they renamed the Communications Subject Area Committee. The council's membership now includes—

- Ken Towers, superintendent (ex officio)
- Rebecca Johnson, assistant superintendent and committee chair
- Bryon Garrett, member, board of education
- Vernon Wilson, member, board of education
- Molly Grover, patron; mother of a high school student
- David Askins, patron; father of an elementary school student
- Barbara Morgan, middle school language arts teacher; committee chair
- Billie Yost, first-grade teacher
- Jackie Smyth, third-grade teacher
- Bob Snyder, fifth-grade teacher
- Mike Hall, high school language arts teacher
- Joan Bell, special education coordinator
- Myra Jackson, elementary school principal
- Jack Dodd, high school principal
- Mary Chapman-Miller, middle school science teacher, science SAC chair designee

- Betty Wilson, high school math teacher, math SAC chair designee
- Don Baker, K-8 music teacher, fine arts SAC chair designee
- Jennifer Mitchell, district technology coordinator /media specialist

Bea Perkins, administrative assistant to the superintendent, serves as the council's secretary and record-keeper. As strongly suggested by consultants, the council's minutes are comprehensive, precise, and regularly reviewed.

Rebecca uses staff development periods to call a two-day meeting of the council. The agenda includes a few updates and reports, mostly dominated by the proposal coming from the Communications SAC.

Rebecca Convenes the Curriculum Council

Before the meeting I (Rebecca) talk with Ken and Barbara. Joining us is Bea Perkins, who prepares all handouts and ensures the proper functioning of the computer projection media. She explains how the meeting records will be maintained and available for future reference.

I review the meeting agenda, including what we accomplished at the beginning: the ad hoc steering committee became the council in accordance with bylaws drafted and later agreed to by the board. As stipulated in the bylaws, council membership was increased by adding two community residents who are parents of students.

Again we discussed the long-range plan, which we could modify as necessary. No changes. Possibly the most important discussion from past meetings pertains to the tentative district mastery statement, which can also be modified, but changes must be made before subject mastery statements are prepared or confirmed. Curriculum is written based on the subject mastery statements. Mastery statement development remains in flux, to be continued in the months ahead. Thus, the first appointed SAC made assumptions. One assumption stated that the tentative version (Mary's draft from her teacher education exercise) was close enough to council intentions to align the subject mastery statement with it.

Ultimately the alignment of intended student outcomes written in district, subject area, and grade-level mastery statements is imperative. But this time we opened the door to unexpected creative thinking. The current district mastery statement came from an outside source, a good document to implement at the beginning of our process. When the district mastery statement is finalized, its overall impact will be realized. After we cover those pro forma items, the council will hear the report from the only currently operating subject area committee. Ken, Barbara, and I know the report will sound familiar to many on the council who also serve on the Communications SAC, but not to Vernon and the two community representatives. For Vernon and the others, the report may appear somewhat startling, even disconcerting. It seems to exceed the authority of a subordinate body. These proposed ideas and practices dramatically change the norm in American education as they align with the New Learning Infrastructure philosophy.

The Council Meeting Begins

After I welcomed new members of the council and introduced everyone, I asked Bea to read the minutes of the last meeting. She quickly summarized the bylaws and the long-range plan. I postponed further discussion of the mastery statement until after we presented and discussed the SAC report. Then I invited Barbara, subject area committee chair, to begin.

"My report needs a little background. According to the model we follow, our first order of business was supposed to gather information about our current language arts curriculum, what has been called the 'walls exercise.' Our current way of doing business is not bad, because we are already professional decision-makers about curriculum. We use it for the benefit of our students.

"But we had not previously aligned the curriculum in terms of scope and sequence. The 'walls exercise' ensured no gaps or unnecessary repetitiveness and was designed to check for appropriateness. The discussion on appropriateness partially led us toward the review of mastery statements *before* we analyzed the current curriculum in the 'walls exercise.' We felt the need to be cognizant of where we headed academically with our students.

"That took us to the tentative district mastery statement, to create a language arts mastery statement aligned with it— to get a sense of direction at the local level. Unlike previous years when we designed curriculum using other techniques, we avoided preliminary alignment with state standards. We reworked the curriculum before checking it against state standards. The old unpacking-of-standards method works top-down, constrained in terms of academic reach. It limits our professional vision of what students should know and do.

"Also, standards tend to use more operational than measurable verbs, such as students will *cover, discuss, review, read,* and *study.* These action verbs do not pertain to a particular skill or knowledge area to be measured."

I asked Barbara if the review of standards was still on the SAC's future agenda. She said yes. Then I asked if our new local mastery statements might make alignment with state standards more difficult.

"Possibly," she said.

"Why?"

"While in the ballpark indicated in the standards, our district's mastery goals for student learning are written using a broader intellectual construct. In other words, our intentions for student learning are written in macro terms, designed to allow teachers to break them down into suitable details. Standards are typically focused on the details themselves, forcing teachers to align instruction with those elements.

Barbara grinned. "That's the difference between micromanagement of education and the New Learning Infrastructure. Besides, our state standards are supposed to be guidelines and not curriculum, not even a specific source for curriculum."

I said we should accept that report for the time being and take a break. Since the district and language arts mastery statements played such a significant role, I suggested that we look at them next and examine their significance.

· · · ● · · ·

Mastery statement development in a district is usually a work in progress. Traditional goals are somewhat understood or evident, and everyone knows how the statement will likely read. But a dramatic shift is coming in the way the district's teaching and learning happen, and everyone knows it.

Barbara allowed discussions associated with mastery teaching and learning, mostly because of Rebecca's urging and ideas. They avoided language based on *if* students meet academic expectations. Instead, students *will* become engaged thinkers and creative contributors in a dynamic twenty-first-century American culture.

Barbara Presents the Basis of the New Learning Infrastructure

Barbara speaks in the curriculum council's meeting as chair of the communications SAC.

Her committee causes the full council to consider making big changes in the academic program. The "bottom-up" change initiative causes serious deliberation.

Now we examined the new communications mastery statement we created. I (Barbara) asked Rebecca to fully participate because she created the programmatic processes to institute genuine mastery. I also turned to Mike Hall and his interpretation of mastery as being closer to adroitness. In abbreviated form, he repeated his definition of *mastery* as the ability to control facts and processes. Adroitness includes that definition but involves more creativity and innovation.

I recorded and transcribed portions of his original comment about Americanism. "We have allowed the assembly-line mentality now used in schools to dominate our essence as a culture. People in economic and political power succeeded in equating efficiency with Americanism, yet efficiency is only a small part of what makes this country great.

"America's real strength comes from uncompromising ingenuity. We invent because we see a need. Then we analyze it, conduct research and development, evaluate it through trial and error, and create something to better meet the need.

"We should use that argument to support the New Learning Infrastructure. The American way of life is in jeopardy because we have allowed shackles to be put on our brains and academic enthusiasm, forcing us to do the same for students we teach. And it is killing our schools."

Ken said he initially disagreed with Mike but now wonders if Mike is right: "I worried about finding some way to sell our patrons and parents on the New Learning Infrastructure. It's possible that approach bridges the political divide in our country and community. America's greatness comes from innovators and ingenious builders. At a certain point in their lives many of those folks became innovators by giving up on the school's curriculum. How can that kind of thinking be acceptable enough for us to keep doing it?"

I said, "We start by redefining curricular categories. The Communications SAC combines language arts and technology, and it emphasizes teaching strategies that include engaging projects and other forms of interaction.

"We suggest this interdisciplinary way of thinking for all future subject area committees. Technology and project-based teaching open the door to the possibility of adroit behaviors, making learning tangential to the quest for new perspectives and answers—a rebuilding of the American spirit."

At that point in the discussion I projected our proposed communications mastery statement on the big screen in front of the conference room.

Life is more than a single dimension. Rather, it is an

assortment of experiences that make it worth living. One experience underscores the ability to communicate expressively both orally and in writing. Students participating in and completing the district's language arts curriculum will master outcomes corresponding with written intentions for learning at grade level. Among those intentions for learning are the following:

- Defining reality in the context of decisions made valid through background knowledge and evidence.
- Gaining insight into human interactions and behaviors as depicted in literature.
- Discussing cultural influences, thereby gaining an appreciation and respect for diversity.
- Interpreting problem-solving as the ability to consider challenges, weigh the accuracy of options found in literature, conduct trial-and-error tests, and work in teams to create and evaluate possible or probable solutions.
- Establishing a working definition of creativity as being an authentic learning goal, characterized by the dynamic nurturance and acceptance of novel ideas, proposals, and behaviors that depict curiosity and devotion to some endeavor.
- Demonstrating responsible behaviors in the context of what is read as valuable. Good taste, logical reasoning, instructive to readers as guidelines for living and learning. Responsible behaviors manifested in written works reflective of the writer's own creativity. The ability to express ideas, opinions, and factual information offered through quality syntax.
- Developing through reading and writing an appreciation for competition. Based on valuable insight, examples of moral/cognitive/physical self-improvement and the willingness to take risks for reasons other than self-aggrandizement.
- Accepting persuasiveness based on conviction.

- Improving the common good as the appropriate model for entrepreneurial enterprise.
- Accepting that reading, writing, speaking, listening, and interacting through language are the basis of lifelong and worthwhile learning.
- Using literature and other media as catalysts essential for making learning a conscious, intentional, and ongoing part of life.
- Making curiosity a fundamental part of living and becoming, through reading or accessing diverse forms of media on a regular and ongoing basis.
- Inquiring appropriately and regularly.
- Participating in the interchange of vigorous and stimulating ideas in which feedback is welcomed.
- Recognizing the acquisition of self-confidence, the result of taking initiatives in widening groups.
- Using insights taken from literature and other media.
- Applying skills in speaking, writing, and listening to the act of reaching out.
- Placing oneself where encouragement of others is given and received.
- Practicing the art of mindfulness.
- Being sensitive to prioritizing actions and responses, particularly through effective oral and written communication.
- Articulating the meaning and practice of self-discipline. The development of personal values, reinforced by reading quality literature and viewing uplifting media.
- Interacting with others based on the art of conversation. Staying engaged with the world and listening carefully.
- Pursuing knowledge and sharing that knowledge with humility and sincerity through both speaking and writing.

Technology is not mentioned specifically in this mastery statement because it achieves the described *ways of becoming*. This mastery statement differs vastly from current standards. It does not dwell on the minutiae of learning, but neither does it ignore the individual skills necessary to become more—*more* in the context of achieving the American dream and spirit.

We know a mastery statement like this is hard to measure in quantitative and concrete terms, but so is anything classified as being high-quality. High-quality music, paintings, books, homes, and cars are more than the mere sum of their parts. Standards, high-stakes tests, and data fall short. They assess mastery in minimum competency and functionality, but America is more than that. So must our education systems be more as well.

· · · **●** · · ·

Reflecting on the Meaning of Accountability

Before continuing the meeting of the curriculum council, we revisit the topic of teacher accountability.

Neither the SAC nor the curriculum council speak directly to the issue, but it underlies everything. The SAC accountability is now aligned with professional performance, individually and collectively—not as civil servants meeting expectations issued by their supervisors.

American industry was built on holding employees accountable for pro-duction quotas, competitive sales, high profit margins, and efficiency. In World War II industrialists understood the overriding importance of quality product and service—the measure of accountability to customers, employ-ees, and the nation's victory. After the war William Edwards Deming proved the importance of quality. He helped Japanese industry rebuild. His man-agement model produced such amazing results that American industry adopted it, which became their attempt to stay competitive. Industrialists learned that holding employees accountable for production efficiency and profit was not as important as creating working conditions that resulted in quality.

Traditional Industrial Processes Influenced American Schools

Our nation's schools were patterned on the nineteenth- and twentieth-century industrial model. Top-down management, efficient assembly line strategies, and accumulation of data measured the meeting of goals. Graduation rates, college acceptance levels, grade-point averages, standardized test scores, and other concrete data measured effectiveness.

Due to compensation and logistical factors, education is expensive. Those who allocate public money continually stress efficiency—how to get the greatest bang for their buck. Data-based accountability becomes the measure of quality, especially significant when standardized test scores are both high and efficiently achieved. Data measure teacher accountability and effectiveness, sometimes used to determine which school districts rate better than others. This theory states that competitive feelings motivate poor or mediocre districts to improve.

What Does Quality Mean? How Does It Relate to Accountability?

Quality means something different in our culture today. The same is true for accountability. Quality autos, homes, and other products are different than in the 1950s. Technological advancements play a role, but consumer expectations have changed. We expect more today. We hold manufacturers accountable for meeting those expectations.

Defining Quality in Schools

Intense academic and intellectual engagement are missing in American schools today. Recent reform efforts rarely mention engagement or determine its meaning: dynamic cognitive interaction between and among human beings. Interactions cause the development of insight and an ability to transfer understandings to meet a wide variety of challenges, to take full advantage of opportunities for academic and personal growth.

Quality today is too often defined as meeting baseline expectations related to skills and knowledge areas. Such skills and knowledge areas can be measured on high-stakes tests as results are quantified and recorded as data. Those data establish norms, make comparisons, and support funding decisions. But a high-stakes test reduces the definition of quality to acceptability or baseline competence. It lowers accountability to the expectation of minimums. It eliminates ingenuity that regularly adds depth to our American culture. It cheapens human living, diminishes personal satisfaction, and affects the quality of life for the communities in which we live.

Defining Accountability in Schools

We define accountability in schools as establishing expectations, ensuring that they are met as stated. But Deming disliked quotas or goals because they seemed too arbitrary. What he liked was to continue the improvement of processes. Quality was not a single dimension to Deming. Rather, the *constant* seeking of quality was the proper measure of accountability. As a statistician, Deming used numbers when it made sense to do so. But using qualitative measures made sense in describing anecdotal evidence associated with student academic and personal development.

Using Deming's definition in schools, quality becomes active as dynamic engagement between and among teachers and students. Evidence constitutes behaviors. Products reflect student thought and academic contributions. Teachers prove accountability by creating these conditions on a regular basis.

Barbara Seeks Consensus

The council meeting now discusses what accountability and quality mean when woven into the decision-making process.

But continuing issues remain in the minds of some council members. Again, Barbara ignites serious discussion at the council level.

After a healthy discussion about quality, accountability, and the proposed communications mastery statement, many on the council appeared nervous. The rationale seemed solid enough.

David Askins and Vernon Wilson shifted in their seats. David said, "All of this sounds good philosophically, but I can't get my head around what it will look like on a day-to-day basis. I know it is a cliché to say, 'The devil is in the details.' But my background as a machine shop owner makes me want to know operational specifics.

"When I hire someone, it's important that the new employee functions proficiently and safely. Frankly, that's all I want to see. I couldn't care less about the person's ability to do all the stuff you folks wrote in the communications mastery statement. For me, education and training have everything to do with performance at the lathe and with other machinery in the shop.

"The arguments in favor of ingenuity and creativity fall flat. Sure, I want that kind of thing for my son. I hope he goes to college and does more than what I ask of my employees. I want employees who are technically competent, can problem-solve, and assume more responsibility, especially as the shop upgrades our computer software. Most employees can be trained for an upgrade."

Vernon responded. "I get what you're saying, David. I agree with you up to a point, but public schools do not train machinists. They don't educate students for Internet technology work. They prepare people for meeting a vast array of challenges, being able to think effectively and creatively in the larger community. You said two things that resonated with me: the ability to problem-solve and the ability to assume greater responsibility over time. In my legal profession I encounter many folks who cannot solve even the simplest problem, so I do it for them. I also deal with men and women who cannot describe the meaning of responsible behaviors, much less live responsibly.

"Common sense is not very common as some people have not been prepared to manage their worlds. They don't have a clue as to how to acquire and maintain good relationships. Consider your machinists and technicians outside the door of your shop. Who they are away from their work impacts what they do inside your building."

• • • ● • • •

Ramifications

Members of the curriculum council realized that responding positively to the Communication SAC's proposal could have serious and far-reaching ramifications. Most evident would be pushback from multiple sources: parents of students, taxpaying patrons of the district, accreditation organizations, the state's department of education, politicians, special interest groups, post-secondary education institutions, and other members of the education profession.

While it feels exciting to be trailblazers, who will step into that role?

Trailblazers accept the certainty they will be challenged, questioned, doubted, even vilified. They must respond with appropriate vigor, accepting the certainty of setbacks, frustrations, occasional missteps, and failures. Predicting the challenges ahead is difficult. Shoring up preparedness requires intrepidness many people lack.

Most of us admire Thomas Paine's "If we do not hang together, we shall surely hang separately" remark which he wrote about the colonies' need for independence from Britain. The colonies gained that independence, but Paine never let up. His ideologies continued to make him controversial. However, today many of his ideas are fundamental to our democracy.

Countless other stories exist about intrepid trailblazers who saw things differently and acted on their beliefs. While greatly admired today, many suffered as Paine did. That level of sacrifice is not expected in the district's implementation of the New Learning Infrastructure, but the controversy may occasionally seem that way. We live in an era filled with a strange amalgam of social pressures, virus-related uncertainties, political divisiveness, economic concerns, loneliness, and media intrusiveness. Our children feel the intensity as much or more than we do, which makes it imperative that we figure out how to make schools better serve their needs now and in the future. Which perspectives associated with the New Learning Infrastructure will likely get pushback?

- CURRICULAR SOURCE. The source of the district's curriculum is local mastery statements. Many in the academic world and public distrust local educators to make curriculum decisions not officially tethered to approved standards, textbooks, or other materials sanctioned by fully qualified academicians. Local teachers and administrators are not viewed with that status. The New Learning Infrastructure is designed to change that perspective.

- INDUCTIVE LEARNING. Mastery statements used by the district are broader in both content and purpose than traditional curriculum, standards, and most textbooks. Such mastery statements are behavioral. They focus on demeanors depicting interactive competence, intellectual depth, investigative mindset, engaging collaboration, and creative experimentation. They operate in the upper categories of Bloom's taxonomy (applying, analyzing, evaluating, creating), yet they recognize the essential building blocks of remembering and comprehending. This approach reverses traditional strategies by emphasizing the importance of inductive teaching and learning, a key element in the New Learning Infrastructure.

- FORMATIVE TESTING. Assessment processes are more significantly based on formative, not local summative or high stakes tests. Teachers measure student learning frequently as part of the instructional process. Results are recorded but might be anecdotal and dependent on teacher opinion. In some cases, empirical evidence may be present based on the structure of tests and objectivity of content. Most classroom tests do not qualify as valid and reliable. They usually focus on student skills in the categories of remembering and comprehending. Parents and patrons often believe current classroom testing is objective and worthwhile, but much of the time it measures incidental material. It fails to promote ongoing retention of key skills and concepts.

● SCHOOL REPORT CARD. One of the biggest problems for those advocating the New Learning Infrastructure is the current school improvement culture based on standardized test scores and other data. Standardized tests, whether high stakes subject-focused or college readiness aptitude, play a less significant role today. But they still exist and remain important in the opinion of the public—as do graduation percentages, college acceptance levels, and grade-point averages. Supporters of the New Learning Infrastructure believe in the real effectiveness of students and graduates—"real" in both vocational and scholarly pursuits that go beyond statistical indicators, descriptors such as *researcher, innovator, inventor, problem-solver, builder, leader*, and *social entrepreneur*. Those more meaningful, richer, and revealing data do not translate well in a superficial weighting system in which numerical scores remain dominant.

Difficult Conditions Add to Challenging Ramifications

Unlike many other American institutions in the last fifty years, public education looks and feels remarkably similar to the middle of the twentieth century in terms of basic organizational and management strategies and in what students are taught. The COVID pandemic modified how students were taught, but that change involved only distance media and methods to retard the spread of the virus.

A few superficial differences emerged over the years: modern buildings and equipment, casual clothing for teachers and administrators, relaxed dress codes for students, security measures that include entrance scanning and uniformed guards, and a profusion of electronic devices. Students own cell phones, computers, and other devices to communicate and entertain. The pandemic introduced distance teaching and confusion—a major disruption in the flow of learning, socialization, and a sense of educational purpose.

As the pandemic waned, getting students back in the buildings proved challenging. Teachers resigned in frustration. Applications plummeted for teacher education programs, and principals felt more pressure than ever before. Teachers' satisfaction with their profession, always an issue, significantly dropped. The pandemic exacerbated the major issue. Teacher exclusion in decision-making made them feel demeaned and undervalued.

A National Imperative Implemented Over Time

Revolutionary change needs a definable cause, one that resonates with enough people to open possibilities. Changes that remain over time are incremental, as in the growth of democratic government and its maintenance. For the New Learning Infrastructure to work, it needs revolutionary momentum—steady growth over time. It needs acceptance by many constituents because the process works well for students and society in general. The curriculum council begins to understand. High school principal Jack Dodd steps up.

Rebecca Reconvenes the Council Meeting

I (Rebecca) asked Barbara to present the proposal from her Communication SAC. That action prompted response from members of the council, but we needed to get back on track and make some decisions.

Vernon dominated the last meeting of the council, so it was not clear how to get discussion rolling again. I wanted to turn everything back to Barbara and let her continue the report from the communications subject area committee. But the council moved past the SAC's report to discuss bigger issues related to the question "What are schools for?"

David and Vernon made interesting contributions but no clear path to launching our version of the New Learning Infrastructure. We needed a broader vision, something more than semantics, specific student proficiencies, and particular kinds of behavior.

Jack Dodd once taught history and government. He leads his school as a bipartisan believer in democratic decision-making. He believes himself to be a teacher currently serving as a building administrator. The title he holds, once known as "principal teacher," deems him responsible for overseeing the routine needs of those working and being served within the building. Jack believes proposed changes in the district are akin to a national imperative. We as a people are influenced by what we learn and become within families, schools, communities, and organizations that give us value and meaning in our lives.

Jack thinks the district's new endeavor underscores democratic practices, as opposed to autocratic processes that seem more purposeful and efficient, but only on the surface. They're like the current mode of improving American schools—the mode that is *not* working.

Jack appreciates Lincoln's famous phrase in the Gettysburg Address, that democracy is government "of the people, by the people, for the people."

Jack said, "Institutions within our American system of governance are always improved when strong collaborative leaders reach out, when they nurture others to be better than they thought they could be. Lincoln might phrase it, 'We are who we believe we are. We have a responsibility to act on those beliefs for the benefit of everyone.'"

Out of that philosophy Jack offers ideas for selling the New Learning Infrastructure by redefining:

- **The source of curriculum** (an amalgam of scholastic knowledge, pragmatic interpretations of that knowledge, and the tapping of insights arising from an awareness of human potential)
- **The primary goal of teaching** (conveying factual information and merging it with the uniquely human ability to reflect on the meaning of those facts in our lives and society)
- **The measurement of human growth and potential** (an ongoing activity that requires those who guide learning to be continually sensitive to the level in which others become more insightful, capable, and effective in their own right)

- **The ultimate goal of education** (to create a human culture that features ongoing improvement of self and society in ways that make life worthwhile and meaningful).

I said, "Those four descriptors need ordinary language for the public to understand what they mean. In our proposed New Learning Infrastructure teachers play a much larger role in determining the source of the curriculum. Students will be taught to think more deeply about what they are learning with testing of student learning the ongoing responsibility of teachers using multiple strategies. Education should be designed to help human beings live more engaged and meaningful lives.

"We suggest the four descriptors above as the opposite of what is happening now. To wit: teachers are mere conduits through which curriculum created by others indoctrinates students. Students are expected to mechanically meet academic standards established by experts. Students parrot back what they learn—on tests created by people other than their classroom teachers. Students are adequately prepared to live and work in a carefully managed society."

The dramatic language used in those bulleted descriptors showed how everything hinged on the quality of teachers and how accountable they would be to achieve the goals of the New Learning Infrastructure. The quality of teachers has always been a major sticking point, but now the issue is paramount. The pandemic induced a shortage of teachers. Replacing them has entailed lowering certification and employment criteria.

How can we upgrade the instructional quality depicted in the New Learning Infrastructure with novice teachers possessing minimal baseline credentials? We involve considerable staff and faculty development in the areas of curriculum-writing and instructional design.

To open the conversation, I shared my perspective on how teachers should be held accountable as a contrast to the methods used now. The suggested method was associated with the teaching and learning contract model I developed for the Communications SAC:

STUDENT:			
PARENT OR TUTOR:			
RESOURCE CONSULTANT (optional):			
COURSE OUTCOME:			
UNIT OUTCOME:			
COMPONENT:			
TEACHING STRATEGIES USED:			
RESOURCES USED:			
LEARNING STRATEGIES USED:			
CRITERION:			
Formative Assessment (type or types): **DESCRIPTION OF FORMATIVE ASSESSMENT:**	Oral (X): Product (X):	Written (X): Performance (X):	
CONTEXT:			
MASTERY PROFILE:			

This contract requires a strong and well-written curriculum with teachers trained to use it effectively. The key idea: *transparency is the basis of true accountability* with no mysteries or hidden agendas. Therefore, I plan to make that process and this template a centerpiece for how we overcome the challenges associated with implementing the New Learning Infrastructure in the face of multiple obstacles.

17

The Curriculum Council's Decision

T he emergence of the New Learning Infrastructure now circles back
to Mary Chapman-Miller.

As a member of the curriculum council, Mary listens intently to the
conversation. She senses that her unique university training places her
in a delicate position. She is a neophyte with skills that older teachers
have not developed—but for the district to implement the New Learning
Infrastructure, teachers must also learn them.

Rebecca Urges the Council to Decide

**Courage means knowing that a decision, made collectively
or not, will have lasting and difficult ramifications.**

Both Ken and Rebecca will need to explain and defend the new
system. Comparisons constitute a classic apples/oranges situation, so
evidence is required. Standardized test scores remain unpredictable.
Those who seek easily generated hard data attempt to prove their
point, claiming any qualitative data coming from the district as

continued

inconclusive. Why wait years for evidence that students emerging from the New Learning Infrastructure are happier and ultimately more successful adults?

Ken and I agree we need a *go/no go* decision from the council with no middle ground and no place to compromise or ride the fence. A vote to "go" means—

- Teachers will play a significantly larger role in creating and implementing curriculum.
- Students will be encouraged to actively reflect on the factual material they learn.
- Student progress will be measured by teachers using multiple methods and strategies.
- Scholarship will be defined as engagement, leading to insightful and creative behaviors.

Current teachers and those to be hired must prepare to work differently. They need thorough instruction and intense on-the-job training—a big commitment. If the council votes to move forward, backed by the school board, the ramifications will be immense. The two most significant pressures are (1) working against current bureaucratic and political perspectives and (2) transforming teachers into fully professional decision-makers and practitioners.

A few days before meeting with the council, I talked with Barbara and Mary. Would Mary be alarmed at the prospect of becoming a key local resource for implementing the New Learning Infrastructure? Our outside consultants would provide leadership both online and in person, but Mary would be recognized as the on-site expert. She accepted the responsibility. Her role includes—

- How the new model is structured.
- How it impacts thinking and planning.
- How to write curriculum with specific kinds of instruction.
- How to write curriculum with specific kinds of assessment.
- How to create lesson plan resource documents.
- How to develop teaching/learning contracts.

Those tasks happen gradually, but they seem gigantic to most teachers and administrators, especially with COVID having caused havoc in almost every aspect of school functioning. Maybe the pandemic and its aftermath will push the curriculum council toward giving the New Learning Infrastructure a thumbs-up.

Everyone is clearly tired of fighting pandemic-related battles. A return to "normal" remains a false dream, now buried under the public perception of educational dysfunction. The two board members serving on the council believe other board members feel the same. Rearranging educational deck chairs will not save this sinking ship. So isn't it time to stop trying to save a program not worth saving, to commit to building something new and better—even if that means stretching folks, however expensive and time-consuming?

Bryon and Vernon, the two board members, want answers as do Molly and David, the two patrons. Their practical and necessary questions follow:

- How will the New Learning Infrastructure overcome pandemic-related problems with teaching and student learning?
- How soon will the new model be in place?
- How will it renew the mission of our schools and regain public confidence?
- How much will it cost?

My challenge was to make the answers straightforward and convincing, but I expected others in the group to offer additional perspectives. Mary wanted to provide an answer for the first question about overcoming pandemic-related problems with teaching and learning.

"I am young and new to teaching," she said, "but my teacher education courses caused me to believe the pandemic did not need to be so problematic. One of my professors used an analogy to explain why. We buy products both in stores and online. Products in stores are seen, touched, tasted, tried on, and operated. With sales personnel dwindling, products are placed on shelves and customers select what they like.

"The same products sold online are pictured, described, and consumer-tested with specific uses and advantages, tools for assessing quality, and policies for making exchanges. Some have sites for a live chat. Delivery is easily available through the post office or other services.

"To compete with online sales strategies, traditional retailers started online services, even if the product was picked up at a brick-and-mortar store. Current on-site school programs compare to traditional brick-and-mortar stores. Their product is available for those interested in them with a sales force (teachers) available to inform, answer questions, or give guidance. That approach does not work with online learning just as store-based marketing techniques do not work with online sales.

"Passive approaches to sales *and* education must be replaced with dynamic methods, carefully designed and assertively implemented. For both online and on-site schooling, we need a dynamic curriculum that is focused, meticulously written, and gauged to work in any kind of delivery system."

Everyone looked at Mary with amazement.

Ken said, "Your professor's analogy makes sense to me, but what exactly is a 'dynamic curriculum'? Is it the kind of thing we've been discussing, one focused on mastery (or adroitness) and constructed with specific intentions for learning, with measurable verbs and specific content fields?"

"Exactly. My training stressed the idea that curriculum is useless as 'topics covered'—just as products in stores are of little interest as 'displays.' The word *dynamic* means action, forcefulness, movement, and engagement."

Ken said, "Developing that kind of curriculum, with teachers fully involved, will take much time and effort. Is that true?"

Mary nodded. "That's true, but I was surprised by how quickly we teacher education students learned how to do it. Because it is logical and makes sense, it's easy to learn."

Logical and makes sense resonated with everyone. But the next two questions remain: *How long?* and *How much?*

It would take a few years and it would be expensive. The consultants said the process would be ongoing, but the first portion would align with the long-range plan already developed—about seven to nine years. The cost would be somewhere between $50,000 and $100,000 per school year. The board could work on assessing the cost after the proposal was presented and approved.

• • • • ● • • •

The Board of Education's Verdict

The board of education endorsed the curriculum council's proposal to implement the New Learning Infrastructure. Ken and Rebecca, working with board members Vernon and Byron and two community members, participated in approving the proposal. Board approval was almost a foregone conclusion. Ken's original worries about state policies and accreditation dictates softened as did his concerns about potentially poor student scores on standardized high-stakes tests. Ken long believed the financial carrot associated with compliance to external regulations was not worth much. Discretionary funds from federal and state sources are always welcome, but they come with too many strings attached. Thumbing his nose at external pressure could have killed his career, but now Ken's district builds a case for using a proven alternative academic model. He thinks about partnering with other superintendents and universities to build a case for the New Learning Infrastructure.

One option opposes outside-the-district pressure for purely personal or political reasons, but a strong case is made for using a valid alternative process—a better way to educate children and young people. The goal is to make them American problem-solvers, entrepreneurs, innovators, and members of an interactive society—doers and leaders, not just people who meet minimum expectations and comply with a stale status quo.

Ken Introduces a New Academic Program Governance Schematic

Making the New Learning Infrastructure work depends on the effectiveness of bylaws, to accept a new way of thinking about decision-making and action-taking authority. With the help of consultants, I (Ken) created a table of organization. It depicts the way decisions will be made in the district. While the new schematic may not look remarkable, it is a significant departure from the standard decision-making structure. Like hospital administration, there is a split between the managerial and professional sides below the level of board and superintendent.

Operationally, the split does not indicate separate leadership. It provides a greater concentration of authority in making decisions concerning what schools are for. Schools are for student learning, yet boards and administrative teams spend inordinate amounts of time on issues such as finance, personnel, facilities, and other important—but merely support—functions. As with a company that concentrates so much on managerial needs, it overlooks the product or service it was created to provide.

In the new table of organization, teachers play an important role. Administrators serve on both sides of the chart. Academic decisions are prevalent and encompassing of all professional stakeholders—as they should be. One of the more challenging aspects of this new way of looking at district governance is the board itself. Citizens become candidates for board membership for many reasons. Even in positive times (unlike the pandemic era) issues arise that involve lengthy, sometimes rancorous debate—democracy at work. I accept being the agent that carries out the board's wishes. But now I ask the board as a group, and each member, to constantly concentrate on what schools are for, to give as much time as possible to academic policy development and maintenance through the continuing education of members and systematic allocation of meeting time to topics related to curriculum, instruction, and learning.

ORGANIZATION FOR ACADEMIC GOVERNANCE

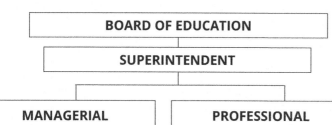

BOARD OF EDUCATION

SUPERINTENDENT

MANAGERIAL

ADMINISTRATIVE TEAM

Make decisions related to management of personnel, finances, facilities, schedules, public relations, legal matters.

PROFESSIONAL

CURRICULUM COUNCIL AND COORDINATORS

Make decisions related to curriculum, instruction, assessment, quality of learning, and accreditation issues.

SUBJECT AREA COMMITTEES

BUILDING PRINCIPALS

MANAGERIAL

- Serve on administrative team.
- Implement decisions made by administrative team.

PROFESSIONAL

- May serve on curriculum council.
- Work as equal partners with teachers in building to implement curriculum in the instructional program.
- Interact with subject area committees.
- Monitor and mentor building-level implementation of decisions made by curriculum council and SACs

All successful superintendents attempt to build a good relationship with their boards. They recognize that we serve multiple roles: being professional resources, providing leadership, serving as

254 | *The New Learning Infrastructure*

spokespeople, and creating conditions in which educators and citizens work together for the good of the community's children and young people.

Now we decide the next steps. Simple enough. Tell the curriculum council that the process moves forward. Direct the administrative team to create a plan for informing parents and patrons. The council under Rebecca's leadership will confirm decisions already made to determine where they stand in meeting other expectations.

Rebecca and I met to go through a checklist for actions to be completed at the council level:

- Review the content and meaning of the academic decision-making bylaws approved by the board.
- Examine the new table of organization. Make certain everyone on the council understands its meaning and implications involved.
- Review the suggestions of the communications subject area committee in terms of their possible influence on the district and subject area mastery statements.
- Review the suggestions of the communications subject area committee in terms of their possible influence on the long-range plan.
- Begin discussion of how the district's staff development should be modified in light of new expectations of current and new teachers.

Most of these actions are pro forma, and the bylaws are in good shape. The table of organization aligns with the bylaws' provisions. Mastery statements are broad, possibly hard to translate into curricular outcomes, but as aligned as possible. Outcomes can be taught and assessed. The long-range plan may need revisions due to the communications committee's recommendation to use an interdisciplinary approach—no hurry.

The biggest challenge is an efficient and effective way to write and teach the New Learning Infrastructure curriculum. Especially at the outset, this plan is likely to be time-consuming, but the commitment has been made. Barbara, Mary, and our consultants will now create the new communications curriculum, which will serve as a stylistic model for all that follow.

• • • ● • • •

Curriculum-Building as the New Learning Infrastructure Begins

The philosophical discussions ended as the district committed to the New Learning Infrastructure. The governance model was in place and the bylaws included in board policy. The table of organization now tangibly underscored the importance of student learning over all other considerations. The decision was to remake the curriculum to be completed locally. Teachers would play a key role in writing the curriculum and an even greater role in executing it in their classrooms.

The curriculum focuses on knowledge and skills, incorporating effective interdisciplinary and practical behaviors, the technological aspects of current life and future possibilities. Student effectiveness focuses on such areas as communication, leadership, productive collaboration (teamwork), responsibility, and resourcefulness. Emphasized are curricular intentions for learning. Teachers will assess student progress formatively and will accept accountability for quality learning.

Parents will benefit from the transparency of the curricular content. They assist in the determination of mastery. Progress reports transition from an emphasis on quantitative indicators (grades) to qualitative descriptors, which paint a more accurate picture of students' abilities and potential. Teaching methods undergo a dramatic change, more than the written curriculum. Methods make use of discipline-focused projects, simulations, and scenarios to depict conditions found in real life.

Barbara Convenes the Next Communications SAC Meeting

Our proposal to the curriculum council was approved through the board of education level. All structural aspects of the New Learning

Infrastructure now fall into place. The curriculum council implements the new model, delegating the hardest parts to the Communications SAC.

Rebecca and Ken talked with Barbara. Ken said, "The whole idea sounds radical because of what Americans believed for decades—that our free society depends on managing public education through use of standards and high-stakes tests.

"That's a social oxymoron," Rebecca said, "that a micromanaged and standardized educational system expects to work in harmony with democracy and free enterprise.

"They have never been compatible. Mark Twain and thousands like him proved that point.

"Not even today's universities and post-secondary training programs rely solely on student test scores and grade-point averages for admissions. They look at applicants' personal qualities and contributions, their sense of purpose, and analytical abilities."

With that backdrop in mind, Rebecca said our committee is now responsible for writing the K–12 communications curriculum. Consultants will help. Mary's experience will be supportive. Nevertheless, it seems like a steep learning curve and a major challenge—wordsmithing to the utmost. Meanings of words and phrases must be exact. Course content must align with the new subject area mastery statement. Explicit and intentional learning outcomes with measurable verbs align with content fields. Precision is required because learning is assessed formatively and qualitatively as part of an ongoing teaching method. No longer do we "cover" a topic and then later test students' abilities to give correct answers.

Rebecca said, "The former methods happen qualitatively in summary fashion to ensure retention of learning and readiness for subsequent study, but they will not be regarded as a summative test for the purpose of assigning grades or for comparing students, or for plugging information into a database used to compare schools and districts. The New Learning Infrastructure is not about competition or making comparisons. The corporate model on which school districts were created is no longer relevant."

Ken said, "Quality is defined as contributions fulfilled, services rendered, ideas shared, and connections made. No distinction will be made between graduates admitted to top universities and those entering trade and vocational schools. Our job in the New Learning Infrastructure is to build student potential by inspiring students and giving them the self-confidence to meet goals they competently set for themselves."

When I (Barbara) convened the communications subject area committee, I conveyed decisions made by the council and board. I also passed on the observations made by Ken and Rebecca. Everyone looked a bit stunned. Mary grinned. Information was recorded on butcher paper taped to the walls. It reflected earlier learning, topics now "covered" in language arts grades K-12. Another paper on the back wall showed "language arts + technology + project methodology = communications." Posters contained mastery statements for the district and a proposed interdisciplinary communications curriculum. Schematics near the door showed examples of a lesson plan resource and a teaching and learning contract. How do we start building an interdisciplinary communications curriculum?

I looked at Mary. Our consultant, Emily Thompson, sat across the room. She looked at Mary, grinned, and gave her a thumbs-up. We all saw it and felt relieved.

Emily said, "We keep our eyes on what our students must know and do, as indicated in the communications mastery statement. Break them down by grade level and course, with scope and sequence in mind. Then do the same in each grade and course, using measurable outcomes and components. Use information from the "walls" exercise to determine the extent our new curriculum aligns with the old.

"We've done this in other districts, so we know it works. It goes slowly at first. But you'll be surprised how quickly you learn how to do it, just as Mary did in her preservice teacher education program."

We ended the meeting on that promising note. The next time we met, our wordsmithing tasks would proceed as never before.

18

The Wordsmithing Begins

F or our purposes, *wordsmithing* means content precision, intentional writing for teaching and learning, and an ongoing qualitative measurement of student progress. Students intrinsically absorb and acknowledge a subject to make its content part of who they are and what they think, but *not* indoctrination.

Rather, this method helps students reflect upon and creatively construct ideas to consciously become more effective and self-assured and to create a better sense of who and what they are as members of a community, culture, and human race, not individualization of instruction used to inculcate specific skills nor a one-way literary interaction between teacher and student, such as teacher comments written on an essay.

Wordsmithing is a dynamic interaction, similar to a Socratic technique in the form of conversation with give and take, employing teacher listening as much as building student skills and understandings. This definition of curriculum goes far beyond information on the walls—what is currently covered in the district's language arts curriculum, only a one-dimensional learning veneer.

"Covering" a curriculum implies teacher dissemination of information that students absorb, a requirement often ignored because they do not understand, are not able to comply, or refuse to accept. For content to be meaningful in a curriculum, there must be a clear expression of what will influence a change—in student perspective, performance, or deep knowledge. Verbs stipulate specific responses, and content fields describe the breadth of those responses.

Quality teacher/student engagement starts with well-written intentions for student learning combined with an understanding of how those intentions are presented, broken down sequentially, and continuously evaluated within a scholastic milieu that acknowledges students are more than empty vessels into which information is poured.

Barbara Guides the Discussion on Curricular Wordsmithing and Validation

Both Mary and I (Barbara) are amazed. The core of the New Learning Infrastructure consists of skills we can convey to older teaching colleagues. We told our SAC members that curricular expression and teacher/student responsiveness are mutual conditions. In plain English, curriculum is taught and learned as written, interpreted by teachers collectively *and* individually. Our Socratic teaching is greater than a smart guy passing on his thoughts to eager young people seeking wisdom. For our purposes, teaching and learning are not just intellectual musings. They are based on specific skills and knowledge areas within a well-designed curriculum and reinforced from year to year.

As I told SAC members, allegiance to curriculum reveals more than teacher intuitiveness about what is scholastically important. Being guided by a curriculum begins with clearly written intentions for student learning. We teachers who create the curriculum must thoroughly understand and interpret it through our interaction with each other and deep personal reflection.

I asked Mary to explain how that worked structurally. "The high achievement unit outcome is a critical part of a grade-level curriculum, a brief but powerful statement that contains many elements requiring teacher background knowledge and reflection. Here's an example:

Students will define and describe each of the six writing traits and produce accurate examples in published original essays incorporated into technological media.

"First, we isolate the measurable verbs and clarify their meaning: *define/describe, produce,* and *published*. The content field for *define/describe* pertains to the six writing traits. The content field for *produce* includes original essays (using those traits) written and published. In this case, *published* means use of available social media such as a blogpost.

"The six writing traits are *voice, ideas, presentation, conventions, organization, word choice,* and *sentence fluency*. They are defined and described, used in essays written by students and posted on a social media platform."

After Mary offered that information, I made sure everyone on the committee understood. This outcome is a multifaceted unit that meets the three criteria we established for a communication curriculum: language arts + projects + technology.

Language arts in this unit pertains to composition skills. *Projects* relates to published essays. *Technology* is the use of electronic social media.

Mary added, "Anything classified as a unit takes time to teach and learn, maybe multiple weeks in one grade level. We might spread that unit through many grade levels, emphasizing individual writing traits. That element is critical if we are honest about teaching something to mastery or adroitness. In our example unit outcome, we break it down by each of the six traits, or we combine them in some way to show compatibility.

"In my field of science, similar traits lie within what we call the 'scientific method.' But it is difficult to treat them separately. Even development and use of a 'hypothesis' bleeds into everything else scientists do to make discoveries, like the gathering, use, and treatment of data."

Bob Snyder added another consideration: "Writing traits are necessary, but aren't styles even more important? Traits are basic tools that make writing effective, whereas styles tell us what our writing is meant to accomplish. What are we trying to do? Tell a story, convince an audience, offer instructions, describe an activity, or offer ideas or personal perspectives? In my fifth-grade class I discuss these styles:

- Narrative
- Descriptive
- Expository
- Persuasive
- Comparative/Contrasting
- Reflective
- Personal

"What if we added styles with traits in a high achievement unit outcome—one that looks like this? *Incorporating the six writing traits and using specific styles, students will produce and publish original essays they incorporate into technological media.*

"Using both traits and styles allows us to individualize over a broad range of communication needs, depending on student interests. Students in the early grades like hearing and telling personal stories. My fifth-graders do as well. Stories are interesting, especially if the six traits are applied effectively—and regarding the type of character telling the story, how interesting the character or storyline is, whether the story's events flow logically and understandably, and the extent to which words and phrases are familiar."

Myra Jackson, elementary school principal, leaned forward: "Maybe it's my background as a first-grade teacher, but I could not agree more. I am a C. S. Lewis enthusiast. Lewis was a theologian who attempted to explain Christian beliefs using analogies such as *The Chronicles of Narnia* series. J. R. R. Tolkien wrote *The Lord of the Rings* fantasy to encourage deeper thinking about human relationships and conflicts. Even J. K. Rowling's *Harry Potter* stories explore topics of relevance to our world. Stories we read and tell are a function of creative thinking—of connecting the mundane aspects of life to reflecting on our existence and purpose."

Ken said, "I like the idea of an explicitly stated curriculum and preparing teachers to use it accurately to cause deep and enduring student learning. I also understand the importance of communication as central to everything else we teach."

After Ken made those observations, I asked him to elaborate. He agreed.

Wordsmithing and Curricular Centrality

Ken brought up an interesting point. Like many other public school educators, he was originally convinced that curriculum should concentrate more on STEM. Reasons for that seem obvious as our world is now more influenced by science, technology, engineering, and mathematics. STEM has become pervasive as a driver for everything else in the curriculum. It dominates the meaning of scholarship. But Ken and others working on the curriculum rethink that bias. Those STEM subjects are tangible and critical to the growth of a twenty-first-century economy, academically challenging and a prerequisite to post-secondary programs. They prepare our nation's inventors, builders, and technical problem-solvers.

Ken still accepts and appreciates that position. He supports his district's efforts to move in such a direction, to the extent it makes sense. To Ken it makes sense to students with the innate ability to build their interest and capacity, to become contributors and leaders in science and technology. It also makes sense to help everyone benefit from scientific research and technological development in terms of richer and more meaningful lives, a kind of Disneyesque Imagineering, communicated to everyone as ways to make their lives more enjoyable. But Ken's thinking is changing because of larger concerns:

- Governance
- Social order
- Family strength
- Individual contentment
- Health and wellness
- Cultural equity
- Mutual understanding and acceptance

Ken sees an erosion of social and cultural relationships within our inability to effectively communicate with each other. Reasoned debate has morphed into biased argument. Helpful convictions have become iron-clad with unchanging opinions. Social problem-solving is replaced with an unbending acceptance of unilateral decision-making.

Ken knows the four elements of STEM disintegrate if scientists adamantly disagree with other scientists, if technical specialists let competitive barriers separate them, if engineers do not work and communicate with each other in teams, if mathematicians confine their logic to numbers and formulas instead of society's welfare.

Real learning is the product of both cognitive and emotional engagement, a kind of connectedness that transforms us, transcending our mundane existence into a panoply of possibilities, a foundation that mitigates against feelings of isolation, loneliness, despair, and worthlessness.

Ken's background as a social studies teacher and coach helps him understand the power of engagement. His students and team members improved only when they felt engaged and when they acted on that feeling.

Like Myra, Ken appreciates the philosophy of C. S. Lewis. Ken believes in the power of connecting imagination with rationality. He used it in his coaching when he told players to imagine what winning looked like and how it happened. In teaching history, he asked students to imagine what it was like to be born in the early twentieth century's age of invention. In teaching government, Ken contrasted argument with reasoned debate as the basis of a true and lasting democracy. Debate rationally examines two sides of an issue, using both researched data and the convincing power of imagination. It is a means of communication that enlightens without offending, inventing ideas in the realm of logic.

Barbara Perpetuates Discussion on the Use of the High Achievement Unit Outcome

At the last SAC meeting Ken said, "I understand the importance of communication as central to much of everything else we teach."

I (Barbara) asked him to elaborate on that comment. He expanded on his feelings about the place of STEM in our curriculum and why it is important only in the context of how well human beings communicate. He spoke about the importance of both cognitive and emotional engagement as the basis of all real learning, of how we need to connect rationality with imagination if we are to fully grasp any subject to the point of long-term retention to the point that our outlook and behaviors are significantly affected. Ken was convincing and open to hearing other points of view. At first no one had more to offer. Everyone seemed to agree.

But special education teacher Joan expanded on Ken's points: "We're talking about a high achievement unit outcome for all our students to accomplish. Most of my students need more time, over time. The key to making that process work effectively as teachers is being different than before. We must transform our thinking as repositories of knowledge to being seekers and students ourselves, and that demeanor needs to be evident all the time, not as a demonstration of ignorance but as thoughtful questioning."

Third-grade teacher Jackie seemed perplexed: "My problem with this kind of discussion is that some of us are influenced by what school meant to us as students. We became teachers because we bought into that old way of doing things. I liked to play 'teacher' as a child and concluded that learning meant I did as expected, what pleased adults. They expected me to do well on pencil-and-paper tests or in reciting back what was required. I learned to do that well, and I felt sorry for those who would not or could not do the same.

"My goal as a teacher revolves around how to make my students be like me, serious about performing properly and staying on track, pleasing teachers who help me meet our prescribed learning objectives. To me when I was a child, communicating meant meeting expectations. Imagination had boundaries. Creativity involved staying inside the lines. Competition of any kind was simply a matter of who best complied with the rules or fundamentals, whether it involved games or anything else in life.

"I'm not sure I can break out of that mold. Call it a security blanket if you wish, but I get queasy when I think about it. Maybe development of a curriculum that centers on the effectiveness of communication will help me make the transition. I hope so. But right now my emotions are tied in knots just thinking about leaving this comfortable cocoon. To venture into an unknown place is scary."

Jackie was not the only teacher with those feelings. To a certain extent, all of us shared her beliefs. The issue needed further consideration.

19

Breaking the Cycle

Changing American schools continues to be difficult for many reasons. We have touched on several with this district trying to implement the New Learning Infrastructure. Breaking the cycle of frustrated attempts at school improvement first requires an understanding of the issues involved.

Jackie's courageous expression of concern is possibly the most significant barrier to school improvement. Unlike other professional groups, Jackie represents all of us who were once young students. The experience of being a student during our formative years imprinted attitudes and aspirations about the school experience, both good and bad. Jackie's was good. Board member Vernon's was bad. Most of us lie somewhere in between.

Certain feelings and perceptions are imprinted by family members. Social experiences such as poverty, relational dysfunction, and other rite-of-passage encounters affect us. We learn from youthful encounters, and we are shaped by them. As with many other teachers, Jackie loved her school experience. Perpetuating what felt good was a no-brainer. Jackie's response to structure, adult guidance, test-taking, and reinforcement from parents and other authority figures felt comfortable. She viewed the world as described in textbooks and media. It all made sense then. It makes sense to her now.

To examine ways to bring Jackie and others like her into accepting the New Learning Infrastructure will not be easy. It requires a review of all the other barriers to change.

Barrier One:
Teacher Education and Expectations of New Teachers

Mary was prepared in a university that advocated a strong link between curriculum and instruction, not just in terms of coverage but also in a well-constructed local curriculum applied through carefully aligned instructional design and execution, instruction that incorporated specific content fields, set out clear techniques for working with students, and assessed their progress continuously and formatively.

Mary's preparation is not the norm for teacher education, and there is not a market for teachers prepared that way. Mary would not fit in most school districts, because they do not use those processes. They represent the traditional American way of teaching and learning. The assembly-line model used in school districts precludes mastery learning, which accepts student proficiency levels on a scale of poor to excellent.

Barrier Two: Micromanagement of School Improvement and the Assembly-Line Mentality

Toward the end of the twentieth century some movement modified the old system, but the implementation of No Child Left Behind and its emphasis on governmental micromanagement of public education worsened everything. Standards, high-stakes tests, data management associated with test scores, and superficial methods to compare districts in terms of compliance destroyed anything related to quality teaching and learning. Modification of NCLB was mostly an effort to move micromanagement to the states, especially with the Common Core initiative.

But micromanagement by politicians, bureaucrats, and others in positions of authority over public education simply does not work. They still believe in the assembly-line method—with efficiencies and productivity—of adding scholastic components to the human brain, the ultimate rollout of citizens and workers who contribute to the effectiveness and wealth of our nation.

Barrier Three: The Pandemic

The pandemic forced schools into the necessary use of electronic media platforms or on-site classrooms that necessitated use of social distancing and masks. As of this writing, the pandemic's effects continue being a problem. Without the curriculum and instructional design advocated in the New Learning Infrastructure, teachers fail to maintain even the status quo. Many teachers are retiring or leaving due to stress caused by COVID-19. This exodus creates tens of thousands of available teaching jobs.

Barrier Four: Superficial or Sidebar Methods of Stimulating an Interest in Improvement

Improved salary and teaching conditions top the list of possible solutions to the current problems, but both remedies are poorly defined in terms of numbers and meaning. Research on the relationship between salary and job satisfaction shows that money does not make employees "happy." It merely makes them "not unhappy." The same neutral feeling comes from good benefit packages, caring supervisors, and easier work schedules. Happiness comes from feelings of being valued and considered essential to the welfare of the organization and its clients—the welfare of a school and its students. Happiness also comes from being recognized by peers as essential to achieving commonly held convictions about meeting organizational goals.

The lack of regular veneration from peers always presents a problem in public education. Most of the day, teachers interact with their students, spending limited time with peers in the workroom or cafeteria. Being appreciated or even loved by students feels wonderful, but adults still need the respect of other adults. In higher education, respect is made more possible through committee meetings, faculty governance activities, research teams, and somewhat lighter teaching loads for tenure or tenure-tracked faculty members. Even with its flaws, tenure and promotion policies in higher education build a scholastic camaraderie not found in public school teaching ranks. Achieving tenure and the rank of full professor is typically the result of peer judgment, with endorsement by administrators who are themselves professors. In addition, the effectiveness of university instructors is usually gauged by service and research as well as classroom teaching.

Attempts to implement merit-based salary processes in public schools usually meet with failure, mostly because they are managed by administrators, laden with complaints about favoritism, types of teaching assignments, competence of supervisors, and how well students perform on standardized tests.

Merit pay is just one of the quick fixes attempted over the decades. Others involve differences in school architecture, class scheduling, team teaching, progress by grade levels, interdisciplinary configurations, and others. One of the most current is the extreme emphasis on the importance of STEM, even to the point of diminishing other critical aspects of a curriculum.

Barrier Five: Politics

Politics makes the situation worse. The New Learning Infrastructure advocates parental partnership in the conduct of school programs, but in a local, systematic, and ongoing way not mandated by legislatures. Current political issues about critical race theory and LGBTQ cause legislators to craft bills and pass laws limiting those subjects in a curriculum. Such initiatives also advocate parental control of curriculum. Enforcing such mandates are techniques that range from salary deductions to other forms of disciplinary action. Instead of local and clear-headed discussion of what should or should not be in a curriculum, lawmakers turn educators and local communities into political footballs.

Parental control via micromanagement from lawmakers or others in governmental authority does not define the New Learning Infrastructure. Rather, the New Learning Infrastructure includes transparency and openness, a willingness of all stakeholders to make reasoned decisions in the best interests of students and the community.

Breaking Stereotypical Perspectives

Jackie is a caring, intelligent, and dedicated third-grade teacher. She loves her students, and they love her. She is dependable, respected by peers and her students' parents. Her principal's evaluations place her in the exemplary category. Jackie maintained an excellent grade-point average on the way to earning her bachelor of science degree in education. She is exploring the possibility of earning a master's degree in elementary education. Jackie's lesson plans are works of art—thorough, organized, and well-researched in terms of meeting state standards. Classroom management could not be better. Students stay motivated, work on task, and accurately complete assignments. Parents repeat positive statements about what their children say about Jackie and her classroom. Standardized test data collected on Jackie's students show them meeting requirements at the eightieth percentile or better. Students needing extra attention readily receive it in the classroom or through referrals to professional support personnel.

Jackie is married to a respected businessman in the community, and they are active in a local church. Their two children attend the school in which their mother teaches. As an alumnus, Jackie regularly supports the sorority to which she belonged as an undergraduate.

But Jackie has concerns about the different ways of thinking linked to the New Learning Infrastructure. Her reactions will impact improvement strategies and may cause a disconcerting effect on the colleagues who respect her. Many of those colleagues share Jackie's competence and concerns but are typically not as open as Jackie. They honestly want to participate in the new way of doing things but will quietly accede to instructions until this innovation disappears like others in the past. It is just TYNT (this year's new thing).

Many secondary school teachers have a similar demeanor as Jackie, but they focus on the subjects they enjoy teaching. As students they excelled at math, science, language arts, or some other subject. They entered education because of their academic passion. Some try to emulate their college professors with inspiring lectures, experiments, and innovative instructional strategies. They build good relationships with students and increase their enthusiasm. They are highly respected by both the young people and their parents.

The Conundrum

Teachers such as Jackie and her elementary school associates, as well as exceptional teachers at the secondary level, are pedagogical stars. Admired and emulated, they receive awards and often media attention—the kind of teachers others want to emulate. This cultural phenomenon, most evident in the United States, praises exceptionality in all walks of life: sports, business, community service, politics, and other kinds of achievement.

Entrepreneurship builds on the admiration of exceptionality, because others feel they want to emulate that behavior. Recognition of exceptional persons drives a nurturing ambition and achievement toward excellence. It also spurs on the foundation of competition: making money, achieving social status, gaining authority, acquiring possessions, receiving recognition, and being admired for certain positive characteristics. Elements of our culture continue to value the benefits of competition, a significant reason for NCLB's development. Pitting schools and teachers against each other theoretically makes them work harder and makes students more successful.

This theory chooses the idea that education improves if evidence shows one school or district doing a better job at causing students to learn. Local boards, real estate agents, patrons, and parents put pressure on deficient schools to do a better job especially if state report cards on schools and districts report data that reflects inferior performance. They believe one way to improve performance is to encourage all teachers to be more like pedagogical stars—a pervasive belief that overlooks conditions in which no one has control, such as—

- socioeconomic factors (poverty and broken homes) that interfere with school improvement initiatives
- authoritarian leadership (usually from building principals) that makes teaching and learning dysfunctional
- internal staff jealousies that create a toxic work environment

Those who believe competition and emulation of pedagogical stars will improve schools created a conundrum. If schools cannot be improved with these theories, what is an acceptable alternative? More money or increased micromanagement are not solutions. What *is* the solution?

Teams

Americans have created a mythology associated with the adulation of individual ability depicted by fictional heroes, comic books, and films. Settings include war, commerce, politics, science, exploration, crime, and a myriad of human interactions. Special people we admire in history and novels seem faultless. They rarely need help. They accomplish the seemingly impossible through rugged individualism, which is inspiring—but nonsense.

Accomplishments are always the product of cooperative endeavors, even when one name rises above the others. Cooperative endeavors involve teamwork, with heroes serving as leaders. Decisions and actions of leaders are always influenced by sidekicks, or someone in the background. Heroic leaders appreciate and acknowledge the help of associates. These associates show their appreciation through their cooperativeness and friendship with the leader. They become a team—one for all and all for one.

Before the imposition of NCLB, schools experimented with teaming. The two most prevalent models were interdisciplinary structure, used in grades six through eight (middle schools), and intradisciplinary organizational systems, in high schools. Middle school theory emphasizes the social and emotional development of young people transitioning from childhood to adulthood based on research proving that social and emotional development intertwines with cognitive, linguistic, and academic progress. Teams of teachers made up of the standard curricular divisions (math, science, social studies, and language arts) meet regularly. They discuss student progress and use project teaching to underscore how previously taught skills apply to real life.

Intradisciplinary teams, usually at the high school level, do much of the same, gauging student progress and making extensive use of project teaching and learning.

The Transition

Pedagogical stars do not need a team. They already serve as part of a faculty team led by a building principal who gives them glowing evaluations. The New Learning Infrastructure utilizes teams at all levels and categories—the kind of teaming that transcends sporadic and fragmented teaming used in earlier years. It absorbs everyone into the fundamentals of curriculum development and implementation. Jackie and other pedagogical stars learn to adapt to this kind of teaming.

Team Building and the New Learning Infrastructure

The New Learning Infrastructure creates effective teams where and when they make a difference in curriculum, instruction, and student learning. Inclusive teams as curriculum councils and subject area committees concentrate on those three academic goals. Council and SAC members include teachers, administrators, school board members, parents, and patrons.

Teamwork in Schools Is Not Always Focused on Academics

In American schools, teams have existed for decades, mostly designed for managerial and operational reasons. Convenient communication systems worked for administrators who wished to appear acceptant of participatory governance—advisory in nature.

- Building faculties are often referred to as team members, supervised by a principal who provides direct and supportive guidance to a subordinate cadre of teachers, most guidance related to policies and procedures, scheduling, student management, discipline, routine assignments, and generalized staff development.
- Smaller teams within a building traditionally function at grade levels or within subject fields concentrating on management concerns.
- Building leadership teams (BLTs) have been used for decades,

typically to advise the principal on school policy and procedures. In larger schools these leaders are subordinate to the principal, grade-level chairs, or subject area department chairs.

While existing or traditional teams remain positive, their main purpose is operational or managerial. Rarely do they consider academic challenges and opportunities.

Academic Teams

Before the NCLB era, many academically focused teams used a curriculum created by team members and rarely linked to what they taught directly. They did not necessarily stay true to a grade-level scope and sequence.

Academic Teams and the New Learning Infrastructure

The New Learning Infrastructure involves academic teaming supported by the district's mastery objectives and total curriculum. The story of Mary, Rebecca, Barbara, Ken, and others shows how a district created such a system. The district moves forward through the use of dialogue. Issues arise that need review and discussion, referred to as barriers, such as—

- Teacher education and expectations of new teachers
- Micromanagement of school improvement and the assembly-line mentality
- The pandemic
- Superficial or sidebar methods of stimulating an interest in improvement
- Politics

Now they concentrate on one of the more perplexing barriers: how to transform pedagogical stars like Jackie into team players, those who accepted "school" as they experienced it and performed as teachers by following the same practices they knew and loved in their youth, uncomfortable with the New Learning Infrastructure. They are cooperative stars but are waiting until this innovative school model disappears like others before it.

Rebecca Addresses Pedagogical Stars, COVID, and the New Learning Infrastructure

As an assistant superintendent, I (Rebecca) stay cognizant of trends and challenges. What I read today frightens me. The average age of today's teachers is forty-two with about seventy-seven percent of those teachers being women. Most entered the profession roughly fifteen years ago when they were between twenty-three and twenty-seven years old. Some were even younger. Even as public school students, they never knew classrooms without—

- External standards
- High-stakes tests
- Data-centric decision-making
- Instructional resources aligned with approved subject content

Prior to COVID, up to forty percent of new teachers left the profession within five years. The reasons they left varied widely. The percentage leaving the profession during the pandemic is reported to be significantly higher while those choosing to prepare for teaching is much lower. COVID may be one reason.

I am forty-nine. After ten years as a classroom teacher, I decided to earn master's and doctoral degrees in education to prepare me as a leader in curriculum and school administration, to qualify me for both building and district-level certification. My work as a building principal and district curriculum director opened my eyes to many challenges—the pandemic being the most destructive. Problems related to masks, social distancing, vaccinations, and virtual/hybrid learning platforms are challenging enough. Even more challenging is the isolation felt by teachers trying to cope with so many issues.

Debilitating feelings of isolation plague teachers, likely because they did not work in academic teams before the pandemic. In addition, they failed to work together in the design of instruction aligned with a well-articulated local curriculum. During COVID, classroom-based instructional platforms needed to be changed dramatically. Most teachers figured it out on their own, because their districts were not organized to give them the help they needed.

Jackie and other outstanding young teachers reported feelings of isolation. School became something other than what they understood. Jackie needed to change but did not possess the professional skills to do it on her own, nor was she part of a team who could help her modify the situation.

A Heart-to-Heart Discussion with Jackie

I decided to talk with Jackie about her remarks during the curriculum council meeting. It was an emotional dialogue. For the first time in her personal and professional life Jackie felt like a failure.

"Jackie, haven't you experienced times in life when mistakes were made, when conditions were not as you wanted them to be?"

"Sure, but most of them were manageable and easily corrected. My supportive family, teachers, and friends helped get me over the bumps in the road. Feelings of success motivated me to continually do better. That's why I build a classroom environment in which my students feel successful. If they feel successful, there's a better chance they will *be* successful, just as I was."

"That was not always true with me," I said. "School was not easy for me, possibly because I was late to mature and felt challenged by subjects like math. Developing friendships with other students became a problem, especially during my middle school years. Sometimes I cried at night and told my parents how upset I was because of my gawky look and stupidity in school. They loved me and tried their best to build my self-esteem, but that rarely helped. During teacher-parent conferences, teachers said I was a challenge in class. They suggested strategies to help me meet my 'potential,' whatever that was supposed to be."

I smiled. "In my younger years, a few teachers like you made me feel better about myself, like a warm emotional blanket. But in later years I wasn't ready to handle the tough challenges on my own."

Jackie looked amazed. "But you've accomplished so much academically compared to the kind of student you were."

"We often learn best when we figure out how to survive, when we make mistakes and struggle to get ahead, or when the deck is stacked against us. It's a problem-solving mentality that comes from an internal strength created by a perceived failure. My best teachers and professors put me through the intellectual ringer. I asked one of my overbearing professors, Betty Bracket, why she picked on me so much. Betty said my potential needed to be probed, something she detected but did not see used. I wondered what specifically Betty detected in me.

"She said, 'Irrepressible curiosity and an almost irreverent ingenuity.' She told me to take to heart two quotes from Albert Schweitzer: 'The path of awakening is not about becoming who you are. Rather it is about unbecoming who you are not. Imagination is more important than knowledge. Knowledge is limited. Imagination encircles the world.'"

Jackie looked puzzled. "How will understanding those perspectives help me become part of what this district is doing to change our curriculum, teaching, and learning? To change what I do in the classroom? To become part of a teacher team that views mastery in a different way?"

I suggested we ask a few more teachers to join our discussion, to seek answers to her questions.

Transforming Pedagogical Stars into Leaders

Albert Schweitzer's quotes relate to the importance of imagination. Imagination is the root of creativity because it comes from a variety of sources linked in unexpected ways. Creativity is acknowledged as being at the top of the learning hierarchy—above evaluating, analyzing, applying, understanding, and knowing.

Maria Montessori promoted a different way of engaging young children in productive learning. In its basic form, her model of education directly related to constructivism, sometimes referred to as inductive as opposed to deductive learning. It built learning through curiosity and experimentation inspired by challenges to meet or opportunities to achieve. The Montessori process eclipsed rote intellectual development and felt more fulfilling, especially when recognized by parents or teachers.

Pedagogical stars in education became stars because of imagination fed by a reality in which they cognitively role-played the kind of people they wanted to be. That reality reinforced their imagination because it was channeled within a classroom setting they liked. But the pandemic and other circumstances modified the setting, and many teachers are distressed by the change. They feel cut off from their cognitive and emotional roots, burdened with feelings of isolation—even incompetence. Nevertheless, fear keeps them from accepting anything different that forces them to leave the arena in which they felt productive and happy. Rebecca's challenge is to help Jackie and others like her become leaders in a different arena.

Jackie Accepts and Expands the Transformation Process

Rebecca asked me (Jackie) to help other teachers who feel frustrated with the current situation, those who accepted and worked with the system before and during the pandemic.

Before accepting any future leadership role, I discussed it with my husband, Ben. He understood my concerns and feelings of despondency. He saw it every day. He recognized parallels to my situation in the company in which he works.

Ben manages an office of twenty people. Before the pandemic, they interacted either in meetings or with each other as they completed various projects. Like thousands of other companies during the height of the pandemic, Ben's company decided to allow employees to work from home. Some functions required Ben and others to be at the worksite, but for almost two years nearly ninety percent of the workday was from employees' homes. The system worked reasonably well. Employees enjoyed the casual dress and avoidance of city traffic. Baseline productivity increased.

Ben and his superiors were pleased, but the executive ranks felt something important had been lost. At first they could not explain it. Then they realized creative problem identification and problem-solving diminished. Work assignments were fulfilled, but outside-the-box thinking and acting were rare. One vice president, trained as an industrial psychologist, concluded that human beings need to be in proximity with each other to effectively problem-solve and create.

I told Ben that my experience with school kids underscored the VP's conclusions. What applies to adults is accentuated among children. Working with students virtually discouraged us because the medium failed to simulate give-and-take, the reinforcement of learning, recognition from others, or enjoying the *aha* moment. These responses happened in the on-site classroom on a regular basis as we problem-solved and created together.

Ben understood my point. "Jackie, you're an excellent teacher. Normally your students benefit from your knowledge and dedication to their learning in a classroom setting. But in some ways you're like the high-functioning people in our office who enjoy their independence. Independently minded folks in my office developed that same kind of demeanor. They protected their precociousness in a subject like math. As students, math came easily to them, which made them feel proud and special. Working with fellow students only slowed them down or resulted in other students stealing their answers. They earned good grades not because of their own ability but because they theoretically *stole* from those who were good at it. Such a perspective carries over to the workplace. As a manager, I often encounter that unwillingness to work in teams, even when we're all together in the office. Virtual meetings only make a bad situation worse. Collaborative brainstorming and discussion that need creative solutions are out of the question.

"I see what Rebecca is trying to do. Unlike Rebecca, the only way I can change the dynamics is to fire and hire—fire those who refuse to work in teams, hire those who embrace teamwork. People I dismiss because of an inability or unwillingness to communicate do not understand my reasoning. They believe their performance is wonderful because they are meticulous and computationally exceptional, but they do not know how to work in a team and show no interest in doing so.

Ben smiled. "Don't get me wrong. Reclusive accountants with exemplary math skills aren't like you. They do not team well because they have unfortunate personality traits.

"Your personality traits are wonderful, and I love you for them. You're also an intelligent and stimulating teacher with terrific people skills. The problem is the system, in which teaming either does not exist or is ineffectual. The system accepts the status quo because that's how schools have always been and how many politicians and the public view schools and learning.

"Your forward-looking district's leaders believe teachers should collaborate in team settings to create and implement curriculum. They believe such teachers will more likely focus on the district's common intentions for student learning and grow professionally through an ongoing review of what does and does not work. They'll improve instructional programs accordingly. Changing the status quo is what your district is attempting, and you play a key role because you're a smart and dedicated teacher. Now you're being asked to leave your professional cocoon and work with others to examine new possibilities."

I looked at Ben in amazement. How had he become so informed about the way schools should work? His analogy associated with his company made sense. "So, Ben—do you think I should participate in leading this project and assisting with staff development?"

"Yes."

The next day I talked with Rebecca and Barbara. "I'm ready to assist in making the necessary changes, which includes learning more about the New Learning Infrastructure. I'll serve as a leader, training other teachers in how to write the new curriculum and how to use it in their classrooms to guide instruction and formative assessment."

20

Training Pedagogical Stars to Become Leaders

Mastery (or adroitness) becomes the teaching/learning goal for all students in this district. The responsibility for meeting that goal falls on the teachers who together create curricular intentions for student learning in multigrade teams. Individual student progress is measured formatively using a variety of assessments. Academic appraisals depend on the declared intentions for learning and personal dispositions of students.

Assessment strategies vary according to student proclivities, teaching methods, and classroom conditions. Determination of mastery is made qualitatively by each teacher, yet within boundaries by cooperatively created action verbs and subject fields within unit outcomes and their components.

Teacher accountability is determined through student personal and academic growth—over time. They use the teaching and learning contract, an agreement created with and for students, parents, and the teacher. Accountability will no longer be measured quantitatively by student performance on local or standards-based high-stakes tests. The district commits to overturning the old viewpoint of public and governmental expectations.

Another change in perspective involves the measure of quality teaching based on the dedication of individuals who sacrifice themselves in the name of a worthwhile "calling." Jackie and other pedagogical stars learn not to think of themselves the way many politicians and others compartmentalize teachers, as society's caregivers and nurturers who perform essential tasks for intangible and heartfelt rewards, as people willing to work hard at a job some think is relatively easy and inherently rewarding, thereby moving it from the category of "professional" to service provider. These stars feel privileged to guide the development of children and young people in ways dictated by society's leaders with monetary compensation commensurate to amounts paid to civil servants.

Jackie now realizes that her dedication and success with students are more than a sacrificial version of civil service. Modifying her role and the roles of others like her means the attainment of a professional stature within an active involvement and opportunity to make decisions as a team member in the areas of curriculum, instructional practice, and the assessment of student learning—to be viewed and respected as a professional leader who participates in forming decisions that make a difference with colleagues, students, community members, and the academic world in general.

Jackie Works with Rebecca to Devise a Plan

After my discussion with Ben, I (Jackie) thought about the difference between being a member of a team of professional decision-makers and action-takers instead of the devoted and compliant civil servant teacher. I know who I want to be. My change in perspective pleased Rebecca. She appreciated my new insights and suggested we devise a plan for helping other teachers understand the importance of establishing team structures. I agreed to help, because I too am convinced that multigrade teaming is at the heart of making the New Learning Infrastructure work.

Changes in process are meaningless if teachers do not feel different about themselves and their work and cannot interact positively and within a community of likeminded educational professionals. I asked Rebecca, "Who among the district's teachers should we include in our discussion? Is a workshop format best?"

Rebecca said, "We'll present a proposal to Ken. Upon his approval, the council and board must sign off on it. Voluntary participation is best if the project's budget is large enough to encourage teachers to attend during off-contract days. Another enticement could be the use of a retreat center. Retreats take us away from school buildings and allow a more casual interchange of views. During the retreat getaway we address the same emotional topic you dealt with. The retreat morphs from a 'how to' event to a 'who I must be' exercise. We must plan it carefully and sensitively."

I wholeheartedly agreed. Inservice staff development was usually laughed at or considered a waste of time. Even though we heard somewhat helpful ideas or funny stories, the events proved to be nothing better than harmless diversions. Such traditional staff development was taken seriously by administrators and boards. They used discretionary state and federal funds to pay substantial fees to outside experts but usually nothing happened in the way of systemic or systematic follow-up. Nothing happens without continual and consistent follow-up that stimulates discernable change.

The one exception was NCLB, at least for a few years. NCLB brought about change through use of quantifiable expectations. Governmental micromanagement ran amuck under the belief that change could be achieved through force. NCLB proved to be a disaster, especially during the pandemic.

The Retreat Format

Unlike old staff development formulas (superficial "in-service days" or NCLB's "do it or else" approach), the retreat process helps teachers discover their professional sides. As Rebecca put it, "It allows the development of a persona in which teachers are encouraged to imagine themselves as more—to be professional somebodies. They are connected to a supportive and dedicated community of knowledgeable and respected colleagues."

I said, "That sounds cool but how does a program like that present structure or anything in the way of definable outcomes?"

Rebecca's reply surprised me. "The teachers involved with our ongoing series of retreats are or will be involved in the work of subject area committees. So the retreat series becomes an emotional support system for working collegially with others, creating and implementing curriculum.

"Joan is an example. She's been teaching fifth grade three years, considered by her principal and the parents of her students to be exceptional. As with other teachers, she has been impacted by the pandemic and related problems. Recently new political issues like CRT and debates about equity stress her out. Talking about those problems with her retreat series' cohorts is helpful. If Joan currently serves on a subject area committee or the curriculum council, procedural decisions feel somewhat easier, more doable. She has a place to talk them out subjectively with trusted colleagues. In other words, the concept of teaming involves more than working with others to make policy. Dedicated teachers need another kind of professional family to air out their emotions and get in touch with their convictions."

Thinking about my own awakening process, I said, "That takes the load off families and significant others who help teachers through the emotional down times. It reminds me of when I was single, a student teacher in a community new to me. My cooperating teacher was great, but I didn't feel free to express some of my deepest feelings. Going home to my little apartment after a particularly stressful day felt like torture. My only outlet was a phone call with my mother or crying myself to sleep. Neither helped. I needed to talk with someone who had insight and the capacity to empathize, someone with the kinds of experiences I was having in the classroom, from deep frustration to feelings of incompetence, anger, and despair."

Rebecca understood. "Yes, teaching is difficult on many levels. Those who have never worked with thirty young students in a public school classroom don't have a clue. What most cannot understand is how an intense sociological and psychological environment like a classroom impacts decisions made about curriculum and instructional design. What you teach and how you teach involve much more than techniques and strategies based on content to be covered."

I agreed with Rebecca and was ready to start writing a proposal.

· · · ● · · ·

Barriers Reviewed and Challenges Presented

The most recent barrier is the hesitancy of excellent teachers who emulate the practices they admired as students. These practices now interfere with new ways to help students learn, new ways to make them contributing members of the twenty-first century with its multiple challenges and opportunities. Overcoming these barriers will take time and effort. A brief recap of obstacles includes the following:

- Inadequate preservice teacher education
- Micromanagement of schools and the assembly-line mentality
- Social ravages caused by the pandemic
- Narrow beliefs about what schools are for
- Political attacks from special-interest groups
- Teacher self-perceptions that limit professional behaviors and outlooks

The sole barrier over which the district has control is teacher self-perception. Other more troublesome barriers exist for these reasons:

- University teacher education that avoids outside influences
- Governmental entities shielded from effective criticisms
- After-effects of the pandemic
- Education's purpose constricted long enough to be pervasive
- Divisive political discourse

The only way the district can move forward is to—

- Modify teacher education locally.
- Ignore governmental micromanagement as much as possible.

- Use the pandemic as a learning experience and adjust accordingly.
- Unilaterally redefine education's purpose.
- Temper the ill effects of divisive political discourse.

That's a lot to ask. Is it possible?

The New Learning Infrastructure depends on districts with the courage to do the right thing—to take positive action in building programs that work best for students and their communities.

With barriers addressed by the district, the next steps challenge the building of local curriculum, instructional processes, and assessment strategies involving the work of the curriculum council and, more specifically, the subject area committees. In the New Learning Infrastructure, councils and subject area committees build curriculum from the ground up using readily available resources that serve as informational tools. Local educational decision-makers create curriculum, design instruction, and assessments.

Why Must the Work Be Done from the "Ground Up"?

Public or church-related American schools have long depended on externally produced resources: "readers" or textbooks, films, digital items, maps, full curricula, and other media produced by states or publishing firms. What was not available could be found in libraries and district resource centers, which are now online. Based on moral and Christian teachings, the McGuffey Readers made a significant impact for a more homogeneous American society. McGuffey materials supported poorly prepared early-nineteenth-century teachers who worked primarily with young students.

As public schools grew in number and enrollment, with better educated teachers, they needed more secular and sophisticated materials. Some states produced their own. A few, such as New York, created standardized tests called the "Regents Exams." Publications were tailored to prepare students accordingly. In the mid-twentieth century most states turned textbook publishing over to corporations. Industries soon dominated public school curriculum. After passage of the Elementary and Secondary Education Act of 1965, school publishing companies prospered. Federal grants gave districts discretionary funds to build or support many improvements to the curriculum. A multitude of associations and for-profit groups produced tangential materials used in tandem with governmentally funded projects. Those groups and entrepreneurs conducted workshops and other staff development programs. They still do.

The secret of their success is formulaic. "Why develop a local curriculum when my company already produces one? Why worry about creating good teaching strategies when my company guarantees to excite students and cause them to learn? Why struggle with assessments when my company sells good ones ready to go?"

Public school teachers become the market for these corporations. Administrators appreciate such resources. The evaluation of teacher performance is either included or made easier because adopted materials include expectations. NCLB was the 2001 version of the 1965 Elementary and Secondary Education Act. It emphasized the use of standards and high-stakes tests, an easier way for corporations to create and market their materials. Everything was aligned with NCLB-designated student learning outcomes, easy for both publishing corporations and districts to replicate standards as if they were curriculum —but not suitable as curriculum. Most gave inadequate attention to logical scope and sequence through the grades. Teachers found them difficult to incorporate into daily lesson plans. Nevertheless, commercial enterprises streamlined convenience for teachers and administrators. These expensive materials cost less than extensive staff development. Corporations were held accountable when politicians and special-interest groups found fault with their content.

Textbooks are created for higher education as well, but individual professors choose resources based on their credibility as scholars. Most "civil servant teachers" in public schools are not given that opportunity. Pedagogical stars like Jackie figured out a way to work around the micromanaged system. They refuse to limit their classrooms to worksheets pulled off the shelf or assessments guaranteed to be aligned with state standards alone. Jackie was exceptionally good at figuring out how to circumvent the barriers and challenges. She acknowledged them, but with a professional flexibility from both intelligence and setting her students' classroom priorities.

These priorities included the following convictions:

- Needs of students must supersede inflexible instructional methodology and unvarying allegiance to the inculcation of prescribed content.
- Student needs must cause unit and lesson plans to be inter-mixed with personalized learning important to all students now and in the future.
- Changes made by the pandemic provide opportunities to try different and more effective teaching and learning strategies.
- Schools are for student learning that emphasizes deep thinking, self-assurance, creative problem-solving, effective communication, quality human relationships, and a deep respect for others.
- General opinion, politicized or not, is an element of free speech. Teachers are as free as any other citizens to present points of view properly labeled as beliefs and not facts. Everything said or done in the classroom should be transparent—open for review by parents, patrons, and others who support the school.
- Teachers have the right and responsibility to perceive themselves as professional decision-makers, to work in partnership with all other educators and lay leaders in the district, to be transparent with and responsive to the public they serve.

Jackie is ready to write the proposal to initiate a retreat program using principles aligned with discerned priorities.

21

Creating an
Enlightened Local Curriculum

Wordsmithing for an enlightened communications curriculum is now possible for the district. The teachers and other educators on the council and subject area committee look differently at the challenges ahead. The curriculum council, board of education, and district administrative leaders accepted changes proposed by the newly named communications subject area committee. The long-range plan has been modified accordingly.

While externally imposed regulatory practices are either acknowledged or followed procedurally, the district decided to pursue a different school improvement framework than the one set in motion by the No Child Left Behind initiative of 2002. NCLB and federally initiated acts are not requirements because they are based on ESEA. Rejecting those stipulations merely means related funds will not be made available. State standards and tests differ because they involve accreditation and state financial support. Some states do not use standards or tests, or they extensively modify them. In the state in which the featured district operates, both standards and tests have been diminished in importance, possibly due to the pandemic's impact. Discord about the importance of standards and high-stakes summative assessments abounds. Journalists and members of the public convince themselves that micromanagement and stringent accountability policies do more harm than good.

Political discussion arises about critical race theory, LGBTQ, curricular transparency for parents and patrons, teacher recruitment and certification, and changes needed because of the pandemic's aftermath. In this era, for a district to move forward on its own is unusual. Politics continues to be a strange phenomenon. NCLB was originated by a party that called for freedom of choice and the importance of local decision-making, yet it became the epitome of governmental micromanagement. Within that party, decision-making authority about education is considered the right of legislatures and governors, because they hold the purse strings and create regulations. Education at all levels remains the most expensive of state functions. The party that micromanages issues fiscally frugal declarations meant to cut back on waste. The biggest target for assumed waste is compensation given to salaried workers, teachers, and others in the business of education.

The other major American political party tends to accept the status quo with periodic exceptions. It fears that equality, inclusion, sufficient local funding, and acceptance of innovative teaching will be hindered without the oversight of the federal government. But the federal government, the originator of NCLB-driven techniques to micromanage, finds itself moved to the back burner by the states.

Similar to what happened with the Common Core, which later morphed into the Every Student Succeeds Act, not all states accepted those standards. Since then, a hodgepodge of other standards emerged, making today's situation confusing. Standards invariably focus on specific disciplines, written by assumed experts in their fields, emanating from various entities.

The characters in our example district find themselves in a quandary. However, they possess the courage to move forward on their own, using principles and actions believed to be best for their students, parents, and patrons. With Barbara's help, Rebecca now works with the curriculum council to move the communications SAC forward and to promote the proposal written by Jackie to start a retreat program.

Rebecca Implements the New Learning Infrastructure

Jackie created a proposal to start a retreat program for those who volunteered to participate. Ken and the board agreed to fund it for one school year. The purpose of the retreat was to help teachers accustomed to excelling as individuals gain skills as team members: in curriculum development, instructional design, and the creation of formative assessment techniques.

During the curriculum council meeting, I (Rebecca) decided to again revisit the tentative district mastery statement. I designed a poster of its contents and tacked it to the wall. Although we saw it before and discussed its content and meaning, it was now our task to use it in nurturing students toward more meaningful tasks, more valuable than simply passing high-stakes tests that concentrated on minutiae sometimes known as minimum competencies.

In this district we accept no minimum competencies. This district produces leaders, doers, thinkers, and creative members of society—adults self-sufficient enough to contribute to the welfare of others. This district's teachers model those characteristics and behaviors. They create dynamic classroom activities in which students sense the value of their own talents as extensions of the society in which they play a significant part.

DISTRICT MASTERY STATEMENT

Students completing the full program of studies at XYZ School District demonstrate skills that expand their understanding of reality and continuously express a deeper understanding of themselves and how they fit into the world.

They solve complex problems, think and act creatively, and manage their own needs responsibly.

Graduates explain and act on principles associated with entrepreneurship, with the ability to become lifelong learners through knowing how to learn and being motivated to do so.

They are curious about ways they can stretch boundaries into new and different realms and reveal an inherent drive to learn continuously, to ask good questions, and become part of diverse communities in which feedback is vigorous and stimulating.

They demonstrate and articulate the importance of self-confidence, gained through experience with widening groups, taking meaningful initiatives (reaching out), and accepting and acting on consistent encouragement from respected associates.

Each day students and graduates will practice mindfulness in terms of clarifying priorities and actions.

They are open to and acceptant of others from different backgrounds. They articulate and work to achieve self-discipline and personal values. They create and maintain the convictions to pursue these values.

Students participating in and completing the full program of studies at XYZ School District will speak and write effectively. They will make people feel at ease, those from every walk of life. Students and graduates will enter conversations with others and show genuine interest in their ideas and activities.

While each academic discipline is important, graduates will grasp the idea that problem-solving usually associates with a complex and interactive system. Solving problems requires collaborative skills that allow all disciplines to work in concert.

Students and graduates exercise and respect the meaning of intellectual passion, not a passion simply for attaining more knowledge but also for comprehending its significance and value.

They communicate expressively both orally and in writing, demonstrating that life is more than a single dimension but also an assortment of experiences that make it worth living.

The district's new mastery statement will confound some individuals and groups because at its center is formational growth, not the mere accumulation of skills and knowledge areas. It focuses more on who students *are* than on what they can do in isolation. Designed to bring teachers and students together, it maximizes their potential and intensifies their unique contributions.

The central idea within the New Learning Infrastructure is that excellence in human beings can be nurtured and continuously reinforced through opportunity. Through the kind of teaching that sees which wonderful qualities exist in students, teachers show them how to find portals to fulfillment and walk through them.

Summary

TECHNICAL ASSISTANCE
FROM EXPERTS OUTSIDE THE DISTRICT

This story about a fictitious district courageously trying to create a New Learning Infrastructure is nothing new, but it is unique. The difference in this story reinforces that something makes the effort cohere, take shape, and slowly become a reality. Such slow change starts with a *cultural reconceptualization*. Who we believe we are underlies anything performed differently.

In this district the cultural reconceptualization contains many parts, the most important being that educators and other stakeholders reconceive the definition of what schools are for. They distinguish between the past goal of *preparing a workforce citizenry* and the new goal of *encouraging entrepreneurial innovation*—a distinction at the core of what constitutes the New Learning Infrastructure.

In addition, they—

- Reclassify themselves as professional thinkers and local entrepreneurs.
- Assert beliefs in terms of actions not necessarily aligned with the prevailing national opinion.
- Reject the civil servant mentality of compliance and replace it

with professional assertiveness.

- Acknowledge and overcome weaknesses of the assembly-line model used for decades.
- Follow up on the increasing need for teachers to work in teams.
- Redefine the meaning and function of teacher accountability.
- Reinstitute formative assessment as a primary way to measure student progress.
- Concentrate on the "creating" category through project teaching.
- Recognize the stressful emotional aspects of teaching and provide ways to deal with them.

Professionals Performing Differently Need Technical Assistance

Early in this story Mary Chapman was enrolled in an exceptional training program. Her professors expected her to achieve professional discipline to define learning mastery in concrete terms, not as an inspiring aspiration but as a well-articulated intention achieved through designing down and delivering up.

Then came wordsmithing—the use of powerful verbs with depth that trigger real scholarship on the part of both teachers and students, verbs preceded with the auxiliary verb *will,* as in *will create,* verbs used in phrases that depict continuous intellectual development, as in *will define, develop, modify, implement, and evaluate,* verbs that cut across all categories of Bloom's taxonomy.

Mary learned the importance of taking seriously the phrases in subject and course purposes, starting with verbs and subsequent follow-up fields of concentration. She came to understand that "design down" is an inverted pyramid with the big-picture scholastic goal on top, broken into component parts underneath. The inverted pyramid becomes the high-achievement unit outcome, and everything below the initial phrase is components.

All outcomes are different, but one example calls for students to define, develop, modify, implement, and evaluate. Component intentions shown below the outcome must expand on the meaning of each verb, such as specifically what must be defined and how that requirement is assessed. At some point in the sequence students are tested over the *entire* outcome, assembling all the pieces into a coherent scholastic understanding intended to be retained and applied.

Mary was introduced to the lesson plan resource, a useful framework for organizing instruction focused on learning goals instead of just what happens each day, as is the case with the standard "daily" lesson plan. Her professors taught that today's public school curriculum cannot be "covered" as many previously assumed.

"Covering" subjects does not suggest mastery. Systematically teaching to mastery takes both time and an ongoing assessment of student learning quality. The lesson plan resource includes strategies for formative assessment, fully aligned with backstory intentions. That instructional approach, with rich content and mastery stipulations, requires much more time than merely covering topics in the hope that students catch what is thrown at them. Mary learned that having more than ten to fifteen high-achievement unit outcomes a standard school year is impossible.

For Mary the term "scope and sequence" gave a substantive meaning, not merely how much content was to be taught in a certain order. To her the term increasingly means the continuous development of academic sophistication, like the difference between playing a piano well and musicianship. One description depicts baseline abilities while the other means artistry.

For Mary, the science teacher, sophistication means more than learning scientific terms and processes. It employs a curious mindset that constantly probes the unknown. For Mary's friend Barbara, expression in writing and speech involves more than information-giving or receiving. It is a richness made possible through creative thought and nimbleness in the use of words and phrases.

Mathematics is being transformed by technology, making most of its applications routine, not the subject that distinguishes intelligence levels. Many now view it as a problem-solving discipline and communications function. Social studies suffered most in the NCLB and standards era. It continues to be seen by some as a concentration on names, places, events, governmental structures, and dates. However, human development and social problem-solving issues and resolutions are key in causing reflection and solution-building.

Preservice Teacher Education Needs an Inservice Boost

Writing high-achievement unit outcomes supported by components and inserted into lesson plan resource frameworks is not a skill taught in most undergraduate teacher education programs, nor are other sections of the form related to instructional strategies and assessment. The district must teach those skills to its teachers to both prepare lesson plan resource documents *and* assist those using them in the classroom. Technical proficiencies will likely require assistance from outside the district. Additional in-service guidance to subject area committees must be provided to work through scope-and-sequence issues, other implementation challenges, and orientation opportunities for the board, parents, and patrons.

The nonprofit Curriculum Leadership Institute (CLI) provides those services both on-site and online. It also offers interim assistance electronically to groups and individuals as needed. The CLI has successfully served hundreds of districts since 1991, using processes that work in moving districts toward meeting criteria associated with the New Learning Infrastructure.

The characters in the story learned a new way to think about curriculum, teamwork, and the all-important goal of educating students. As more districts consider the New Learning Infrastructure and work with helpful organizations such as CLI, it is possible to reform education and teach the next generation how to think and act creatively.

Resources

• • • ● • • •

Curriculum Leadership Institute: cliweb.org. Contact directly at info@cliweb.org or 620-412-3432.

LPR: Lesson Plan Resource

NCLB: No Child Left Behind

A Nation at Risk: The Imperative for Educational Reform, https://edreform.com/wp-content/uploads/2013/02/A_Nation_At_Risk_1983.pdf

SAC: Subject Area Committee

Common Core: Common Core State Standards Initiative of 2006

STEM: science, technology, engineering, mathematics

BLT: Building Leadership Team

CRT: Critical Race Theory

ESEA: Elementary and Secondary Education Act of 1965

PBL: project-based learning

Acknowledgments and Inspirations

ACKNOWLEDGMENTS

The ideas in this book, *The New Learning Infrastructure*, come from hundreds of educators, friends, students, clients, and family members with whom I lived and worked the last sixty years. If I could, I would acknowledge them all.

The person who taught me to listen thoughtfully and responsively to all those contributors was my wife of fifty-seven years. Barbara helped me understand the importance of reshaping ideas I thought were my own into viable insights accumulated and shared by others.

The most significant of those insights coming from Barbara and hundreds of others is that true education is above all a relational enterprise. Knowledge and ability are not simply cognitive functions or behavioral characteristics within individuals. Education involves the process of a person becoming fundamentally different over time within a human community that benefits from the contributions of its members.

INSPIRATIONS

I am also inspired by many courageous educators with whom I have worked over the years.

Four of them were and still are my greatest source of inspiration. Who they are and the reasons they inspire me in the realm of authentic school reform are listed below.

Doug Christensen
Commissioner Emeritus
Nebraska Department of Education

Nebraska's STARS (School-based, Teacher-led Assessment and Reporting System) is an assessment and reporting system created to support efforts to improve the local schools of the state. The foundation of STARS is three dimensional. It (1) originates in the classroom and at the school level, not the state level; (2) focuses on teaching and learning, not test scores; and (3) provides the data and evidence to support the work of educators and policymakers in improving the quality of decision-making and improvement initiatives.

STARS and its minimal "regulations" built partnerships between the state and the local schools to strengthen curriculum, instruction, and assessment for improved student learning. The STARS system used a different set of philosophies, policies, and practical ideas than the federal No Child Left Behind initiative, which resulted in conflicts and uneasy compromises that have taken center stage since 2001.

Doug Christensen courageously fought imposition of the federal mandate. Eventually he needed to compromise in order to receive federal funds for discretionary school improvement. Nonetheless, Nebraska was the last state to accede to federal pressure to receive ESEA support. Elements of the STARS program still exist in Nebraska.

Carol S. Roach
President Emeritus
Chairperson, Board of Directors
Curriculum Leadership Institute

Courage is best reflected in the willingness to accept significant challenges, even when circumstances prove vague and not especially promising. It is more remarkable when the ongoing effort to achieve results is full of obstacles and complicated problems such as client acceptance of new ideas and strategies or significant changes in personal and organizational behaviors.

Carol Roach authored and implemented excellent public school curricular guides for law-related education. She worked closely with the Kansas Joint Commission on Public Understanding of the Law. Carol later created a series of effective training workshops for community college extension programs, businesses, and public agencies, known as Effective Methods of Teaching/Training Seminars. In 1991 she was cofounder of the Curriculum Leadership Institute (CLI). She coauthored *The Curriculum Leader* book and dozens of other materials used by public schools throughout the United States and overseas. Carol conducted workshops in hundreds of locations and was a consultant to many school districts and other educational entities, such as Consortia.

Every project Carol led involved courage to advocate out-of-the-box thinking and acting. Most important is her service as role model to those now employed by or associated with the Curriculum Leadership Institute. After 30 years, CLI continues to provide nationally recognized nonprofit assistance to the nation's schools. Carol's legacy is exceptional, as is her unparalleled service based on courage and unselfish dedication.

Dan Lumley
Retired District Administrator
Researcher, Motivational Speaker, Change Agent
Kansas and Missouri/National

Courageous service is often a product of a leader's fascination with history and the exploration of the "what ifs" of human existence. Often those thoughts result in exploring ideas that serendipitously seem to work for no predetermined reason, something like Arnold Toynbee's observation: "History is just one . . . thing after another."

The genius of Dan Lumley's courageous service is detailed in his leadership of curriculum and instruction in three school districts in Kansas and Missouri. He is fascinated with how people interact intellectually, thereby becoming more engaged and motivated. Dan's service is also based on an ability to give the ordinary a novel and even humorous twist, a skill that makes students and his workshop attendees see the world through a different lens. It is difficult to write into a public school curriculum because it is anything but unidimensional with just one correct answer.

Dan's approach to learning aligns well with the new emphasis on *creativity* as being the preeminent learning outcome in the new taxonomy of educational objectives. Today's learning theorists avoid the term *learning objectives.* They view learning as a dynamic process, more suitable to twenty-first-century work and living. Dan has advocated that idea for decades, which stimulates students and fellow educators to become more than they thought was possible.

Ken Weaver
Dean Emeritus
The Teachers College
Emporia State University

In 2010 the Kansas State Department of Education sponsored a committee that wrote Teacher Leader Standards. School district support was sought for teachers to defray expenses of earning the endorsement and a $1,000 permanent addition to base salary provided by the legislature. Ken Weaver ensured that Emporia State University would be the first to sign on to the project by offering a teacher leader endorsement. Although lack of funding caused by the 2009 recession stopped project development, ESU continues to have an area of concentration in teacher leadership, five "domains" that emphasize professional collaboration in using research to improve teaching, learning, and use of data for school improvement.

Although the original project is dormant, Ken's interim leadership of the National Teachers Hall of Fame is now connected with the National Network of State Teachers of the Year, a strategic plan built on teacher leadership. Ken encourages the members of the National Teachers Hall of Fame to use their National Teachers Hall of Fame platform to elevate the awareness of the bold initiatives they established as dynamic and creative teacher leaders to change schools.

Ken has provided courageous service in previous endeavors as a Peace Corps volunteer, public school teacher, professor of educational psychology, department chair, and college dean. All those contributions bode well for his exercise of leadership in an organization that for thirty years contributed much to the betterment of American schools and is poised to do even more in the years ahead.

About the Author

S tu Ervay is a retired university professor and a consultant to public schools. Prior to his work in higher education, he served as a unit commander in the United States Army and taught history and government in secondary schools.

During his forty-three years of university service, Stu wrote professional books, including *The Curriculum Leader* and *Common Sense about the Common Core.* His articles have been published in many educational journals: *The Oxford Round Table Review, NASSP Bulletin, Malaysian Journal of Education, The Rural Educator, Educational Considerations, The Teacher Educator, Occasional Report, American Middle School Education, Journal of the Kansas Council for the Social Studies, Focus, Kansas School Board Journal, The Teacher Educator, The Educational Forum, Phi Delta Kappan, Action in Teacher Education, Educational Leadership, Clearing House, Kansas Teacher,* and *Arizona Teacher.*

Stu was founder and first editor of *The Kansas Teacher Education Advocate* and conducted hundreds of workshops and presentations at multiple professional conferences. He was also an executive board member in the Association of Teacher Educators.

As director of the Emporia State University Office for Professional Education Services, Stu chaired the ESU Department of School Leadership and was executive director of the ESU Center for Educational Research and Service. He also served as assistant dean of The Teachers College. While at ESU, Stu led research and development activities that resulted in the 1991 development of a nationally recognized school improvement service, the

Curriculum Leadership Institute. CLI is a nonprofit publication and service organization that has served hundreds of school districts throughout the nation. Information about the institute can be found at https://cliweb.org/. CLI leaders are now developing systems to help teachers become more effective as virtual instructors.

Since retirement Stu has written journal articles and a book on school improvement, *The Teacher as Somebody: Skills that Make Teaching a True Profession*. He is now a state AARP volunteer leader and recipient of the *2020 Ann Garvin Award for Excellence in Community Service.* Stu is leading an effort to create an AARP Lifespan Planning Course for use in postsecondary institutions and higher education. His book *Confronting Dementia: A Husband's Journey as an Alzheimer's Caregiver* is available on Amazon and other bookseller websites.

His late wife, Barbara, was also a retired educator. In addition to many years of teaching middle school science, she played a significant role as an advocate for women in church leadership. Barbara also worked closely with Stu in the development of the Curriculum Leadership Institute

Stu has two sons and three grandchildren. Barbara was diagnosed with Alzheimer's disease in 2014 and died February 5, 2021.

Made in the USA
Monee, IL
30 May 2023

34711969R00174